EVIDENCE-BASED PRACTICE IN SOCIAL WORK

The role of evidence-based practice is one of the most central and controversial issues in social work today. This concise text introduces key concepts and processes of evidence-based practice whilst engaging with contemporary debates about its relevance and practicality.

Evidence-Based Practice in Social Work provides both an argument for the importance of evidence-based practice in social work and fresh perspectives on its controversies and organizational prerequisites. It gives an accessible overview of:

- why evidence-based practice is relevant to social work
- the challenges that the realities of social work practice present to models of evidence-based practice
- concepts of evidence-based practice as a process and professional culture
- the role and nature of evidence
- how evidence-based practice can be implemented and the importance of the organizational context
- the globalization of evidence-based practice, including issues of cultural diversity and adaptability of evidence-based interventions
- controversies and criticism of evidence-based practice.

Written by internationally well-respected experts, this text is an important read for all those with an interest in the area, from social work students to academics and researchers.

Haluk Soydan is Associate Dean of Research and Director of the Hamovitch Center for Science in the Human Services at the University of Southern California, USA.

Lawrence A. Lomas Feldman Professor of Social ern California, USA.

EVIDENCE-BASED PRACTICE IN SOCIAL WORK

Development of a new professional culture

Haluk Soydan and Lawrence A. Palinkas

School of Social Work
University of Southern California
Los Angeles, California

Routledge
Taylor & Francis Group

LONDON AND NEW YORK

First published 2014
by Routledge
2 Park Square, Milton Park, Abingdon, Oxon OX14 4RN

and by Routledge
711 Third Avenue, New York, NY 10017

Routledge is an imprint of the Taylor & Francis Group, an informa business

© 2014 Haluk Soydan and Lawrence A. Palinkas

The right of Haluk Soydan and Lawrence A. Palinkas to be identified as the authors of this work has been asserted in accordance with sections 77 and 78 of the Copyright, Designs and Patents Act 1988.

British Library Cataloguing-in-Publication Data
A catalogue record for this book is available from the British Library

Library of Congress Cataloging-in-Publication Data
Soydan, Haluk, 1946-
Evidence-based practice in social work : development of a new professional culture / Haluk Soydan and Lawrence A. Palinkas.
pages cm
1. Evidence-based social work. 2. Social service. I. Palinkas, Lawrence A. II. Title.
HV10.5.S677 2014

ISBN: 978-0-415-65733-4 (hbk)
ISBN: 978-0-415-65734-1 (pbk)
ISBN: 978-0-203-07710-8 (ebk)

Typeset in Bembo
by Swales & Willis Ltd, Exeter, Devon, UK

*This book is dedicated to our children and grandchildren:
Olof and Jonas; and Eleanor, Bill, and Gustav;
Ashleigh, Jonathan, Caitlin, and Heather; and
Kiran and Tazneem.*

CONTENTS

FIGURES

TABLES

PREFACE

This book is about evidence-based practice in social work. Since the introduction of evidence-based medicine more than two decades ago, the establishment of the Cochrane and the Campbell collaborations, and the gradual diffusion of evidence-based practice into the social and behavioral professions, social work has been at the very core of this development. From a global perspective, both evidence-based medicine and evidence-based practice are processes of innovation diffusion and adoption; perhaps it will take another two decades for evidence-based practice to establish itself and become sustainable in most of the countries in which these processes are currently developing.

As we see it, with the social work field embracing evidence-based practice, the profession is in the midst of developing a new professional culture, a mind-set that combines the profession's traditional values, such as dedication to the underserved and impoverished populations and social justice, with the awareness and willingness to make use of high-quality scientific evidence. The outcome of this fusion in social work is currently unknown; however, the results of the preceding 10–15 years are encouraging. This book has been prepared at a historical juncture during which the evidence-based practice movement is shifting from being perceived as individual-level interaction to a view of evidence-based practice as a professional culture shared by a collective of professionals embedded in defined institutional and organizational settings. Developments within the social work profession have contributed heavily to the perspective shift. By its nature, social work is aptly suited to adopt and adapt innovations, and is not opposed to combining and integrating components once perceived as incompatible (such as evidence-based practice and practice-based evidence).

In this book, we provide a holistic perspective of the last 20 years of development in evidence-based practice, but we also trace the historical roots of humankind's propensity to seek progress, strive for betterment, and embrace the experimental mind—phenomena that create the backdrop to evidence-based practice. Naturally, we outline the basics of evidence-based practice such as its definitions, scientific components and sources, and its locus in professional organizations. We have paid special attention to controversies concerning evidence-based practice, as well as challenges that will in various ways affect its ultimate destiny. We dedicate a chapter to recent developments in globalization, international translation, and transportability of evidence-based interventions. As the title of this book indicates, the issue of creating a professional culture for evidence-based practice is one of the core components of this book.

We wish to acknowledge the inspiration and guidance provided by many colleagues over the years, including Greg Aarons, Robert Boruch, Hendricks Brown, Patti Chamberlain, Bruce Chorpita, Charles Glisson, Kimberly Hoagwood, Sally Horwitz, John Landsverk, Dorothy de Moya, Edward Mullen, Lisa Saldana, Karin Tengvald, and John Weisz. We also want to thank the William T. Grant Foundation for providing partial support for this project (grant no. 10648), and to Vivian Tseng and Kim Du Mont for their thoughtful suggestions on conceptualizing the role of use of research evidence and academic–community partnerships.

We are thankful to the faculty members of the University of Southern California School of Social Work for their dedication to evidence-based practice and collective role as partners in scholarly conversations. We would like to acknowledge the tireless and careful efforts of Eric Lindberg of the Hamovitch Center for Science in the Human Services in improving the editorial quality of this book.

1

INTRODUCTION

In this book, we use the terms *evidence-based medicine* (EBM) and *evidence-based practice* (EBP) interchangeably depending on the context being discussed. Both terms adhere to similar principles, although the former is typically used in health-related contexts and the latter in social and behavioral contexts. However, to the extent possible and without losing track of the chronological and disciplinary evolution of these concepts, we use the term EBP in this book, which is designed for social workers and other professionals in social and behavioral human services.

EBP has two mainstream meanings. One refers to interventions supported by robust empirical evidence, in which *robust* is defined not only by agreed-upon and shared methodological standards but also the current state of the art in a specific knowledge and practice field; in other words, as robust as possible under the current circumstances. The other meaning of EBP refers to a process of applying evidence-based interventions in a specific sociocultural context. We see this process as a professional culture, a state of mind in performing professional work.

As described later in this book, there is ample debate regarding what EBP is and is not. In this book, we remain loyal to the definition and intention of the term as conceived by its originators (Sackett, Rosenberg, Muir Gray, Haynes, & Richardson, 1996). Most importantly, we emphasize that the EBP process model is designed to support professional activities in an imperfect world, in which real-life conditions change in terms of time and space and our methods of capturing the reality of that social and behavioral world have shortcomings. EBP prescribes use of the best available evidence, recognizing that this evidence is not the ultimate truth but only a temporary estimate of causal relations in real-life situations.

Exploring more than two decades of EBP development in its modern form, we note that much progress has been accomplished in advancing EBP. During this period, we advanced our ability to develop and use sophisticated means of searching, retrieving, assessing, synthesizing, and disseminating rigorous evidence on effective interventions in social work practice and other human services. Yet we believe that EBP is still in its initial stages of development and we expect much more to come. There are good reasons for expecting continued progress.

First, the success and failure of the EBP process model are interconnected with the translation and implementation of evidence-based interventions in diverse settings framed by organizational and cultural factors. In our previous book (Palinkas & Soydan, 2012), we elaborated on translational and implementation research, noting that this field of research is in its initial stages but has great potential for understanding underlying mechanisms of successful translation and implementation of not only evidence-based interventions but also scientific knowledge in a broader sense. Efforts are being invested in infrastructure development, organizational research, cultural exchange mechanisms, and global transportability. Advances in all those fields will have an impact on the EBP process model.

Second, there has been a return of the experimental mind to the social sciences. As described later in the book, advancing knowledge through experimentation has long and deep roots in human history. Most researchers in the natural and physical sciences have designed and conducted experiments to probe the mysteries of the physical and biological world. This experimental mind-set was later recognized and implemented by the social and behavioral sciences, partly because of the need to address social and behavioral aspects of biological diseases and partly because social scientists understood the benefits of reducing bias in scientific estimates via experimentation. This development culminated in "the experimenting society" envisaged by Donald Campbell. In conjunction with the establishment of the Cochrane and Campbell collaborations, and the subsequent need for high-quality evidence in estimating causal relationships in social and behavioral interventions, there has been an increased worldwide interest in experimentation. The return of the experimental mind to the social sciences is promising, especially if we consider that it may take more than a generation to fully produce a cultural shift in established institutional structures of research and higher education. From this perspective, we must assume that we haven't yet seen the full impact and outcomes of the changes of the last two decades.

Third, we expect further increased understanding and appreciation of the opportunities that *big data*, which capture many dimensions of large populations, can provide in the future. Large-scale and longitudinal datasets, as developed in countries such as Sweden, will open new horizons in epidemiological tracking of many types of diseases and societal dysfunctions.

However, what is perhaps more exciting is the possibility of using big data-sets to understand collective behavior in ways that have yet to be conceived. One can only speculate about how this may enhance our understanding of yet unknown patterns of collective behavior across national and cultural boundaries in this increasingly globalized world. Big data are contingent upon and propelled by advances in computational sciences. It was only a few decades ago that most scientific institutions did not have access to computers or had to handle data with punch cards and massive, low-powered computers. Now we can sit in our offices, at home workstations, or on the run and compute huge amounts of information. Collection and use of big data are now possible, and can be done at a low cost.

Fourth is the "biological hurricane" as described by Nicholas Christakis (2012) and his Harvard-based research team:

> Discoveries in biology are calling into question all kinds of ideas, historically important ideas, in the social sciences—everything from the origin of free will, to collective expression and collective behavior, to the deep origins of basic human behaviors. All of these things are being challenged and elevated by discoveries in biology. . . . So, a conversation is taking place between our behavior and our culture, on the one hand, and our biology on the other. But rather than it being the biology which guides or dictates the culture or the behavior, it's the culture or the behavior which guides or dictates the biology. We domesticate animals, and this gets internalized down at the level of our genes. We change as a species as a result.
>
> *(para. 3, 16)*

Social work scholars, especially in advanced research hubs in the United States, have been well aware of the intersection between biological and social work sciences. As a result, social work is home to evidence-based interventions developed and tested at the intersection of biology and social and behavioral sciences. In other words, social work as a science has some degree of preparedness, perhaps more than some other disciplines, to take advantage of interdisciplinary and transdisciplinary research pertaining to EBP.

Fifth is the globalization of the world and expansion of cultural exchange among nations, regions, ethnic groups, and organizations. Cultural exchange was defined by Palinkas and Soydan (2012) as "a transaction of knowledge, attitudes, and practices that occurs when two individuals or groups of individuals representing diverse cultural systems (ethnic, professional, organizational, national) interact engage in a process of debate and compromise" (p. 175). Cultural exchange in the context of EBP as an innovation has diffused at an amazing pace. This process of global diffusion of EBP was aptly described by Gray, Plath, and Webb (2009). Today, there are several international networks that promote EBP and EBP-related devices such as national guidelines, research cooperatives, and clearinghouses. Within the Cochrane Collaboration alone, more than 28,000 people from more than 100 countries contribute to the advancement of EBM and EBP. This group of countries includes high-income as well as low- and middle-income countries across the world.

In sum, we embrace the idea that research on EBP, educational infrastructures available for EBP education and training, and application infrastructures for EBP worldwide are all in their early stages of development, and that this book only reflects the state of the art at this time in EBP's historical trajectory. It is apparent there are good reasons for expecting more advances in EBP.

Ethics of evidence-based practice

One of the most important factors that explains our dedication to EBP in both of its meanings, and which has been a driving factor in the authorship of this book, is the importance of the ethical dimension of EBP.

"The concept of value refers to beliefs that human beings as individuals or human societies as collective systems internally and cohesively maintain, cherish and expect others to accept" (Soydan, 2010a, p. 132). Ethics are based on value judgments of our actions as good or bad, right or wrong, and acceptable or not. In a nutshell, the most central ethical rule of social work can be expressed as follows: Do no harm! Doing harm to clients is bad, wrong, and not acceptable. The question is, how can we prevent common causes of harm to our clients? We believe that operating with weak evidence combined with a lack of transparency and client input may put social work in jeopardy and harm clients. Exposing clients to interventions that lack evidence would mean experimenting with clients without knowing possible outcomes, thus ignoring ethical considerations. Due to ignorance, we might at times use interventions that have questionable evidence and most probably cause harm. Those cases may lead to violations of our most dearly held professional ethics.

Ethics of EBP practice should be studied on two levels: Ethics pertaining to the knowledge base of EBP and those pertaining to the process model of EBP. One of the most prominent social workers who has consistently returned to ethical aspects of social work in general and evidence-based social work practice in particular is Eileen Gambrill. In an article (Gambrill, 1999), she contrasted EBP with authority-based practice. Her characterization of the differences of knowledge used in these two contrasting models revealed the ethical foundations on which these models are based. In applying EBP, practitioners are expected to conduct systematic searches for the best available evidence and critically appraise the information at hand (or, as described later in this book, rely collectively on the infrastructural resources of the organizational setting in which implementation is taking place). Such processes will reveal: (1) beneficial forms of interventions supported with clear evidence obtained by controlled studies; (2) interventions likely to be beneficial or promising; (3) interventions with a tradeoff between beneficial and adverse effects; (4) interventions with unknown effects; (5) interventions unlikely to be beneficial; and (6) interventions likely to be ineffective or harmful (Gambrill, 1999).

In contrast, authority-based practice is supported by inert knowledge, false knowledge, and pseudoscience. Gambrill (1999) defined inert knowledge as content knowledge that lacks the procedural grounds required to use it in practice. False knowledge refers to beliefs that are not true, not permissive of questioning, and that have very little direct bearing on reality. Pseudoscience, Gambrill observed, refers to information that makes scientific claims but provides no supporting evidence. She attributed the following characteristics to pseudoscience: reliance on anecdotal experiences, discouragement of critical appraisal of assertions, lack of substantiation, lack of skepticism, ignoring or explaining away falsifying evidence, use of ambiguous language, and delivering of untestable assertions.

> Relying on pseudoscientific methods to inflate and promote claims is a common propaganda method in the professions. Classification of clients into psychiatric categories lends an aura of scientific credibility to this practice, whether or not there is any evidence that such a practice is warranted or it is helpful to clients.
>
> *(Gambrill, 1999, p. 345)*

Thus, finding, retrieving, appraising, matching, and implementing the best available evidence and evaluating outcomes become a necessary but not sufficient precondition of ethically justifiable and acceptable social work. Furthermore, ethically defendable interventions require a process of vetting the best available evidence in relation to client values, preferences, and circumstances and assessing the entire treatment process in the context of clinical and other circumstances pertinent to the situation.

The EBP process model and its scientific standards represent an ethical tool for navigating professional uncertainties to the best possible benefit of clients. This is in strong alignment with the ethical codes of social work's professional organizations. The code of ethics of the National Association of Social Workers (2008) in the United States reads: "The mission of the social work profession is rooted in a set of core values. These core values, embraced by social workers throughout the profession's history, are the foundation of social work's unique purpose and perspective" (para. 3). These core values pertain to service, social justice, dignity and worth of the person, importance of human relationships, integrity, and competence. Similarly, the code of ethics of the British Association of Social Workers (2012) states:

> Ethical awareness is fundamental to the professional practice of social workers. Their ability and commitment to act ethically is an essential aspect of the quality of the service offered to those who engage with social workers. Respect for human rights and a commitment to promoting social justice are at the core of social work practice throughout the world.
>
> *(p. 5)*

Social workers cannot compromise the ethical codes of the profession and must avoid authority-based social work practice.

Cost-effectiveness and cost–utility analysis

Cost-effectiveness analysis in the context of effectiveness studies of interventions is a historical offspring of the EBP paradigm and becomes meaningful when comparing the outcomes of different interventions for the same or similar diseases, threats to public health, and social problems. Cost-effectiveness studies were originally developed to compare health-related interventions and services. Later, they were applied to public health prevention programs. Although the implementation of cost-effectiveness analysis in social work has been limited so far, we expect that social work interventions will be increasingly subject to such scrutiny.

Cost-effectiveness analysis can be defined as the study of expected benefits, harms, and costs of alternative interventions and programs to improve health conditions. Cost–benefit analysis measures outcomes of interventions in natural units such as number of lives saved, life years gained, cases prevented, pain-free days, cases successfully diagnosed, and complications avoided. In this sense, cost-effectiveness analysis is different than cost–benefit analysis, which measures monetary values attributed to program outcomes, and cost–utility analysis, which is a type of cost–benefit analysis that includes a quality-of-life variable pertinent to morbidity using health indexes such as quality-adjusted life years (QALYs).

Because different health care interventions are not expected to generate the same outcomes, it becomes crucial to understand and assess both the costs and consequences of alternative interventions (Robinson, 1993a). If comparisons can be made, resources can be redirected to achieve more with less input. Cost-effectiveness information is crucial for decision makers to make appropriate use of public taxes and other national resources. However, it is

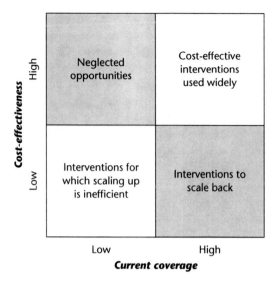

FIGURE 1.1 Efficiency of interventions

Adapted from Jamison et al., 2006.

essential that cost-effectiveness information is communicated in the context of the burden caused by a specific disease. Figure 1.1 illustrates how cost-effectiveness and the burden of disease are related.

Highly cost-effective interventions that cure diseases that highly burden a population are the most efficient from a resource and burden perspective. For example:

> Antimalarials and insecticide-treated bednets are cost-effective measures that, in certain countries, would avert a large burden of disease. If possible, countries would finance all measures that would improve health, but as every country faces a tight budget or constrained capacity to deliver services, the avertable burden of disease is an essential piece of information that policy makers require when choosing between otherwise similarly cost-effective interventions.
>
> *(Jamison et al., 2006, pp. 52–53)*

On the other hand, treatment for leishmaniasis, a parasitic disease that occurs in the tropics and subtropics, is cost-effective but applicable only to a limited number of people. Scaling up such a treatment would be inefficient and unlikely in countries that must use very limited resources to address the significant burden of other diseases such as malaria.

The shortcomings of cost-effectiveness studies have been debated among economists. Consider the case of an intervention with long-lasting effects.

That intervention would become relatively more cost-effective if it was discounted over time. Currently, cost-effectiveness analysis considers costs but not time. As an alternative, cost–utility analysis is recommended. Cost–utility analysis uses the QALY, a utility-based unit, as the outcome measure when comparing the cost of different intervention methods. "To calculate the number of QALYs resulting from a particular intervention, the number of additional years of life obtained are combined with a measure of the quality of life in each of these years to obtain a composite index of outcome" (Robinson, 1993b, p. 859). However, critics of cost–utility analysis have suggested that it discriminates against elderly people, makes illegitimate interpersonal comparisons, disregards equity considerations, and infuses bias into quality-of-life measures. In light of the current debate, cost–utility analysis is considered the best method of assessment but cost-effectiveness analysis remains a promising tool and should be used with due sensibility (Robinson, 1993b).

At this point, it may be unclear how cost-effectiveness or cost–utility analyses may be useful in social work. Consider some of the social plagues of our times and the number of people affected. For example, violence is a huge problem in many societies. Offenders are incarcerated and large amounts of taxpayer funds are spent on the criminal justice system. Offenders, victims, and their families are affected perhaps for a lifetime, causing not only human suffering but also significant expenditures for treatment of mental health problems and lost employment revenues. Understanding the relative cost-effectiveness of violence prevention interventions and programs in contrast to postviolence interventions is crucial for the well-being of individuals and the society in which they live. We believe cost-effectiveness and cost–utility analysis must go hand in hand with effectiveness studies of social, behavioral, and educational interventions.

The structure of the book

The objective of Chapter 2 is to explore and describe EBP as a process and professional culture. We provide an account of its origins, aims, and mission. We also provide a historical perspective because we believe historical accounts are helpful to understand the evolution of EBP from a linear perception of the relationship between sources of scientific evidence to a complex, interactive, and dialectical model in which various components interact. A generic model of EBP as first envisioned is presented. The creation of EBP in the context of interaction between the best available scientific evidence; client characteristics such as values, traditions, and acceptance; and organizational and professional factors such as worker skills and values and organizational structures is explored. EBP is related to other concepts such as EBPs and interventions and evidence-informed practice.

Expanding upon the generic EBP models introduced in the previous chapter, in Chapter 3 we describe one of the three components of EBP: scientific evidence. We define scientific evidence and elaborate on the concept of evidence hierarchy. In this context, we also provide an account of scientific validity and factors that threaten internal validity. Scientific evidence is generated using various types of study design; we describe various types of experimental and nonexperimental study designs that are commonly employed. We also describe methods of synthesizing results of outcome studies, including systematic research reviews and meta-analyses. As the originators and leading generators of systematic research reviews, the Cochrane and Campbell collaborations are presented and their approach described. Methods of evidence dissemination, particularly evidence-based clearinghouses, are described. This chapter concludes with an important note on the limits of knowledge.

In Chapter 4, we explore the organizational context of EBP, including staff motivation, leadership support, resource allocation, and dedication to a learning organization culture. The locus of the social work profession in modern societies is the organization. EBP takes place in the context of human services organizations. However, organizational factors may or may not facilitate the EBP process; as research and experience show, organizational factors may at times be barriers to successful EBP. Using this examination of organizational context as a backdrop, we then elaborate on issues of evidence dissemination, translation, implementation, and sustainability—components without which EBP would be a hollow promise.

Chapter 5 discusses the challenges and controversies pertaining to the use of EBP in social work practice settings. In this chapter, we identify and describe challenges of the profession as a backdrop to the emergence of EBP. The social work profession has historically defined its mission as operating in the service of individuals and communities, the underprivileged, the oppressed, and the neediest in society. However, supporting, empowering, and treating clients is a professional activity that takes place in real-world conditions subject to limitations and constraints. In this chapter, we explore some of these limitations and constraints, including the complexity of social and behavioral problems; the conceptual models that govern social work practice and their capacity to accommodate or challenge EBP; the limits of knowledge, even under the best circumstances provided by enhanced access to better scientific evidence; organizational constraints; and problems associated with evidence-to-action processes.

Chapter 6 outlines controversies pertaining to EBP. We provide an account of the most frequent objections and elaborate on points made by opponents of EBP. These include a shortage of coherent and consistent scientific evidence, difficulties in applying evidence to the care of individual patients and clients, and barriers to the practice of high-quality medicine and social work, as well as factors unique to EBP such as the need to develop new skills, limited time and resources, and a paucity of evidence that EBP works. There are also misperceptions that EBP denigrates clinical expertise, ignores patient values and preferences, promotes a cookbook approach to practice, is a cost-cutting tool or an ivory-tower concept, is limited to clinical research, and leads to therapeutic nihilism in the absence of evidence from randomized trials.

The objective of Chapter 7 is to examine globalization of evidence from the perspective of transportability. We begin the chapter by relating global transportability to general scientific issues of external validity and generalizability. We describe the role and challenges of replication studies, which constitute the classic backbone of generalizability, and therefore validity, of evidence across boundaries. We address recent developments in implementation of interventions in culturally diverse societies and connect those efforts to the translation and transportation of evidence in light of globalization. In this context, we introduce the concept of country prototypes. We conclude the chapter with a case description borrowed from the work of one of the authors, who is engaged in a project to bring evidence-based interventions to China.

The final chapter summarizes the main themes covered in the book. We elaborate on future directions based on challenges that EBP currently faces and may face in the future. Chapter 8 also addresses opportunities for disseminating and implementing EBPs through the creation of a new professional culture in social work, beginning with the training of social work students in academic and community-based settings, as well as the development of academic–community partnerships dedicated to the translation of research into practice.

2

EVIDENCE-BASED PRACTICE

In this chapter, we explore and provide an account of evidence-based practice (EBP) as a process and professional culture, including its origins, aims, and mission. A historical perspective is necessary to understand the evolution of EBP from a linear perception of the relationship between sources of scientific evidence to a dialectical model in which various components interact. Generic models of EBP are presented. The creation of EBP in the context of interaction among the best available scientific evidence; client characteristics such as values, traditions, and acceptance; and organizational and professional factors such as worker skills and values and organizational structures are explored. EBP is related to other concepts such as EBPs and interventions and evidence-informed practice.

As noted in Chapter 1, in this chapter we use *evidence-based medicine* and *evidence-based practice* interchangeably depending on the context being discussed. Both terms refer to similar principles, although the former is commonly used in health-related contexts and the latter in social contexts.

Let us start by defining EBP. At this stage of its evolution, the concept of EBP has two main components:

- First, EBP is an intervention supported by empirical evidence.
- Second, EBP is a process of applying an evidence-based intervention in a specific sociocultural context.

In this chapter, we examine various aspects of each of these components. However, at this point we would like to clarify that we view both of these components as important and indispensable aspects of EBP, which differs from most (but by no means all) literature on EBP. In many instances, particularly in the everyday language of professionals and laypersons, EBP is conceptualized according to the first component. As outlined in this chapter, this component has been the primary historical focus of EBP. EBP as a process is a more contemporary concept, introduced first as a standalone process and later in the context of other human services professions, such as social work, education, and law enforcement.

The second component of the definition is as fundamental as the first. The idea of EBP as a process is a new and innovative attempt to develop a professional culture; if further advanced, it carries the promise of radically changing the work culture of professionals and others, as well as the context of client–patient treatment. In this sense, EBP is a professional mind-set or culture of professional practice, as indicated by the title of this book.

Origins of evidence-based practice

EBP doubtlessly has its background in evidence-based medicine (EBM). Perhaps the most-cited definition of EBM was coined by Sackett and his colleagues as follows:

> Evidence based medicine is the conscientious, explicit, and judicious use of current best evidence in making decisions about the care of individual patients. The practice of evidence based medicine means integrating individual clinical expertise with the best available external clinical evidence from systematic research.
>
> *(Sackett, Rosenberg, Muir Gray, Haynes,*
> *& Richardson, 1996, para. 2)*

Most interpretations of this specific definition begin by emphasizing a process—the interaction between, and integration of, evidence, patient characteristics, and clinical (structural) circumstances in an intervention. Later in this chapter, we do the same. Similarly, in our view, EBM as a process is the translation of the best available scientific evidence to implementation and practice. However, we start with the concept of evidence itself as we seek a historical understanding of the origins of EBM and EBP.

The concept of scientific evidence in therapeutic interventions or in more general terms is related to the truth of a theoretical assertion or the validation of an assertion in real-life practice and experience. From a universal and historical perspective, it may be interpreted in the realm of the human inclination and desire to know the truth and explain phenomena in a valid fashion. In Western traditions, evidence is related to a great extent to experimental thinking. However, it would be false to assume that the experimental mind is exclusively a Western virtue, given the historical emphasis of Eastern traditions in China and India on wisdom and cosmology.

Although the modern concept of EBM is relatively very young, the concept and practice of medicine based on the best available evidence have existed in some form for a very long time. Paradoxically, the experimental mind and the authoritative mind seem to have existed side by side both in the history of scientific progress and in terms of therapeutic intervention. As illustrated by the James Lind Library (www.jameslindlibrary.org), our knowledge has been successively progressing from the fallacy of making misleading claims toward the practice of making insightful, valid claims about the effects of therapeutic intervention. Seen in this perspective, the modern concept of EBM is a promising step in this very direction.

In his 1951 doctoral thesis, J. P. Bull (1959) provided numerous anecdotal as well as verified accounts of experimental thinking and practice in the known history of human societies. Claridge and Fabian (2005) described the historical development of EBM in four stages—the ancient, Renaissance, transitional, and modern eras—which in our view is a reasonable way of structuring historical events. In the following section, we briefly characterize these four developmental stages. These brief, chronological presentations highlight the work of various scientists and practitioners. However, our presentation is far from a comprehensive historical exposé and does not include numerous other figures that deserve mention as contributors to our collective heritage of the events leading to the modern understanding of EBM in the 21st century.

EBM during ancient times

For obvious reasons, knowledge of this period is limited to anecdotal studies. Nevertheless, as illustrated in Bull's 1959 article, there are many accounts of the existence of an experimental mind among ancient humans. We borrow two meritorious examples from Claridge and Fabian (2005), which they retrieved from the James Lind Library.

The first anecdote is an early sign of experimental thinking 2,000 years ago in one of the precursors to modern Western civilization; the second example is from China more than 1,000 years ago. Both anecdotes provide an indication of early awareness of the merits of comparative, experimental approaches in understanding the causes of differential effects.

> Then Daniel said to the guard whom the master of the eunuchs had put in charge of Hananiah, Mishael and Azariah and himself. "Submit us to this test for ten days. Give us only vegetables to eat and water to drink; then compare our looks with those of the young men who have lived on the food assigned by the king and be guided in your treatment of us by what you see." The guard listened to what they said and tested them for ten days. At the end of ten days they looked healthier and were better nourished than all the young men who had lived on the food assigned them by the king.
>
> *(Claridge & Fabian, 2005, p. 548)*

The second example of interest comes from the Song Dynasty. In 1061, Ben Cao Tu Jing reportedly said, "In order to evaluate the efficacy of ginseng, find two people and let one eat ginseng and run, the other run without ginseng. The one that did not eat ginseng will develop shortness of breath sooner" (Claridge & Fabian, 2005, p. 548).

Between ancient times and the Renaissance, around 1000 AD, an important series of books was published by an Iranian scientist, Ibn Sina, known as Avicenna in the West. Ibn Sina's *Canon of Medicine* summarized and synthesized medical knowledge, albeit in a relatively crude fashion, into a comprehensive review of literature and experience. His approach to testing of medications became famous because of its experimental orientation. Ibn Sina suggested the substance being tested must be pure, it should be tested on an uncomplicated disease, the dosage must match the strength of the disease, and the outcome must be consistent. Furthermore, he argued that testing substances on animals may not be an accurate substitute for human tests (Bull, 1959). The *Canon of Medicine* remained the authoritative source of knowledge for many centuries, and many of the basic approaches advocated by Ibn Sina still stand today as components of controlled studies.

EBM during the naissance of modern science

From an evolutionary perspective, the 17th and 18th centuries constituted a period of significant advancement in the foundation of modern science. Especially in continental Europe and the British Isles, innovative methods in physics, statistics, and surgical sciences began emerging concurrently. This evolution included the emergence of modern social science methodology during the second half of the 18th century among a group of economists in Edinburgh, Scotland (Soydan, 1999).

James Lind, a surgeon with the British navy, is considered the pioneer of the first controlled clinical trial, which was conducted in 1747. Lind is the namesake of the James Lind Library, a depository of literature illustrating and explaining the development of treatment trials in health care. Lind published *A Treatise of the Scurvy* in Edinburgh, the current home of the James Lind Library, in 1753.

Characterized as a severe vitamin C deficiency, scurvy plagued populations that lacked adequate access to fruits and vegetables for centuries. Sailors were especially affected, given that perishable food could not be stored properly and consumed during lengthy naval expeditions.

The following is a key passage from Lind's treatise (adopted and edited by Claridge & Fabian, 2005; some of the original language is not modernized):

> On the 20th May, 1747, I took twelve patients in the scurvy on board the Salisbury at sea. Their cases were as similar as I could have them. They all in general had putrid gums, the spots and lassitude,

with weakness of their knees. They lay together in one place, being a proper apartment for the sick in the fore-hold; and had one diet in common to all.

Two of these were ordered each a quart of cyder a day. Two others took twenty-five gutts of elixir vitriol three times a day upon an empty stomach, using a gargle strongly acidulated with it for their mouths. Two others took two spoonfuls of vinegar three times a day upon an empty stomach, having their gruels and their other food well acidulated with it, as also the gargle for the mouth. Two of the worst patients, with the tendons in the ham rigid (a symptom none the rest had) were put under a course of sea-water. Of this they drank half a pint every day and sometimes more or less as it operated by way of gentle physic. Two others had each two oranges and one lemon given them every day. The two remaining patients took the bigness of a nutmeg three times a day, of an electuray recommended by an hospital surgeon made of garlic, mustard seed, rad. raphan, balsam of Peru and gum myrrh, using for common drink barley-water well acidulated with tamarinds, . . . with the addition of cremor tartar, they were gently purged three or four times during the course.

As I shall have occasion elsewhere to take notice of the effects of other medicines in this disease, I shall here only observe that the result of all my experiments was that oranges and lemons were the most effectual remedies for this distemper at sea.

(p. 549)

Besides being an example of an early well-documented and controlled trial, the story of scurvy also illustrates complications during the journey from *bench to trench*, or from research to application. The practice of using citrus as an anti-inflammatory remedy was common among the Portuguese by the 1500s. During a long expedition in 1601, Sir James Lancaster, commander in the British navy, observed:

Here two of our men, whereof the one was diseased with skuruie, and other had bene nine moneths sicke of the fluxe, in short time while they were on the iland recoured their perfect health. We found in this place great store of very holesome and excellant good greene figs, oranges, and lemons very faire.

(Markham, 1877, p. 18)

Unintentionally, it seems, Lancaster observed a quasi-experiment when sailors on one of the four vessels under his command received several teaspoons of lemon juice as extra nutrition during a period of food scarcity on board. Later, he observed that many sailors had fallen sick on the other three ships.

However, it wasn't until the mid-1700s when James Lind conducted his experimental study that a causal relationship was established between a regimen of citrus and recovery from scurvy. It would take another 40 years before Sir Gilbert Blane was able to convince British naval authorities to adopt a preventive diet for their sailors (Claridge & Fabian, 2005).

As Claridge and Fabian (2005) summarized, the James Lind Library is rich with many other examples of experimental thinking, notably in surgical science and practice during this historical period. For example, British surgeon William Cheselden's records of surgical techniques to remove bladder stones (lithotomy) during the early 1700s included outcome differences (mortality) based on the age group of the patients—an example of one method to fairly assess medical interventions. In France, the surgeon Ambroise Paré experimented with different treatments for burns on the human body:

> Treatment with standard medical practice vs. that recommended by a "country woman." The country woman stated that . . . I should lay two raw Onions beaten with a little Salt; for so that should hinder the breaking out of blisters or pustules . . . the next day found those places of his body whereto the Onions lay, to be free from blisters, but the other parts which they had not touched, to be all blistered.
>
> *(Claridge & Fabian, 2005, p. 549)*

Obviously, there exists not only a significant span of time but also tremendous advances in methodology between the treatment of burns using onions during the early 1700s and today's understanding of EBM, represented by the international Cochrane Collaboration; contributions by Sackett and his colleagues on EBM processes; advanced, mandatory, or recommended evidence guidelines; and user-friendly evidence-based clearinghouses. As so meritoriously noted by Claridge and Fabian (2005), a transitional period bridges this temporal and scientific gap.

EBM during the transitional era

This era began during the 1800s and ultimately led to the modern era of medicine, the beginning of which arguably is directly related to the British physician Archie L. Cochrane's 1972 book, *Effectiveness & Efficiency: Random Reflections on Health Services*. As described by Soydan (1999), the foundations of scientific methodology, including comparative methods and statistical measures, rapidly developed during the 19th century. Social and statistical analysis became the central concern of scholars from all scientific communities, including social workers. A review of pioneering medical scientists during this period reveals their advocacy for and practice of medical and behavioral information collection, systematization, and comparison as methods of understanding medical issues and improving medical treatment and other interventions.

Kenneth W. Goodman (2003) traced the intellectual birth of EBM to Thomas Beddoes, an English physician who in an 1808 letter to Sir Joseph Banks proposed two strategies to address "the prevailing discontents, imperfections, and abuses, [*sic*] in medicine" (p. 4), namely the systematic collection and indexing of medical facts and increased publication of research results. Goodman (2003) poignantly interpreted the approach as follows:

> Thomas Beddoes is suggesting a moral link between information management and medical practice. He is proposing outcomes research and fantasizing about systematic reviews; demanding databases and hoping for data mining; insisting on broader dissemination, and doing so two centuries ago, or before the World Wide Web would, at least in principle, put every publication on every desktop.
>
> *(p. 5)*

In 1834, a French physician by the name of Pierre Charles Alexandre Louis published his *Essay on Clinical Instruction*, introducing his *numerical method* as a tool for clinical assessment and establishing his legacy as the founder of modern epidemiology. As quoted by Goodman (2003), Louis asserted:

> As to different methods of treatment, it is possible for us to assure ourselves of the superiority of one or other . . . by enquiring if the greater number of individuals have been cured by one means than another. Here it is necessary to count. And it is, in great part at least, because hitherto this method has not at all, or rarely been employed, that the science of therapeutics is so uncertain.
>
> *(p. 5)*

In the United States, Dr. Benjamin Waterhouse conducted the first smallpox vaccination trials around 1800. The concept of inoculation was controversial and it took time to introduce the smallpox vaccine as a public health procedure. When Waterhouse published his first essay in 1799, *New Inoculation*, his ideas received mixed reactions; some applauded, some doubted, and many, especially his physician colleagues, criticized and ridiculed (Cohen, 1980). In June 1800, with a vaccine he received from England, Waterhouse successfully vaccinated his 5-year-old son—the first case of vaccination in the United States. To publicly verify that the vaccine worked, he wanted to test it on a larger scale. He wrote to the Small-Pox Hospital in Brookline, Massachusetts:

I have collected everything that has been printed, and all the information I could procure from my correspondents, respecting this distemper (cow-pox), and have been so thoroughly convinced of its importance to humanity that I procured some of the vaccine matter, and therewith inoculated seven of my family. The inoculation has proceeded in six of them exactly as described by Woodville and Jenner, but my desire is to confirm the doctrine by having some of them inoculated by you. . . . If you accede to my proposal, I shall consider it as an experiment in which we have co-operated for the good of our fellow citizens, and relate it as such in the pamphlet I mean to publish on the subject.

(Cohen, 1980, p. 92)

Waterhouse was supported by Presidents Jefferson and Madison, both of whom were very interested in the vaccination issue, and ultimately received honors from medical societies both at home and abroad.

Advancement of knowledge on topics such as the relationship between microorganisms and infections, coupled with the introduction of anesthesia and the discovery of X-rays, provided the immediate chronological backdrop to further developments in methods of randomized controlled studies and the first explicit shift from opinion-based medicine to medical care based on the systematic measurement of patient treatment outcomes. Perhaps no one represents this transition more so than Ernest Amory Codman (1869–1940), an American physician who developed the *end result idea*. His approach emphasized the collection of systematic information on 5- by 8-inch cards, including preoperative and postoperative data, representing an early version of outcome studies. Furthermore, Codman strongly advocated for making the information cards available to the public to ensure transparency.

For example, from 1911 to 1916, he recorded data for 337 patients who were discharged from his hospital and reported 123 medical errors that were not properly reported. He sent copies of his records to other hospitals and requested they implement the same policy to create standards for benchmarking (Swensen & Cortese, 2008). Codman's end result idea gained much opposition in the medical community. He advocated for professional advancement and primacy to be based on proven systematic knowledge and specialization, whereas the medical community practiced seniority as the principle of decision making (Kaska & Weinstein, 1998). The controversy prompted him to resign in 1914 from Massachusetts General Hospital, where he practiced surgery. However, Codman's ideas were ultimately recognized and manifested in the establishment of the American College of Surgeons' Committee for Hospital Standardization in the late 1920s, which later became the Joint Commission on Accreditation of Hospitals, then the Joint Commission on Accreditation of Healthcare Organizations, and now simply the Joint Commission. Several modern researchers credited Codman as the pioneer of EBM (Claridge & Fabian, 2005; Kaska & Weinstein, 1998; Swensen & Cortese, 2008).

The advent of the randomized controlled trial (RCT) was an important step in the development of EBM. Perhaps one of the earliest examples of a well-conducted RCT is a study conducted in 1931 by J. Burns Amberson and colleagues (Diaz & Neuhauser, 2004). The researchers conducted a clinical trial testing the use of sanocrysin to treat pulmonary tuberculosis and reported their findings in the *American Review of Tuberculosis*. They divided 24 patients into two pair-matched groups of 12 and used a single coin flip to assign the subjects to sanocrysin treatment or a control treatment. To reduce observer bias, treatment assignments were only known to two of the authors of the report and the nurse in charge of the ward. The researchers followed the patients for between 16 months and 3 years, and ultimately concluded that use of sanocrysin was not justified (Diaz & Neuhauser, 2004).

In 1937, G. W. Theobald reported findings of an experiment on the effects of calcium and vitamins A and D on incidence of pregnancy toxemia. Women in their 24th week of pregnancy were randomized (by each subject drawing a bead from a box that contained equal numbers of blue and white beads) into two groups. The experiment group received calcium lactate and vitamins A and D in predesigned daily dosages, whereas the other group served as a control. Results indicated that those receiving dietary supplements experienced fewer incidents of hypertension, headaches, insomnia, edema, and other negative outcomes. Theobald (1937) concluded that "the difference in the incidence of 'complications' between the two groups must, if not due to chance, be attributed to the substances given" (p. 1399).

Another early example of an RCT involved streptomycin, an antibiotic originally used to treat pulmonary tuberculosis that was isolated at Rutgers University in 1943. Beginning in the mid-1940s, the Medical Research Council in the United Kingdom conducted clinical trials that featured randomized allocation of patients, although the term *random allocation* was rarely used at the time. The trials were based on British physician Austin Bradford Hill's series of articles in the *Lancet* in 1937 describing principles of random allocation. Patients were assigned to different treatment groups using a statistical series based on random sampling of numbers at each medical center involved in the study. In the treatment group, patients received streptomycin and bed rest, whereas those in the control group received only bed rest. The details of the random allocation series were unknown to the coordinator and the investigators, and kept in sealed envelopes. After a patient was accepted for treatment and before admission to the streptomycin treatment hospital, the envelope was opened and the card in the envelope indicated to which group the patient was assigned. Patients were not told before admission that they would receive special treatment. Control patients did not know at any time while receiving treatment that they were in a control group—in fact, they received the same treatment they would have experienced under normal circumstances. Streptomycin and control patients were largely kept in separate wards. These randomized controlled studies of streptomycin in the mid-1940s have been recognized as a milestone in the history of random allocation of patients, although most of the principles were not as novel as many believe (Yoshioka, 1998).

Before proceeding to an overview of the advancement of EBM during the last few decades, let us summarize the lessons learned from historical events discussed in the previous sections. What historical experience and insights have been gained during centuries of human civilization to form the backdrop to the emergence of a modern understanding of EBM?

It seems obvious that at least three fundamental components of EBM were developed during a lengthy historical period; namely, the intellectual provinces of the comparative mind, the experimental mind, and the numeric mind. These components seem to be embedded in the human experience and were developed alongside the advancement of complex skills. James Lind's experiments stand as glorious and sophisticated historical examples of comparative and experimental methods. With the birth of modern statistical principles, an understanding of how numbers may be structured and used for better explanation and knowledge of medical phenomena has developed. Later, principles of random allocation and control mechanisms were developed and became increasingly sophisticated, creating the vital operational tool of EBM. It appears to us that all foundational components of EBM were in place by the 1960s and 1970s, albeit after a long and painful historical development. The publication of *Effectiveness & Efficiency: Random Reflections on Health Services* by Archie Cochrane (1972) served as a simple but necessary trigger of our modern understanding of EBM.

Modern era

Modern EBM has been characterized by two events. The first, as previously mentioned, was the publication of Cochrane's *Effectiveness & Efficiency*; the second, an almost parallel event, was the development of a new approach to training medical students launched in 1967 by David Sackett and colleagues at McMaster University in Canada. Interestingly, the former referred to EBM as the use of *gold-standard* evidence (evidence-based interventions) in medical practice, whereas the latter referred to EBM as a process of effective and sustainable implementation of evidence-based interventions in real-life situations.

Archie Cochrane, an epidemiologist, was commissioned by the Nuffield Provincial Hospitals Trust to write a book evaluating Britain's National

Health Service. Cochrane focused his attention on more informed and equitable health care. As a backdrop to his perspective, he declared in the book that his professional career was affected by early life experiences; first traveling in Europe during the 1930s as a medical student and observing poverty and disparities, and then spending 4 years as a medical officer in German prisoner-of-war camps. He served in a camp in which more than 20,000 prisoners had a daily diet of approximately 600 calories each. Prisoners faced epidemics of typhoid, diphtheria, infections, and jaundice. Medication was limited to aspirin and skin antiseptics. The young physician thought many would die of diphtheria in the absence of specific therapy. However, only four deaths occurred during the outbreak, three of which were due to gunshot wounds inflicted by the Germans. He concluded:

> This excellent result had, of course, nothing to do with the therapy they received or my clinical skill. It demonstrated, on the other hand, very clearly the relative unimportance of therapy in comparison with the recuperative power of the human body.
>
> *(Cochrane, 1972, p. 5)*

The second experience of importance during these formative years was in another camp for prisoners with tuberculosis. Many died. During World War II, there was no evidence or knowledge that streptomycin was an effective therapy for tuberculosis. Cochrane experienced the reality of a lack of evidence-based therapy. Although he had clinical freedom to use various treatments, he noted:

> My trouble was that I did not know which to use and when. I would gladly have sacrificed my freedom for a little knowledge. I had never heard then of "randomised controlled trials," but I knew there was no real evidence that anything we had to offer had any effect on tuberculosis and I was afraid that I shortened the lives of some of my friends by unnecessary intervention.
>
> *(Cochrane, 1972, p. 6)*

Cochrane's book, powered by his historical experiences, became the modern document of EBM, in which Cochrane returned to Sir Austin Bradford Hill's principles of random allocation and defined the RCT as the best tool for producing high-quality evidence. In this book, Archie Cochrane emphasized the importance of access to high-quality evidence as the foundation of accurate, effective, transparent, and equitable health care.

The impact of Cochrane's book cannot be emphasized enough. It led to the establishment of the evidence-based Cochrane Centre, which in

March 1993 became the UK Cochrane Collaboration. The concept of the Cochrane Collaboration was presented at a conference organized by Kenneth Warren and Fredric Mosteller at the New York Academy of Sciences and in October 1993, and the international Cochrane Collaboration was formally launched at its first colloquium in Oxford, England. Today, the Cochrane Collaboration is the single most influential international network dedicated to locating, appraising, and synthesizing effectiveness studies (RCTs and quasi-experimental designs) of health interventions. The Cochrane Collaboration publishes the Cochrane Library, perhaps the most focused and comprehensive source of evidence on health, mental health, and public health. In 2012, the number of reviews in the Cochrane Database of Systematic Reviews exceeded 5,000. Its impact factor in 2011 was 5.715. More than 30,000 people work with the network in more than 100 countries, including more than 70% who are authors of Cochrane reviews. A dozen regional centers and nearly 20 center branches organize training, review production, and other related activities. The scientific standards of the collaboration have affected and elevated the standards of many evidence-producing organizations, scientific communities, and agencies that produce professional guidelines. Since 2011, the collaboration has maintained an official relationship with the World Health Organization. As discussed later in this chapter, the Cochrane Collaboration also has served as the role model for the international Campbell Collaboration, a clearinghouse focused on education, crime and justice, and social welfare.

Published in 1997 by David Sackett, Scott Richardson, William Rosenberg, and Brian Haynes, *Evidence-Based Medicine: How to Practice and Teach EBM* is widely viewed as the bible of EBM. In 1995, Sackett and Rosenberg published a small article in which they declared the need and rationale for EBM. They defined the issue as follows:

> Given the extremely rapid growth of randomized trials and other rigorous clinical investigations, the issue is no longer how little of medical practice has a firm basis in such evidence; the issue today is how much of what is firmly based is actually applied in the front lines of patient care. For although we clinicians really *do* need to keep up to date with clinically-important information, direct observations suggest that we usually fail to do so.
>
> *(Sackett & Rosenberg, 1995, p. 620)*

They based their assessment in part on their experiences since the late 1960s at McMaster University, where Sackett helped develop a new medical program. In their article, Sackett and Rosenberg reviewed available empirical studies demonstrating the gap between a growing amount of evidence and the absence of this evidence in medical practice. Specifically, they conducted

a study of the self-reported information needs of 47 physicians. They concluded that, during an average half-day of medical practice, four decisions
would have been changed if clinically useful evidence had been available
and used. Only 30% of information needs were met in clinics. The physicians reported three barriers to adequate access to evidence: lack of time to
keep up to date with current evidence, out-of-date textbooks, and disorgan-
ized patient records. Another study (Antman, Lau, Kupelnick, Mosteller,
& Chalmers, 1992) employed a comprehensive meta-analytic approach
and revealed that most textbooks failed to recommend thrombolytic therapy, even for well-defined indications of heart attack, 6 years after the first
meta-analysis showed it to be efficacious. As a result of these and other
insights, Sackett and his colleagues (1997) outlined EBM as a professional
work model. Essential professional components of evidence-based medical
practice included lifelong and continuing education; seeking and applying
evidence-based medical summaries developed by others; and learning about,
accepting, and using evidence-based protocols developed by colleagues.

The classic EBM model and its offspring are presented later in this chapter. However, at this point we elaborate on the relationship and continuity
between EBM and EBP as designed for social work and other related professional fields, such as education, rehabilitation of criminals, mental health,
public health, and policy development.

Evidence-based social work practice

Although the term *evidence-based social work practice* has been a direct adaptation
of *evidence-based medicine* for the last decade or so, it would be a mistake not
to recognize the longstanding scientific tradition in the social and behavioral
sciences that has significantly paralleled the tradition in medical sciences, as
described in previous sections. The adaptation of language was pioneered by
scholars such as Eileen Gambrill and Leonard Gibbs (Gambrill, 1999, 2001;
Gibbs, 2003; Gibbs & Gambrill, 2002) in the United States and Geraldine
Macdonald (1999) and Brian Sheldon (2003) in Europe, and internationally
by a group of scholars associated with the Campbell Collaboration (Boruch,
Soydan, de Moya, & the Campbell Collaboration Steering Committee,
2004; Gray, Plath, & Webb, 2009). However, there was a prelude to these
developments of the early 2000s, including the work of Edward Mullen and
James Dumpson (1972) in *Evaluation of Social Intervention*. In this section, we
briefly present the historical underpinnings of EBP in the social sciences.

Scientific analysis of society, human behavior, and the foundations of
action for societal change was established in the 18th century through several mostly concurrent developments. Most notably, the writings of a group
of scientists and economists in Scotland that included Adam Smith, Adam
Ferguson, and John Millard, as well as the work of Enlightenment pioneers

in France, made major contributions to our current understanding of scientific analysis of society and human behavior (Soydan, 1993a, 1993b, 1999, 2012).

For instance, Adam Ferguson reformulated an old concept about human progress in his *law of progression*, a basic assumption that human nature integrates a desire to improve the conditions of society and humankind. Although the 18th century served as the period during which the foundations of social scientific methodology were developed, the 19th century was the era of formulating how this scientific knowledge (evidence) could and should be used to improve human behavior and change societal and human circumstances for the better. In general, the concept was that problem-generating social and human conditions could and should be addressed by employing scientific analysis, the central concern of the post French Revolution era. During the early 19th century, Henri Saint Simon pioneered a science-based model of societal betterment (Soydan, 1999). Many others followed, including figures such as August Comte (positivism) and Karl Marx (Marxism).

If we had to cite one important development during the modern era that significantly influenced EBP, our choice would be the idea of the *experimenting society* developed by Donald Campbell, the namesake of the international Campbell Collaboration. This concept represents an accumulation of several decades of thought and scholarship that combined the development of scientific methodology and techniques with a longstanding dedication to the use of social sciences in public policy. Campbell (1988) dedicated a book chapter to the idea.

The experimenting society

It is critical to point out the fundamental resemblance between Donald Campbell's professional experience and that of many of the pioneers of experimental medicine whose work has been described in previous sections. Campbell was a methodologist who developed the modern principles of applying experimental and quasi-experimental research designs in the social and behavioral sciences. In this sense, he was a true frontline scientist who understood the merits (and deficits) of experimental designs in terms of scientific knowledge production. He wrote: "They know me for my lists of threats to validity in quasi-experimental research and for my list of design alternatives that will help render these threats less plausible" (Campbell & Russo, 1999, p. 10). Campbell continued:

> Since 1969 (Campbell, 1969e) at least, this concern has been focused on applied social science, on treating the ameliorative efforts of government as field experiments. In the American social science community,

this falls within the designation of *policy research*. My aspect of it is known as *program evaluation*. I am reporting here on our experience in developing methods for program evaluation and their implications for the question, "Can the open society be an experimental society?"

(Campbell & Russo, 1999, p. 11)

Campbell's idea of the experimental society was influenced by Karl Popper's philosophy of science. Popper advocated falsifiability and not verifiability as the decisive criterion of empirical science, or in other words, scientific evidence. He famously stated that "it must be possible for an empirical scientific system to be refuted by experience" (Popper, 1972, p. 41). Interestingly, Popper was also an arduous defender of the *open society*, a democratic and transparent society, in contrast to the one advocated by Karl Marx and others (Popper, 1962). Not surprisingly, as much as Campbell viewed the methodology and technique of experimentation as the gold standard of scientific evidence and as an important component of the experimenting society, he also expressed a certain degree of pessimism, doubting that his utopian model would persist given the historical absence of such a society. However, he also modified his pessimism by pointing out that, in his model, utopia is a process rather than a social structure or a goal in and of itself, as many historical concepts of utopia have been.

The most fundamental characteristic of the experimenting society, Campbell stated, is its scientific, problem-solving, and self-healing orientation. The human environment is loaded with endless correlations. Positivists once assumed it was possible to establish and accumulate evidence about all correlations, ultimately creating a map of everything in the human environment. However, this assumption proved to be impossible in a dynamic, interactive, and ever-changing environment. Campbell wrote:

> From among all the observable correlations in the environment, humans and their predecessors focused on those that were manipulative correlations. From this emerged the human predilection for discovering "causes" rather than mere correlations. In laboratory science, this search is represented by experiment, with its willful, deliberate intrusion into ongoing processes. Similarly for the ameliorative scientist: Of all of the correlation observable in the social environment, we are interested in those few that represent manipulative relationships, in which—by intervening and changing one variable—we can affect another. No amount of passive description of the correlations in the social environment can sort out which are "causal" in this sense. To learn about the manipulability of relationships one must try out manipulation.

(Campbell & Russo, 1999, pp. 23–24)

The best possible way of obtaining evidence on how interventions work and what outcomes they produce, Campbell concluded, is randomized assignment models. "Although I am a strong advocate of good quasi-experimental designs in which randomization is not possible, detailed consideration of specific cases again and again reinforces my belief in the scientific superiority of randomized-assignment experiments" (Campbell & Russo, 1999, p. 24).

In terms of the philosophy of the experimenting society, Donald Campbell reiterated the wisdom of Karl Popper and some of his contemporaries. It is, of course, a scientific society "in the fullest sense of the word 'scientific.' The scientific values of honesty, open criticism, experimentation, willingness to change once-advocated theories in the face of experimental and other evidence will be exemplified" (Campbell & Russo, 1999, p. 16). Furthermore, it is an active society (modeled after Etzioni) that promotes exploratory innovation as opposed to inaction; a learning society (modeled after Dunn); and a society that is honest, self-critical, egalitarian, and committed to testing reality.

In sum, although EBP is an adaption of EBM, the idea of EBP has its own historical foundations embedded in the dedication of humankind to societal betterment and scientific development. The idea of using scientific evidence to remedy societal problems dates back at least to the late 1700s and developed significantly beginning in the early 1800s. We find the most explicit and influential progress in the early advancement of modern EBP in the work of Donald Campbell. This history represents the linear perception of the relationship between scientific evidence and problem solving—the connection of a problem to a scientifically supported solution. A more sophisticated stage, the dialectical model of EBP in which various components interact, is the focus of the following sections of this chapter.

Evidence-based practice as a process

As noted earlier in this chapter, EBP as a process was first formulated as EBM by Sackett and his colleagues in the mid-1990s as a way to help medical professionals make better-informed, conscientious, explicit, and judicious decisions. This also encouraged, or in fact presupposed, patient participation in treatment decision making. Several decades later, the original definition of EBM and EBP stands exceptionally intact and strong. However, the original definition has been the subject of debate, opposition, distortion, and clarification. A definition that captured all essential dimensions of EBP as a process with great applicability in social work practice was suggested by Allen Rubin, an American social worker:

> EBP is a process for making practice decisions in which practitioners integrate the best research evidence available with their practice

expertise and with client attributes, values, preferences, and circumstances. When those decisions involve selecting an intervention to provide, practitioners will attempt to maximize the likelihood that their
clients will receive the most effective intervention possible in light
of the following: (1) the most rigorous scientific evidence available;
(2) practitioner expertise; (3) client attributes, values, preferences, and
circumstances; (4) assessing for each case whether the chosen intervention is achieving the desired outcome; and (5) if the intervention is not
achieving the desired outcome, repeating the process of choosing and
evaluating alternative interventions.

(Rubin, 2008, p. 7)

The essential message of this model is that the three elements of EBP are all
important and necessary dimensions of making the best possible intervention
decision. In essence, achieving the best possible client outcome is contingent
on the best possible integration of practitioner expertise, client values and
expectations, and the best available evidence.

Later, this model was slightly revised, given a more user-friendly and
realistic characterization, and illustrated (Figure 2.1).

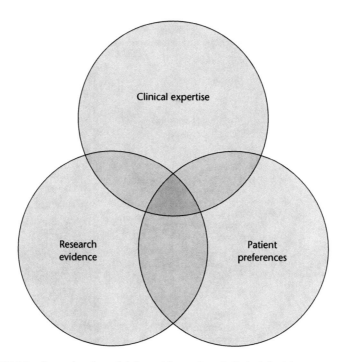

FIGURE 2.1   An updated model for evidence-based clinical decisions

Adapted from Haynes, Devereaux, and Guyatt, 2002.

This definition of EBM may be seen as a simple modification of the original model, but it emphasizes the prominence of the organizational setting in which EBP takes place. *Clinical state and circumstances* refers to the conceptualization of a service organization that may function both as a facilitator and moderator of any evidence-based intervention being implemented (see Chapter 4). *Clinical expertise* represents expertise in integrating research evidence with client preferences and actions in the specific setting of the organization. This model does not necessarily indicate that the service organization itself exists, functions, and strives to survive in larger settings that include components such as social policy arrangements, legislation, economic structures, and cultural patterns. However, it would be correct to stress that the Haynes, Devereaux, and Guyatt (2002) model of EBP operates in a macro environment whose impact is not always very clear.

Later, Sholonsky and Wagner (2005) adapted the Haynes et al. model and detailed all three components to demonstrate the cyclical nature of EBP when applied to an individual client (Figure 2.2). During the cyclical process, current best evidence is integrated with assessment of risk, and resources are directed to clients at highest risk. Action is taken in the context of the clinical state and circumstances as well as client preferences.

We characterize this model of EBP as a dialectical model—a system in which interacting components may not always be harmonious and may have contradictory perspectives and values. For example, even if evidence

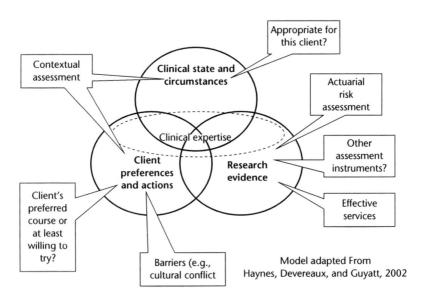

FIGURE 2.2 The cyclical nature of evidence-based practice

Reproduced from Sholonsky & Wagner, 2005, with permission.

indicates that an abortion is necessary for the survival of a patient, this intervention method may conflict with the patient's value system and ultimately her personal preference, or may be prohibited by law. A dialectical model of EBM advances beyond earlier conceptualizations of evidence-to-practice models that were linear or characterized by simple feedback mechanisms. In a complex dialectical model, a decision is contingent on the specific client, organizational, and cultural context.

The EBP model was originally implemented in clinical settings, first in medical practice and later in other human services. In its simplest form, clinical application of the model involves a client or patient and a professional. However, real-life situations may involve more than two individuals. A social worker in a school environment may have a student client whose parents and teachers become a part of the treatment program, the social worker may consult a supervisor and colleagues, and so on.

However, the EBP model is applicable in many other settings. For example, a job creation intervention may involve several neighborhoods or communities and an antiviolence intervention may involve all classes in a school or all schools in a district. On an aggregate level, evidence-based policy may involve entire subpopulations (e.g., all teenage girls in a state, all households under a certain income level).

Steps in applying evidence-based practice

The EBP model (Sackett et al., 1997) was formulated as a five-step process of working with patients. Although various aspects of this model have been modified over the years, it is our assessment that the five-step model remains a lasting and standard EBP approach. This model is conceptualized as a very flexible tool that presupposes critical thinking, willingness to pursue lifelong learning, openness to new ideas, mindfulness about new and strong evidence, and avoidance of the fallacy of authority-based information. We briefly review the steps of the model and point out some critical issues related to applying the model in social work practice.

Step 1: Formulating an answerable question

Like scientists and other professionals, social workers are confronted with problems that need a solution. Problems that clients experience or issues that a troubled community faces may come in various degrees of complexity—they may be apparent or vague, simple or perplexing, at least at first glance. The initial task of the social worker is to systematize and assess the many aspects of a problem and narrow them to an answerable question. Even at this stage, it is good practice to consider what effective evidence-based interventions are available. After all, a problem becomes treatable only when there is an effective or promising intervention available to be implemented.

As any professional knows, problem formulation is a process and may take some time in real-life settings. The professional may need to use a trial-and-error method and revise the problem several times before establishing a solvable question.

Step 2: Finding the evidence

This step of the EBP process is typically perceived as the process of reviewing all sources of knowledge for evidence-based interventions using Internet-based search engines. However, conducting a comprehensive and complex data search can be time consuming and beyond the skills of many professionals. Although we would agree with the need for an evidence search on a broad platform, we would hope that most organizational settings will offer support to individual workers on a daily basis. In other words, EBP can be implemented optimally if social work takes place in organizations that maintain an infrastructure that helps individuals or groups of workers simplify this stage. In Chapter 4, we describe organizational structures that promote and routinize implementation of EBP and point out advances in service delivery organizations to eliminate the burden of exhaustive data searches.

Furthermore, since the launch of the first models of EBP, much progress has been made in bringing evidence to end users. At one time, individual practitioners were expected to conduct time-consuming data searches nearly every time they had to find a solution to a client problem. Over the years, various types of data support systems have been developed and tailored to efficiently address the needs of individual workers and service delivery organizations. Practitioners and their organizations can now easily access and navigate tailored tools such as authorized guidelines, advanced sites such as the Cochrane and Campbell libraries, and evidence-based clearinghouses. These and other evidence sources are reviewed in Chapter 3.

Step 3: Critically appraising evidence quality

In rational, open, democratic societies of the modern world, scientific knowledge is given great prominence in comparison to other sources, such as religious or normative knowledge. Although as scientists we take a similar position, we also want to emphasize that scientific knowledge is associated with problems that often mislead professionals.

First of all, all scientific and good evidence is merely an estimate of an assumed truth. Estimates are probabilities and not absolute truths. Strong scientific evidence provides the probability of a given event, such as when

X (independent factor) occurs, Y (dependent factor) will follow. This specific scientific circumstance, a condition of scientific evidence production, limits our knowledge and mandates caution.

Furthermore, production of scientific evidence is always threatened by factors that undermine the quality and strength of the evidence. Most of these factors are identified as threats to validity of evidence and widely described in the literature. However, scientists continue to produce biased evidence and journals and other scientific media continue to publish biased studies, not necessarily intentionally but often due to practical difficulties, lack of skills, and negligence. This type of threat and others such as publication bias and other biases have been identified and described by both the Cochrane Collaboration and the Campbell Collaboration. Since the emergence of these two international evidence production networks, there has been an increased awareness of evidence quality and strength, which represents a positive step for EBP.

However, from the perspective of service delivery, either as an individual worker or an institution, the risk of flaws in scientific evidence will always be present. Social workers and service delivery organizations need to exercise caution, particularly when considering interventions with weak, flawed, or nonexistent evidence.

Acquiring the skills to independently appraise the quality and strength of evidence is necessary. Such training not only involves the basic ability to read and understand threats to validity, but also the ability to separate good- and high-quality sources of evidence from those with less acceptable qualities.

Step 4: Matching evidence and client

One of the greatest innovations of EBP is the enumeration of conditions in which scientific evidence can or may be implemented. In the original model of EBP (Sackett et al., 1997), the locus of EBP was identified as the interaction of the best scientific evidence, client values and expectations, and the professional expertise of the practitioner. In a revised and refined model by Haynes et al. (2002), EBP was defined as the adaptation and integration of the best available scientific evidence, client preferences and actions, and clinical conditions and circumstance as shaped by the practitioner's expertise and interaction with all involved parties. Later in this book, we further expand and elaborate on the component of clinical conditions and circumstance by highlighting the organizational settings in which service delivery takes place. A specific aspect of matching the evidence with the client is the discourse on translation and implementation of evidence-based interventions, which we addressed in a previous book (Palinkas & Soydan, 2012).

As the EBP models referred to in this book imply, the ultimate implementation of an evidence-based intervention is a result of trade-offs, interactions, and negotiations orchestrated by the social worker. The process of
EBP is the best possible optimization of all components of the model, as
agreed to by all parties, in the pursuit of the best possible outcome for the
client. This process requires transparency and is contingent on the professional skills of the social worker to derive the best model of EBP in each
individual situation.

Step 5: Following up on outcomes

The purpose of any evidence-based intervention is the betterment of clients,
be they individuals, family members, a secondary school, or a neighborhood.
Outcomes of EBP need to be monitored to observe and assess whether the
intended results occurred and if any unintended (and potentially harmful)
results were produced.

Follow-up and measurement of outcomes can be formally accomplished
in several ways and complemented with informal observations and conversation. Rubin (2008) described the use of behavioral recording forms, individ-
ualized rating scales, and standardized scales, in addition to providing sources
of such tools.

EBP and related concepts

During a 2006 conference titled Improving the Teaching of Evidence-Based
Practice in Social Work, a group of researchers addressed challenges facing
EBP (Proceedings of the Conference, 2007). One of the obstacles discussed
was the revision of the original definitions and intentions of EBP. Changing
definitions of scientific concepts over time, and even changing terms for
scientific concepts, is a common practice in the social sciences. These shifts
might be an expression of scientific refinement as well as distortions of original intentions embedded in definitions and terminology.

Whatever the case may be, EBP proved to be no exception. Over the
years, the terms *evidence-informed practice* and *evidence-supported practice* in
particular have been used as alternatives to EBP in both literature and everyday language. During the evolution of EBP, some scholars at one point or
another have used alternative terms such as *evidence-informed practice* without
redefining the concept (e.g., Bowen & Zwi, 2005; Chalmers, 2005; Gambrill,
2008). At times, evidence-informed practice seemed to represent a broader
perspective of the research base of professional practice that included various
types of research designs, or simply acknowledged that available evidence is
not always the best and thus loosened the rigorous rules required by the gold

standard of EBP (see Chapter 3). Although proponents of EBP consider the gold standard as the desired basis for professional practice, they also realize that such an approach is not always possible or feasible in real-life situations, particularly because of the scarcity of rigorous and high-standard research in various practice fields (e.g., Bowen & Zwi, 2005; Rycroft-Malone, 2008). These issues remain unsettled, and whether or not the gold standard of evidence—represented by randomized controlled studies of the outcomes of social and behavioral interventions—should or could be the only basis of EBP will be for future developments to determine.

However, the term *evidence-informed practice* may also take unexpected turns. For example, Arnd-Caddigan (2011) borrowed from one of the core competencies prescribed by the Council on Social Work Education, the certifying institution of schools of social work in the United States, and noted that such a "broad term can encompass a great deal of difference in interpretation" (p. 372). She defined *practice-based evidence* as a form of evidence-informed practice and developed an epistemology that may legitimize practice-based evidence in therapeutic interventions. In her conclusion, Arnd-Caddigan (2011) stated:

> Much of this knowledge is on an implicit level. When trained in reflective practice and adept at entering an intersubjective field with a client, the therapist may be able to discern, even if not articulate, that it *feels* different to be with a client. Much of this implicit knowledge can be brought to the symbolic narrative domain. Therefore, the next step is to push for articulation, exploring how it feels different. These feelings become the evidence that change is occurring. While the direction and nature of the important changes that occur in therapy are usually not predictable, it does not mean that they have not occurred, or that they are not discernible post hoc.
>
> *(p. 376)*

Similarly, practice-based research (PBR) has been presented by a number of researchers as an alternative to EBP throughout the years (e.g., Dodd & Epstein, 2012; Nevo & Slonim-Nevo, 2011). One of the strongest proponents of PBR is Irwin Epstein, a prominent professor with Hunter College's Silberman School of Social Work (Dodd & Epstein, 2012; I. Epstein, 1996, 2001). In introducing the agenda of their book, Dodd and Epstein (2012) referred to a 2001 book chapter by Epstein in which PBR is defined as "the use of research-inspired principles, designs and information gathering techniques within existing forms of practice to answer questions that emerge from practice in ways that inform practice" (p. 11). Furthermore, they characterized PBR as:

research conducted by practitioners for practice purposes. The goal is to inform practice and practitioners throughout the research process. Thus, PBR emphasizes immediate practical applications by practitioner-researchers who conduct PBR studies. These studies may be conducted by individual social workers, teams of social workers or multi-disciplinary teams, with or without research consultation. When that consultation is available however, it is fully collaborative rather than dominated by research considerations.

(Dodd & Epstein, 2012, p. 5)

Dodd and Epstein (2012) made it clear that PBR is conceptualized "as a reaction to conventional ways of thinking about, writing about and teaching social work research" (p. 13). The authors differentiated between EBP and PBR, with EBP representing prior research that is deductive, privileges RCTs, and is driven by academics, whereas PBR represents practice wisdom that is inductive, rejects RCTs, and is driven by practitioners.

It is not an objective of this book to critique the concepts and definitions related to or developed alongside EBP. However, we want to note that, although EBP and PBR are not compatible on a number of issues, notably their approach to and appreciation of the value of scientific designs and scientific rigor in determining outcomes of social work interventions, they agree significantly in terms of the role of professional practice and practitioners. For instance, the classic definition of EBP as a process suggests that a practitioner's professional judgment and skills are vital components of the process. Without the professional judgment to integrate and harmonize all components of the EBP process, there would be no EBP. Furthermore, it is notable that EBP acknowledges the importance of client involvement and client characteristics. Gambrill (2006) aptly indicated how and in what ways EBP involves clients, including: (1) taking into consideration client differences when implementing tested and generalized interventions powered by scientific vigor; (2) supporting clients to develop critical appraisal skills; encouraging client input in the design and critique of research related to practice; (3) involving clients as informed participants in decision making (as strongly promoted by the Cochrane and Campbell collaborations); and (4) involving clients to take advantage of their firsthand and unique knowledge in the translation and implementation of EBPs.

Similarly, before rejecting RCTs as a rigorous research design, it is necessary to properly understand and assess the context in which RCTs and similarly useful research designs are tailored to operate. Randomized controlled effectiveness studies, when conducted properly with enough statistical power, generate the best possible or least biased estimates of the effects of social work interventions. However, they can only do so in a context of generalizability, which means implementation and replication in diverse, real-life conditions. Furthermore, there are limits to evidence generation and knowledge, as any proponent of EBP would agree (Soydan, 2008b).

3

EVIDENCE AND ITS SOURCES

Expanding upon the previously introduced generic models of evidence-based practice (EBP), in this chapter we describe one of the three components of EBP: scientific evidence. Scientific evidence is available in various forms. Historically, the most established source of scientific evidence has been primary research, traditionally a responsibility of universities and academic institutions. However, primary research is no longer restricted to universities. New, important evidence producers include think tanks, private industry-based laboratories, government agencies, and nonprofit organizations. Their products are published in books, scientific journals, graphic media, and online.

For the last 15–20 years, particularly following the development of the Cochrane and Campbell collaborations, systematic research reviews and meta-analyses of primary research have widely influenced our sources of knowledge and challenged the limits of primary research. Systematic research reviews and meta-analysis reports, as well their plain-language summaries, are disseminated by Cochrane and Campbell collaborations and other institutions that have assumed responsibility for specific topic areas.

Besides sources of primary research and institutions that develop and disseminate systematic research reviews, new resources such as evidence-based guidelines and high-quality clearinghouses have been developed to tailor and disseminate scientific evidence in increasingly accessible and comprehensive ways to defined clients or end users.

In this chapter, the concept of the hierarchy of evidence is introduced. Based on a typology of evidence hierarchy, various experimental designs are examined. The chapter is organized in two main sections: (1) primary research, including systematic reviews and meta-analyses and (2) tailored or packaged evidence.

Primary research subsections include randomized controlled studies, quasi-experimental studies, time-series designs, cohort designs, and case-control studies. In addition, we elaborate on the role and merit of qualitative designs in the context of EBP. In this context, we also describe systematic research reviews including meta-analysis. Evidence packages specifically tailored for professionals are explored with a focus on evidence-based clearinghouses.

Scientific evidence and questions in EBP

The rationale for developing a broad variety of scientific methods of data collection and analysis is the diversity of real-life problems and scientific questions that garner our interest. Scientific designs of inquiry are specially tailored to solve specific types of questions. They represent tools in a tool box and serve different purposes. In many instances, they work parallel to and in conjunction with one another in the pursuit of the most valid answers to our questions. In social work practice, real-life problems are diverse and complex; therefore, questions that emerge in EBP are similarly diverse and complex. Social workers may need to know not only how effectively a specific intervention or treatment works but also other important issues, such as the acceptability of a treatment among different client populations; the social epidemiology of a certain problem in communities or specific client groups and their families; the socioeconomic conditions of a neighborhood; the migration history of a specific population and how that background generates opportunities and constraints; and many other questions pertinent to successful social work. No single research design can tackle all of these problems alone. Various research designs are needed. Additionally, all research designs are legitimate for the purposes for which they are designed and tested.

In EBP, different types of evidence may be needed in different contexts. However, because a major concern of EBP is to bring about change and betterment based on well-informed decisions, there is a primary focus on and interest in what works for which clients under what circumstances. This specific focus of social work practice and EBP necessitates a quest for the best possible research designs to generate evidence of the relative effectiveness of social work interventions. This is the gateway to what is known as *evidence hierarchy*. Evidentiary hierarchy refers to the rigor, validity, and conclusiveness of evidence in the context of the efficacy and effectiveness of social, behavioral, and other interventions (Rubin, 2008). In EBP, evidence hierarchy (or evidentiary hierarchy) doesn't refer to the general and unspecified supremacy of one research design over another. Evidence hierarchy refers to a ranking of research designs that measure the efficacy and effectiveness of interventions (treatments, programs) in terms of their ability to control for biases that may distort estimates of outcome measures, and therefore may misguide end users and cause harm.

Evidence hierarchy

A simple Internet search for images that represent evidence hierarchy yields an incredible number of images and typologies developed by individual authors and institutions. They are based on an understanding of how research designs control for and decrease bias, and the conclusiveness of results they may yield. See Figures 3.1 and 3.2 for several examples of how evidence hierarchy is illustrated.

In the following section, main research designs that occupy different levels of the hierarchy are described. As evident in the figures, systematic reviews and meta-analyses occupy the highest rank of the evidence hierarchy. It is assumed that systematic reviews (and meta-analyses, when included in reviews) provide stronger and more trustworthy evidence than individual studies. This assumption is based on several factors. First, by definition a systematic review includes results of more than one study, and therefore

FIGURE 3.1 Research evidence hierarchy in the health sciences

Adapted from http://ebp.lib.uic.edu/nursing/node/12: retrieved November 13, 2013.

Rank	Methodology	Description
1	Systematic reviews and meta-analyses	**Systematic review:** review of a body of data that uses explicit methods to locate primary studies, and explicit criteria to assess their quality.
		Meta-analysis: a statistical analysis that combines or integrates the results of several independent clinical trials considered by the analyst to be "combinable" usually to the level of re-analyzing the original data, also sometimes called: pooling, quantitative synthesis.
		Both are sometimes called "overviews."
2	Randomized controlled trials (finer distinctions may be drawn within this group based on statistical parameters like the confidence intervals)	Individuals are randomly allocated to a control group and a group who receive a specific intervention. Otherwise the two groups are identical for any significant variables. They are followed up for specific end points.
3	Cohort studies	Groups of people are selected on the basis of their exposure to a particular agent and followed up for specific outcomes.
4	Case-control studies	"Cases" with the condition are matched with "controls" without, and a retrospective analysis used to look for differences between the two groups.
5	Cross sectional surveys	Survey or interview of a sample of the population of interest at one point in time
6	Case reports	A report based on a single patient or subject; sometimes collected together into a short series
7	Expert opinion	A consensus of experience from the good and the great.
8	Anecdotal	Something a bloke told you after a meeting or in the bar.

FIGURE 3.2 Evidence hierarchy

Adapted from Shadish et al., 2002, p. 12.

a larger body of evidence should be stronger. It is a question of the whole being greater than the sum of its parts. Second, systematic reviews appraise the quality of individual studies and exclude those that do not qualify based on quality criteria. Third, systematic reviews are conducted with strict transparency, making procedures, limitations, and biases explicit and allowing the reader to fully and independently assess the quality of the review.

In the bottom ranks of the hierarchy we find expert opinion, anecdotal evidence, and editorials. Prior to the emergence of the Cochrane and Campbell collaborations, it was common practice to rely on expert opinion as the ultimate evidence to establish the truth of a scientific proposition. Expert opinion refers to the judgment of a group of distinguished experts in a specific scientific field. This practice was historically characterized by a lack of evidence, a lack of rigor in the available evidence, and scientific controversies resulting from ignorance within the scientific community. Expert opinion is by definition based on authority and leaves little room for independent and transparent examination and critique. Expert opinion is still practiced, albeit not as a mainstream vehicle of establishing evidence, and is often necessitated by inevitable limits of knowledge and uncertainties embedded in estimates of scientific outcomes. However, in the evidence hierarchy, expert opinion is placed near the bottom and is not recommended; if used, expert opinion should be employed with great caution and transparency by established institutional sources of evidence such as the *Community Guide* (www.thecommunityguide.org), which is maintained by the Centers for Disease Control and Prevention. Other variations of expert opinion include anecdotal evidence and opinions expressed in editorials and other venues, and are subject to the same critique.

Validity

Validity is evaluated in terms of two major criteria. First, and as a basic minimum, is what can be called *internal validity*: Did in fact the experimental stimulus make some significant difference in this specific instance? The second criterion is that of *external validity*, *representativeness*, or *generalizability*: to what populations, settings, and variables can this effect be generalized (Campbell, 1957)?

In his seminal 1957 article, Donald T. Campbell introduced the backbone of the concept of scientific validity in experiments in social settings. Throughout the years, Campbell's original framework regarding the validity of estimated effects was expanded upon by a number of scientists, foremost among them being Campbell and Stanley (1963), who further elaborated on internal and external validity, Cook and Campbell (1979), who expanded the validity typology into four types (internal, external, statistical conclusions, and construct validity), and Cronbach (1982), who worked extensively to develop our understanding of and ability to measure unbiased estimates of generalizability. More recently, Shadish, Cook, and Campbell (2002) elaborated on modern elements of experimentation, including counterfactual inference and variation and treatment dosage. A modern typology of various forms of validity was generated as an outcome of this development (Table 3.1).

TABLE 3.1 Modern typology of validity

Statistical conclusion validity	The validity of inferences about the correlation (covariation) between treatment and outcome
Internal validity	The validity of inferences about whether observed covariation between X (the presumed treatment) and Y (the presumed outcome) reflects a causal relationship from X to Y as those variables were manipulated or measured
Construct validity	The validity of inferences about the higher-order constructs that represent sampling characteristics. This type of validity is a measure of the applicability of the inference based on the population represented by the sample
External validity	The validity of inferences about whether the cause–effect relationship holds despite variation in participants, settings, treatment variables, and/or measurement variables

Adopted and revised from Shadish, Cook, and Campbell (2002).

Validity refers to the approximate truth or correctness of an inference (a conclusion that has been drawn from empirical evidence). An inference involves assessing empirical evidence on the basis of previous knowledge and available theories to support the conclusion; thus, the validity of an inference is contingent on human judgment and subject to uncertainty.

With reference to evidence hierarchy, introduced earlier in this chapter, it is important to remind ourselves that a higher-level research design does not guarantee more truthful inferences. Several other aspects of rigor related to the planning and execution of a study are involved and affect the validity of the study. We are cautioned by Shadish and his colleagues (2002):

> Validity is a property of inferences. It is *not* a property of designs or methods, for the same design may contribute to more or less valid inferences under different circumstances. For example, using a randomized experiment does not guarantee that one will make a valid inference about the existence of a descriptive causal relationship. After all, differential attrition may vitiate randomization, power may be too low to detect the effect, improper statistics may be used to analyze the data, and sampling error might even lead us to misestimate the direction of the effect.
>
> *(p. 34)*

Internal validity and threats to internal validity

The main concern when making an inference between X (a cause) and Y (an effect) is to confirm that X, and not any other event or variable, caused Y. A causal relationship will have internal validity when all other factors that might have caused the effect are accounted for and the relationship between X and Y is established. Interference of any other event or factor that might have caused Y is considered a threat to internal validity. In his famous 1957 article, Campbell outlined the threats to internal validity as history, maturation, instability, testing, instrumentation, regression artifacts, selection, experimental mortality, and selection–maturation interaction. Later, these threats were elaborated on by Shadish et al. (2002):

Ambiguous temporal precedence refers to confusion about which variable occurred first to produce an outcome. Causation may be bidirectional or reciprocal. Experiments are designed to create unidirectional causation by manipulating X to yield Y, which would be measured after X has occurred.

Selection is perhaps the most familiar threat and refers to differences between an average person in the intervention group and an average person in the control group at the onset of the experiment. This threat is known as selection bias. Random placement of subjects in different groups allocates subjects by chance, thus controlling for selection bias.

History refers to all real-life events that take place between the implementation of the intervention and the postintervention test that could have produced the measured outcome in the absence of the intervention. Although this type of threat can be eliminated in highly controlled efficiency studies, it becomes a challenge in field studies (i.e., effectiveness studies) that are conducted in real-life circumstances.

Maturation is a natural process most individuals experience as years pass and they age and see and do things differently. Maturation processes could produce the same outcome that the intervention is expected to produce, and thus threaten internal validity. This threat can be controlled to some extent by selecting subjects from same age group.

Statistical regression occurs when the subjects, especially in quasi-experiments, are selected because they score high or low on a given measure. When this occurs, the subjects tend to score closer to the mean on other measures, giving the impression that the measured effect is due the intervention.

Attrition occurs when subjects drop out of the experiment for various reasons, resulting in different sets of participants at the posttest and pretest stages. When fewer subjects remain in the posttest group as compared to the original sample, outcome measures may be distorted and attrition bias is possible.

Testing bias occurs when subject responses during a follow-up test are revised on the basis of an earlier test. The outcome of the follow-up test consequently can be confused with the outcome of the intervention.

Instrumentation bias is caused by shifts in the meaning of the instrument over time. Particularly in longitudinal studies, measurement items may change their nature or meaning for subjects over the life span of the study, thus creating confusion about whether or not the outcome is a result of the change in the instrument or a treatment effect.

Additive and interactive effects of threats occur when different threats interact with or inflate effects or both. Such interaction effects are very difficult to control in experiments in real-life situations.

In sum, there are many serious threats to internal validity in any experimental study. This is a major challenge and too often a pitfall for researchers undertaking experimental studies. As a result, it seems reasonable to us to conclude that not conducting experimental studies is better and safer for end users than experimental studies conducted with poor adherence to safe internal validity and poor scientific rationale.

Primary research

Randomized experimental designs

Randomized experimental designs are perceived as the prime tool for generating *gold-standard* estimates of intervention effects. What is the rationale for this perception? How are randomized experiments designed and conducted?

As evidenced in Chapter 2, the *experimental mind* has lengthy historical roots. The concept of a scientific experiment is to systematically measure effects of an action (intervention) taken for some specific purpose. Experimental study designs are perceived as having the unique ability to describe the relationship between a variation in treatment and its consequences. This ability is known as *causal description* in scientific literature (Shadish et al., 2002). However, experimental designs are not very apt at identifying the conditions under which causal descriptions occur. Understanding the underlying mechanisms of a causal description is called *causal explanation*. This condition is also known as the *black-box phenomenon*, a term often used by opponents of experimental studies to point out this specific limitation of experimental study designs. Nevertheless, experimental studies are very central to science, as explained by Shadish et al. (2002):

> First, many causal explanations consist of chains of descriptive causal links in which one event causes the next. Experiments help to test the links in each chain. Second, experiments help distinguish between the validity of competing explanatory theories, for example, by testing competing mediating links proposed by those theories. Third, some experiments test whether a descriptive causal relationship varies in strength or direction under Condition A versus Condition B (then the

condition is a **moderator** variable that explains the conditions under which the effect holds). Fourth, some experiments add quantitative or qualitative observations of the links in the explanatory chain (**mediator** variables) to generate and study explanations for the descriptive causal effect.

(p. 11)

And, very importantly for the social work profession, they add:

> Experiments are also prized in applied areas of social science [such as social work], in which the identification of practical solutions to social problems has as great or even greater priority than explanations of those solutions. After all, explanation is not always required for identifying practical solutions.

(p. 11)

Interestingly, many scientifically supported social work interventions that benefit individual clients, groups of clients, or communities work without precise information about what is happening in the black box. After all, in practical life, airline passengers are not necessarily concerned with how exactly an aircraft takes off, remains airborne, and lands safely, but rather the fact that it does so. Similarly, a medical patient is not necessarily interested in what mechanisms make a coronary bypass surgery successful but rather the fact that it is successful, allowing the patient to survive. What matters to parents supported by social services is not necessarily how a social work intervention helps their child quit using drugs, but the fact that the therapeutic intervention worked and their child is sober.

Although in all types of experiments, control and manipulation of the treatment are necessary, experiments may vary in terms of the control conditions under which treatments are administered. Table 3.2 shows the typology of experiments.

The logic of random assignment in experiments in which different groups are compared to one another is to ensure that subsamples are similar. This is achieved by using an appropriate procedure, such as a coin toss or specially designed software that ensures units are assigned to different conditions by chance. The rationale of random assignment is that randomization reduces the risk of alternative explanations for intervention effects and promises to deliver unbiased estimates of average treatment effects. If comparison groups are similar before the intervention but differ after the intervention, then postintervention differences could not have been caused by pretest selection differences. Under such circumstances, the control group serves as *counterfactual*, i.e., representing what would have happened if there was no cause to affect.

TABLE 3.2 Modern typology of experiments

Randomized experiment	An experiment in which units are assigned to receive the treatment or an alternative condition by a random process such as a coin toss or selecting from a table of random numbers
Quasi-experiment	An experiment in which units are not randomly assigned to conditions
Natural experiment	A study that contrasts a naturally occurring event such as an earthquake with a comparison condition (this often does not represent a true experiment because the cause typically cannot be manipulated)
Clinical trial	An experiment in clinical settings in which subjects are randomly assigned to a treatment group or groups and compared to a control group. These experiments are usually used to test clinical treatments and drugs, and may use small samples (providing lower statistical power)
Randomized field trial	A community-based experiment in which units are assigned to receive the treatment or an alternative condition; essentially, another term for a randomized experiment
Correlational study	Usually synonymous with a nonexperimental or observational study; a study that simply observes the size and direction of a relationship among variables

Adopted and revised from Shadish, Cook, and Campbell (2002).

There are good reasons why randomization works:

- It ensures that alternative causes are not confounded with a unit's treatment condition.
- It reduces the plausibility of threats to validity by distributing them randomly over conditions.
- It equates groups on the expected value of all variables at pretest, measured or not.
- It allows the researcher to know and model the selection process correctly.
- It allows computation of a valid estimate of error variance that is also orthogonal to treatment (Shadish et al., 2002, p. 248).

In medicine, nursing, education, and social work, randomized experiments are often referred to with terms such as randomized clinical trials (RCTs) and randomized field trials. These experiments are designed to maximize internal validity, i.e., the average estimates of effects of an intervention or treatment under the given conditions and for specific samples of the experiment are as free from selection bias as possible. Randomized experiments are designed to be conducted in highly controlled environments (also called *efficacy studies*), and as such are subject to criticism about their potential lack of generalizability to other populations without large-scale retesting in real-life conditions, which is considerably more complex and difficult to control. Therefore, multiple replications of RCTs at multiple sites (also called *effectiveness studies*) are designed to provide information about external validity, or the extent to which an intervention or treatment is valid and useful in real-life situations for different populations and sociocultural settings. This concept is addressed in more detail in Chapter 7.

Despite some inherent drawbacks, randomized controlled effectiveness studies, when conducted properly, generate the best possible or least biased estimates of the effects of social work interventions.

Quasi-experimental study designs

Although randomized controlled studies are perceived to deliver the least biased estimates, especially if they have robust statistical power and are conducted properly, they may not be feasible in real-life situations. Numerous and unmanageable obstacles may contribute to this limitation. Randomized controlled studies may be unethical to conduct, practical issues might render the approach unusable or even impossible, there might be methodological problems, or there might be funding issues.

Different quasi-experimental designs have been developed for use when RCTs are not feasible. Quasi-experimental designs are very similar to RCTs but with an important difference—they lack random assignment of subjects to different conditions. This means that selection bias may affect estimates generated by the study.

Various methodological principles have been developed to try to control bias to the greatest extent possible in quasi-experimental studies. Shadish and his colleagues (2002) elaborated on three tools. First, they recommended the identification and close study of plausible threats to internal validity to estimate the likelihood that these threats will influence the average effects of the intervention. Second, researchers could employ sophisticated procedures such as the use of multiple control groups or multiple pretests to identify and generate information about the plausibility of threats or to prevent the confounding of a certain threat to validity. Experts highly recommend controlling bias by design as a first step and saving statistical controls for later stages of the study. Third, coherent pattern matching is another strategy:

> A complex prediction is made about a given causal hypothesis that few alternative explanations can match. . . . The more complex the pattern that is successfully predicted, the less likely it is that alternative explanations could generate the same pattern, and so the more likely it is that the treatment had a real effect.
>
> (Shadish et al., 2002, p. 105)

To what extent design and statistical tools can compensate for possible bias in average estimates of quasi-experimental designs is ultimately an empirical question. For some years, researchers have taken on the task of empirically comparing relatively biased estimates produced by alternative designs to estimates of randomized controlled studies. To examine these differences among various study designs, researchers conduct between-study and within-study comparisons.

In between-study comparisons of experimental and nonexperimental studies, researchers typically include several studies executed using different research designs. Then, bias in estimations is calculated by examining the relationship between the design and the estimates of intervention effects. For example, Reynolds and Temple (1995) compared three studies, Shadish and Ragsdale (1996) compared dozens of studies, and Lipsey and Wilson (1993) compared 74 randomized and nonrandomized studies. Results have been mixed. Between-study comparisons have been criticized for not being able to determine whether differences between estimates are due to study design or other factors (Glazerman, Levy, & Myers, 2003).

Within-study comparisons estimate a treatment's effects by employing a randomized controlled group and one or several nonrandomized comparison groups. The method employed in such studies is design replication, which can be described as a reestimation of the effects by using one or several comparison groups. This method allows researchers to determine whether differences in average estimates among randomized and nonrandomized study designs are due to differences in study design or other factors such as differences in treatment environments, investigator bias, or the implementation process. Glazerman et al. (2003) conducted a within-study comparison of 12 labor market-related studies and found that measured estimates of quasi-experimental designs sometimes came close to replicating RCT-generated results. However, quasi-experimental designs often produced estimates that differed with margins of importance for policy making. This is considered an estimate of bias. Glazerman and his colleagues (2003) concluded that "although the empirical evidence from this literature can be used in the context of training and welfare programs to *improve* [nonexperimental] research designs, it cannot on its own justify the use of such designs" (p. 63). Boruch (2007) also offered a thoughtful perspective on this problem.

Observational studies

An umbrella term for another group of research designs is observational studies. When conducting randomized controlled studies or quasi-experimental studies in which random allocation is not possible, an alternative is to conduct an observational study, which is restricted by the inability to manipulate variables. At times, some observational designs are also called correlational studies. Because of different methodological problems and validity issues, observational studies typically produce more biased results than nonobservational studies, particularly randomized controlled studies. In the following section, we describe several common observational designs: the single case-study design, the cohort study design, and the case-control design.

Single case-study design

Single case-study designs involve measurements of specific variables or characteristics of an individual or a group before an intervention occurs. Following the intervention, measurements are taken of the same variables or characteristics. This study design provides baseline values that can be compared with postintervention outcome measures. As its name indicates, this design relies on observations of single subjects, such as a client in a mental health clinic. In actual studies, the sample may include a larger number of subjects, but the most common approach is to include a limited number of subjects, such as the client population of a social work agency. This design is also known as *single-system design* because the sample is often a group of people (e.g., a family, an agency's client population, a community) rather than a single person. This design has been strongly advocated for by some scholars (Kazi, Mantysaari, & Rostila, 1997; Kazi & Wilson, 1996a, 1996b) as appropriate for social workers to evaluate client progress and to use the data on an aggregate level to evaluate intervention outcomes for groups of clients.

In defining the design, Kazi and Wilson (1996b) suggested the following:

> The first step is to identify the target problem. The social worker must come up with an operational definition that will allow the client's problem to be objectively measured, and select an appropriate measurement tool. Continuous assessment over time is used as a basis for drawing inferences about intervention effects. The measurements must be regular, systematic and standardized across all phases in the single-case design. In all cases, reasonable steps should be taken to maximize the reliability and validity of the measurement procedures used.
>
> *(p. 701)*

This design usually allows inferences to be made by comparing measurements taken at different times during the life course of the same subject or system. These designs are sometimes called *time-series designs* (Rubin, 2008) because they use data observed at multiple points in time. As Gray, Plath, and Webb (2009) suggested, this design may be too intrusive in social work because of its repeated measurements, especially for vulnerable clients.

Cohort study design

Cohort study designs have existed for a long time. The underlying concept is that, during a given time period, a certain group of people exposed to a specific event would have different outcome characteristics than another group that was not exposed to the same event either during the same time period or during another period. Early examples of cohort studies include generational studies of disease prevalence among populations born in different periods, born in the same region, or with the same occupation. Later, cohort study designs became increasingly influential tools used to track the causes of various conditions in medical and social epidemiology. Although most early cohort studies were retrospective, prospective cohort studies eventually became widely used. To achieve robust inferences, cohort studies require very large samples that must be followed longitudinally, which necessitates support from complex and costly research infrastructures. Among the best cohort studies are those based on large databases such as national cancer registries or national income maintenance registries that contain extensive population-level data collected over several decades. Cohort studies have also been developed as an alternative to randomized controlled studies when RCTs are not possible or feasible.

In this study design, cohorts must be selected from similar but separate populations, and individuals in each cohort may be matched to decrease the effect of bias on inferences. In smaller samples, attrition may be a serious problem and can dramatically increase bias in results (very large samples allow better control of attrition bias). For example, attrition was not a significant issue in a cohort study of care outcomes (Lindenauer et al., 2007) that included 76,926 patients (ages 18 years and older) who were hospitalized in the United States between September 2002 and June 2005 for heart failure, chest pain, stroke, urinary tract infection, and several other conditions at 45 hospitals.

Case-control study design

Case-control study designs are similar to cohort studies in their general approach. However, the sample in a case-control study is defined by outcome characteristics among subjects rather than exposure to an event, intervention, or life experience, as in cohort studies. For example, a case–control study might compare individuals who are homeless in Los Angeles with those who are not homeless, or those who experienced trauma as a result of a major earthquake to those who were not traumatized.

To establish possible causes of an outcome (e.g., homelessness or trauma), researchers start by comparing outcome characteristics of the affected sample with a control group that does not have those characteristics and evaluating possible causes generated by exposure to certain situations. However, the complexity and quantity of possible background factors in real-life situations often cannot be controlled for or measured with precision.

Qualitative study designs

In a classic book, Strauss and Corbin (1990) stated:

> By the term *qualitative research* we mean any kind of research that produces findings not arrived at by means of statistical procedures or other means of quantification. It can refer to research about persons' lives, stories, behavior, but also about organizational functioning, social movements, or interactional relationships. Some of the data may be quantified as with census data but the analysis itself is a qualitative one.
>
> *(p. 17)*

Qualitative research designs are often attached to theoretical and paradigmatic assumptions that justify those designs. This category includes grounded theory, ethnographic approaches, historical analysis methods, phenomenological approaches, constructivist and interpretivist approaches, and action research. In social work, action research and grounded theory, as well as personal narrative (client life stories) and client–social worker conversation analysis, are among most popular qualitative approaches.

Let's examine grounded theory as an example of a qualitative design, in contrast to randomized controlled designs. Strauss and Corbin (1990) wrote:

> A grounded theory is one that is inductively derived from the study of the phenomenon it represents. That is, it is discovered, developed, and provisionally verified through systematic data collection and analysis of data pertaining to that phenomenon. Therefore, data collection, analysis, and theory stand in reciprocal relationship with each other. One does not begin with a theory, then prove it. Rather, one begins with an area of study and what is relevant to that area is allowed to emerge.
>
> *(p. 23)*

It is assumed that an interpretive theory may emerge from empirical data, but the researcher must employ four criteria for this theory to be valid: fit, understanding, generality, and control. Strauss and Corbin (1990) described these criteria as follows:

If theory is faithful to the everyday reality of the substantive area and carefully induced from diverse data, then it should fit that substantive area. Because it represents that reality, it should also be comprehensible and make sense both to the persons who were studied and to those practicing in that area. If the data upon which it is based are comprehensive and the interpretations conceptual and broad, then the theory should be abstract enough and include sufficient variation to make it applicable to a variety of contexts related to that phenomenon. Finally, the theory should provide control with regard to action toward the phenomenon.

(p. 23)

At times, proponents of qualitative research designs argue that qualitative analysis is a powerful tool for assessing causality. In their classic book on qualitative methodology, Miles and Huberman (1994) were critical of quantitative designs, particularly randomized controlled studies, suggesting that they do not reveal anything in the so-called black box. They argued that qualitative designs can tell us what is actually occurring in the black box by virtue of their approach.

Qualitative analysis, with its close-up look, can identify *mechanisms*, going beyond sheer association. It is unrelentingly *local*, and deals well with the *complex* network of events and processes in a situation. It can sort out the *temporal* dimension, showing clearly what preceded what, either through direct observation or *retrospection*. It is well equipped to cycle back and forth between *variables* and *processes*—showing that "stories" are not capricious, but include underlying variables, and that variables are not disembodied, but have connections over time.

(Miles & Huberman, 1994, p. 147)

In the context of scientific evidence and the gold-standard paradigm used by proponents of quantitative methods—in particular, the Cochrane and Campbell collaborations—the research designs assembled under the umbrella term of qualitative research tend to fall in the lower echelons of the evidence hierarchy. However, this issue remains highly contested by proponents of qualitative research designs (e.g., Denzin & Lincoln, 1994; Miles & Huberman, 1994; Strauss & Corbin, 1990). Others have sought to resolve the historical duality and contradiction between qualitative and quantitative methodologies. For example, British social scientist Ann Oakley, in her excellent treatise *Experiments in Knowing: Gender and Method in the Social Sciences* (2000), argued for eliminating the paradigm controversy. Her introductory paragraph cuts straight to the point:

My main argument goes as follows: that in the methodological literature today, the "quantitative"/"qualitative" dichotomy functions chiefly as a gendered ideological representation; that within this gendering of methodology, experimental methods are seen as the most "quantitative" and therefore as the most masculine; that these processes of methodological development and gendering cannot be separated from the ways in which both science and social science developed, and the social relations in which they were embedded; and that the goal of an emancipatory (social) science calls for us to abandon sterile word-games and concentrate on the business in hand, which is how to develop the most reliable and democratic ways of knowing, both in order to bridge the gap between ourselves and others, and to ensure that those who intervene in other people's lives do so with the most benefit and the least harm.

(p. 3)

She continued:

One crucial strategy for bringing to a close our current paradigm war is to drop the language of "quantitative" and "qualitative" approaches altogether. These terms are relative, rather than absolute, in any case: "quantitative" research often measures quality, and numbers are a frequent occurrence in "qualitative" research.

(Oakley, 2000, p. 303)

Our belief is that both quantitative and qualitative methods of scientific inquiry serve the purposes for which they were designed and each has advantages and disadvantages in terms of understanding and explaining social reality. The concept of a hierarchy of evidence was developed primarily to assess bias in the measurement of causal relationships in the context of estimating the effects of interventions. Qualitative study designs were not constructed for the measurement of effect estimates. Therefore, by definition they are located in the lower echelons of the evidence hierarchy but are certainly not devalued as scientific methods. Results of qualitative analysis often shed new light on findings of randomized studies. In fact, good researchers often look for opportunities to complement quantitative effectiveness studies with high-quality qualitative research, as argued by proponents of mixed-method research (Palinkas & Soydan, 2012).

Research reviews

Production of summaries, reviews, and critiques of previous theories, empirical results, and conclusions has been a mainstream approach in the long history of scientific exploration. In the European tradition of social sciences, *discourse analysis*, which represents a summary and critique of views, thoughts, and facts related to a given topic, has been a sign of good scientific craftsmanship. Today, discourse analysis is often limited to theoretical conversations in the social sciences, whereas a research review is employed to summarize the empirical research results of multiple studies. Traditionally, such reviews have been prepared by or under the leadership of high-profile experts in specific topic areas. However, scientific prestige may not be a good indicator of the quality of scientific evidence reviews.

Petticrew and Roberts (2006) provided several examples of biased literature reviews that misled other experts and the public. One illustrative example of the deficits of traditional research reviews is the case of vitamin C as a preventive treatment. In 1986, Nobel laureate Linus Pauling published a book that outlined the extensive literature on the benefits of vitamin C in prevention of the common cold in which he concluded that large amounts of vitamin C did in fact prevent the illness. However, it was later shown that Pauling's approach was not systematic. Paul Knipschild (1994) conducted a systematic research review involving an exhaustive search of pertinent databases, including a manual search of both unpublished and published literature that had not been indexed. He found 61 trials, of which 15 passed his strict methodological standards. On the basis of the literature, Knipschild concluded that not even massive doses of vitamin C could prevent a cold. He also noted that five of the 15 qualified trials, as well as two other studies, were not included in Pauling's review.

Many scientific journals continue to publish articles subtitled "A research review"; yet a careful examination of these articles may reveal that they were conducted without a systematic approach, lacked an adequate description of the method as to blur transparency, or simply did not adhere to high scientific standards.

Systematic research reviews and meta-analysis

The systematic research review is of much more recent vintage. It represents a response to the challenges and deficits of primary research production and utilization, and was made possible thanks to modern advances in information technology. The rapidly increasing number of publications, deficits of databases, publication bias, poor quality of published research, public desire for high-quality information, and advances in information technology are the main factors that have spurred development of systematic research reviews.

More than 50 million journal articles

Using the search terms *academic/scholarly*, *referred*, and *active*, Arif Jinha (2010) estimated the number of journal titles to be 26,206. He also estimated the number of journal articles published between 1726 (when a steady growth of journals began) and December 31, 2009, to be 50,712,009, with a margin of error of 5 million. This is consistent with estimates calculated by Björk, Roos, and Lauri (2009) the previous year. The pace of production of journal articles after World War II has been staggering and continues to rapidly increase. Although these are estimates, they provide a sense of the volume and rapid growth of journal publications. Developers and supporters of systematic reviews believe that systematic reviews can organize and synthesize research publications in well-defined topic areas for readers who otherwise could not feasibly follow the enormous influx of publications.

Deficits of electronic databases

After World War II, the number of electronic databases increased dramatically. Users no longer need to go to libraries and sift through index cards in catalog rooms. They can sit at home, in their office, or anywhere with Internet access and search electronic databases. Although journals are indexed in electronic databases, it can still be very difficult to track down all existing and relevant studies on a given topic. In a systematic Cochrane research review, Hopewell, Clarke, Lefebvre, and Scherer (2008) synthesized comparative results of electronic research and handsearching, a method developed by the Cochrane Collaboration that involves manually and systematically searching for eligible articles in identified journals.

> Thirty-four studies were included. Handsearching identified between 92% to 100% of the total number of reports of randomized trials found in the various comparisons in this review. Searching MEDLINE retrieved 55%, EMBASE 49% and PyscINFO [sic] 67%. The retrieval rate of the electronic database varied depending on the complexity of the search. The Cochrane Highly Sensitive Search Strategy (HSSS) identified 80% of the total number of reports of randomized trials found, searches categorized as 'complex' (including the Cochrane HSSS) found 65% and 'simple' found 42%. The retrieval rate for an electronic search was higher when the search was restricted to English language journals; 62% versus 39% for journals published in languages other than English. When the search was restricted to full reports of randomized trials, the retrieval rate for an electronic search improved: a complex search strategy (including the Cochrane HSSS) retrieved 82% of the total number of such reports of randomized trials.
>
> *(Hopewell et al., 2008, p. 2)*

They concluded that handsearching is a valuable tool that compensates for the deficits of electronic searches.

Publication bias

This term refers to the submission and acceptance of manuscripts for publication based on the strength or direction of the study outcomes (e.g., authors only seek to publish results that support their hypotheses). When this bias occurs, important information tends to be removed from the immediate reach of the reader and may negatively affect intervention and policy decisions. Hopewell, Loudon, Clarke, Oxman, and Dickersin (2009) assessed "the extent to which publication of a cohort of clinical trials [was] influenced by the statistical significance, perceived importance, or direction of their results" (p. 1). In their systematic review, five studies qualified for inclusion. They found that trials with positive outcomes were published more often and more rapidly than studies with negative outcomes. Furthermore, two other studies reviewed by Hopewell and colleagues (2009) showed that trials with positive findings tended to be published after 4 to 5 years, compared to 6 to 8 years for those with negative findings.

To remedy this deficit, the Cochrane Collaboration developed a method of searching unpublished *grey literature* databases, as well as a communication system for specialists worldwide to locate information about unpublished studies.

Deficits in quality of published research

It is common knowledge that many, perhaps too many, research articles are published despite deficits in the underlying research (e.g., attrition, contamination between treatment and control groups, sampling bias, statistical analysis problems). It is assumed that editorial peer review processes will identify such problems and lead to either correction of problems before manuscripts are accepted for publication or rejection of low-quality submissions. However, a systematic research review of 28 qualified studies found that "little empirical evidence is available to support the use of editorial peer review as a mechanism to ensure quality of biomedical research" (Jefferson, Rudin, Brodney Folse, & Davidoff, 2008, p. 2). Furthermore, authors are not always required to properly report their methods in scientific journals in a way that allows for transparency and independent appraisal. This is a serious problem that disqualifies many articles and reports from being included in systematic research reviews.

To remedy this problem, a variety of standards have been recommended to journals and authors, including:

- Consolidated Standards of Reporting Trials (Moher, Schulz, & Altman, 2001) for reporting the outcomes of randomized experiments;
- Journal Publication Practices in Social Work (Society for Social Work and Research Presidential Task Force on Publications, 2008);

- Transparent Reporting of Evaluations with Nonrandomized Designs (Des Jarlais, Lyles, & Crepaz, 2004) for reporting results obtained in nonrandomized investigations; and
- Standards for Reporting on Empirical Social Science Research (American Educational Research Association, 2006).

Public desire for high-quality information and accountability

The genesis of systematic research reviews coincided with a growing awareness of and desire for transparency and accountability among the public and elected representatives across democratic countries. Incidentally, this is partly an echo of Campbell's advocacy for the use of rigorous science to guide public policy (Campbell & Russo, 1999). This awareness cuts across all sectors of modern society, including health, social welfare, education, crime and justice, the labor market, and sustainable development (Papanagnou, 2011; Solinís & Bayá Laffite, 2011). The desire to effectively utilize social research is associated with increasing pressure for not only greater transparency and accountability but also effectiveness, cost efficiency, and quality in service delivery.

Advances in information technology

Systematic research reviews would not have been able to develop and prosper as they have without the technical platforms provided by modern information technology. These platforms have enabled instantaneous global communication among contributors to systematic reviews, utilization of search engines, the application of information technology in library services, the development of software necessary for processing of reviews, and effective tools of knowledge distribution.

The concept of systematic research reviews was developed by the Cochrane Collaboration for health-related sciences and practices and later adopted by the Campbell Collaboration for social sciences and practices. Today, many other public and private agencies conduct systematic research reviews, at times using Cochrane and Campbell standards. The concept of systematic research reviews has continued to evolve throughout the years, becoming a scientific specialty of sorts. Systematic review production is multidisciplinary and involves contributions from various specialties such as scientific methodology, topic expertise, information search strategies, professional editorial skills, dissemination strategies, and lobbying. The foremost authoritative source of systematic reviews is the *Cochrane Handbook for Systematic Reviews of Interventions* (Higgins & Green, 2011).

A systematic research review can be defined as a synthesis of all available empirical evidence that matches predefined eligibility criteria and pertains to a specific question or topic of interest. The methodology of systematic reviews was developed and undergoes constant refinement to identify, control, and eliminate all possible biases that may threaten the quality of the systematic review. When there is sufficient evidence (effect sizes of the impact of interventions), systematic research reviews include meta-analysis, an umbrella term for statistical methods of synthesizing effect sizes of multiple and compatible effectiveness studies. Good guidance regarding meta-analysis can be found in several books (Cooper & Hedges, 1994; Hunter & Schmidt, 2004; Lipsey & Wilson, 2001).

The Cochrane and Campbell collaborations define the core elements of systematic research reviews as follows:

- a clearly stated set of objectives with predefined eligibility criteria for studies;
- an explicit, reproducible methodology;
- a systematic search that attempts to identify all studies that would meet the eligibility criteria;
- an assessment of the validity of the findings of the included studies, for example through the assessment of risk of bias; and
- a systematic presentation, and synthesis, of the characteristics and findings of the included studies (Higgins & Green, 2011, section 1.1.2).

The example given in Table 3.3 describes a systematic research review of the effectiveness of a crime prevention intervention for juvenile delinquents known as Scared Straight. The program is widely used in several countries, despite the fact that this systematic review indicated the intervention fails to deter crime and can even increase criminal offenses.

Cochrane and Campbell collaborations

The international Cochrane Collaboration (www.cochrane.org) was formally established in October 1993 by British obstetrician Iain Chalmers and his colleagues to "help people make well-informed decisions about healthcare by preparing, maintaining and promoting the accessibility of systematic reviews of the effects of healthcare interventions" (Petrosino, Boruch, Soydan, Duggan, & Sanchez-Meca, 2001, p. 24). Chalmers became the first chair of the international network. In the early 1990s, the National Health Service in the United Kingdom initiated a research and development program with the purpose of exploring development of a national infrastructure for evidence-based health care. Chalmers and his group, which had

TABLE 3.3 Effectiveness of Scared Straight programs

Campbell collaboration research review policy brief—November 28, 2003

Does taking juveniles on tours of prison deter them from future crime and delinquency?

The policy question

A recent Illinois law mandated the Chicago Public Schools to identify children at risk of future criminal behavior and take them on tours of adult prison facilities. The law revisits the long history of using programs such as Scared Straight, which involve organized visits to prison facilities by juvenile delinquents or children at risk of becoming delinquent. The programs are designed to deter participants from future offending by providing first-hand observations of prison life and interaction with adult inmates. Do they work to reduce crime and delinquency by participants?

Results of the Campbell Collaboration review

Results of this review indicated that not only do such programs fail to deter crime but actually they lead to more offending behavior. Government officials permitting this program need to adopt rigorous evaluation to ensure that they are not causing more harm to the very citizens they pledge to protect.

Methods

Review authors conducted a vigorous search for randomized (or seemingly randomized) studies evaluating the effects of Scared Straight or similar programs on subsequent offending. They located nine randomized studies, in which seven provided outcome data making it possible to include them in a quantitative procedure known as meta-analysis. It was only possible to do this for the first posttreatment effect because most studies did not report measurements at subsequent time intervals. Unfortunately, little information on incidence, severity, and latency measures was provided, so the meta-analysis was completed using prevalence data only (the proportion of each group that failed or succeeded).

In the graph below, the seven studies used in the meta-analysis are analyzed and plotted using a Forrest graph. The study's author(s) are provided in the left column, followed by the number of participants who were arrested (or committed a new offense) compared to their total number for treatment and control groups. Treatment groups received Scared Straight or a similar program whereas control groups did not receive the intervention. Odds ratios more than 1 favor the control group whereas odds ratios less than 1 favor the experimental group. In nearly all of the studies, the odds ratios favored the control groups, and the overall meta-analysis is negative for the program (Petrosino, Turpin-Petrosino, & Buehler, 2004).

(Continued)

TABLE 3.3 *(continued)*

Scared Straight Campbell systematic review findings

Study	Treatment n/N	Control n/N	OR (95% CI Random)	Weight %	OR (95% CI Random)
Finckenauer 1982	19/46	4/35		9.8	5.45 (1.65, 18.02)
GERP & DC 1979	16/94	8/67		14.7	1.51 (0.61, 3.77)
Lewis 1983	43/53	37/55		15.3	2.09 (0.86, 5.09)
Michigan D.O.C 1967	12/28	5/30		9.5	3.75 (1.11, 12.67)
Orchowsky & Taylor 1981	16/39	16/41		15.2	1.09 (0.44, 2.66)
Vreeland 1981	14/39	11/40		13.9	1.48 (0.57, 3.83)
Yarborough	27/137	17/90		21.6	1.05 (0.54, 2.07)
Total (95% CI)	147/436	98/358		100.0	1.72 (1.13, 2.62)

Test for heterogeneity chi-square = 8.50
   df = 6 p = 0.2
Test for overall effect z = 2.55 p = 0.01

```
        .1  .2    1    5 10
       Favours      Favours
       treatment    control
```

n = number of reoffending participants; N = number assigned to group; OR = odds ratio; CI = confidence interval; Weight = amount of weight given to study in analysis.

been identifying and reviewing randomized trials pertaining to childbirth and prenatal interventions, were asked to expand their efforts to other areas of health care. Chalmers' Pregnancy and Childbirth Group was registered as a Cochrane Centre affiliate in Oxford, England, and was soon followed by other groups, such as the Stroke Group, the Canadian Cochrane Center, the Baltimore Cochrane Center—which became the New England Cochrane Center at Providence and subsequently the United States Cochrane Center— as well as the Nordic Cochrane Centre and the Musculoskeletal Group, all of which were established in late 1993.

The Cochrane Collaboration is named after British epidemiologist Archie Cochrane, who advocated using the best available scientific evidence in health care practice. In 1972, Cochrane published a persuasive book, *Effectiveness & Efficiency: Random Reflections on Health Services*, arguing that, although randomized trials had shown some treatments to be effective and others to be harmful, medical workers were often unaware of or ignored the evidence. In 1979, he proposed organizing information from pertinent trials based on medical subspecialties to make them more accessible to medical workers.

The Cochrane Collaboration is based on ten key principles (Cochrane Collaboration, 2014), paraphrased here:

1. *collaboration* with the purpose of fostering good communication, transparent decision making, and teamwork within and outside the collaboration;
2. *building on the enthusiasm of individuals* by welcoming and involving worldwide individuals with different skills and backgrounds;
3. *avoiding duplication* in a world of resource scarcity by promoting coordination and maximizing economy of effort;
4. *minimizing bias* through scientific rigor, broad and transparent participation, and avoidance of conflict of interest;
5. *keeping up to date* by ensuring that new evidence is integrated in Cochrane reviews in a timely manner;
6. *striving for relevance* by prioritizing assessment of health care interventions that matter to patients, health workers, and policy makers;
7. *promoting access* through dissemination of Cochrane reviews and other products worldwide in collaboration with other networks and in user-friendly formats;
8. *ensuring quality* by using the best methodology, being responsive to criticism, and developing quality assurance systems;
9. *maintaining continuity* by applying organizational mechanisms such as good editorial processes, statistical support, and upgrading of reviews;
10. *enabling wide participation* in the network by encouraging diverse participation, providing support, and maintaining a global presence.

Although these principles may not always be implemented without error throughout the expansive global Cochrane Collaboration, they are frequently observed in its day-to-day operations and the quality of its products. In 2011, the Cochrane Collaboration network featured more than 28,000 pro bono contributors from more than 100 countries. The Cochrane Library includes more than 4,600 contributions on the effectiveness of health and mental health interventions. Between April 2010 and March 2011, Cochrane Collaboration participants prepared 550 new protocols for forthcoming reviews, 389 new reviews, and 449 updated reviews. Full-text downloads of Cochrane reviews totaled nearly 4 million in 2010. That same year, the top five most accessed reviews were downloaded by users more than 40,000 times, and the Cochrane Library achieved a top ten impact factor. In the 2010–11 fiscal year, funders worldwide contributed more than 16 million British pounds (nearly $26 million) to support the work of the Cochrane groups. As of January 2013, there were 21 registered Cochrane Collaboration groups worldwide (www.cochrane.org).

In sum, the Cochrane Collaboration is in the vanguard of preparing, maintaining, and disseminating what works and what is potentially harmful in health, mental health, public health, and to some extent, social welfare. Its influence on quality of care extends beyond the prominence represented by its impact factor.

The establishment and success of the Cochrane Collaboration have been an inspiration and template for the development of the Campbell Collaboration in the fields of education, crime and justice, social policy, and social care. As an early expression of this effort, then-president of the Royal Statistical Society Adrian F. M. Smith (1996) stated:

> We are, through the media, as ordinary citizens, confronted daily with controversy and debate across a whole spectrum of public policy issues. But, typically, we have no access to any form of systematic 'evidence base'—and, therefore, no means of participating in the debate in a mature and informed manner. Obvious topical examples include education—what does work in the classroom?—and penal policy—what is effective in preventing reoffending? Perhaps there is an opportunity here for the Society—together with appropriate allies in other learned societies and the media—to launch a campaign, directed at developing analogues of the Cochrane Collaboration, to provide suitable evidence bases in other areas besides medicine, with the aim of achieving a quantal shift in the quantitative maturity of public policy debates.
>
> *(pp. 369–370)*

A group of individuals returned to this challenge in April 1997 during a conference titled Social Work as a Tool in the Development of Social Work Discourse, held near Stockholm, Sweden (Soydan, 1998). Two years later, several exploratory meetings—notably one headed by the School of Policy at University College London and another by the Swedish National Board of Health and Welfare in Stockholm—were held in 1999 to establish the Campbell Collaboration (www.campbellcollaboration.org), which was officially launched in February 2000 in Philadelphia, Pennsylvania. The inaugural meeting was attended by more than 80 individuals from 12 nations. An international eight-member steering group was elected and it was decided that the secretariat of the Campbell Collaboration should reside at the University of Pennsylvania (Gray et al., 2009; Petrosino et al., 2001).

The collaboration is named after Donald T. Campbell, who advocated the idea that social reforms should be based on societal experiments using rigorous scientific rules of evidence. He also believed that rigorous methods should be employed to produce estimates of the effects of societal reforms. Robert Boruch and Haluk Soydan cochaired the collaboration for its first 6 years, guiding the network's early development.

The Campbell Collaboration was established on the same principles as the Cochrane Collaboration, and its aim is to help "people make well-informed decisions by preparing, maintaining and disseminating systematic reviews in education, crime and justice, and social welfare" (Campbell Collaboration, n.d.). In January 2013, there were 82 Campbell reviews, 129 Campbell protocols, and 209 Campbell titles (brief descriptions of the first stage of reviews in development) in the Campbell Library. This is a very modest track record of systematic reviews compared to the output of the Cochrane Collaboration, but in the world of social sciences and social practices—which in many ways differs from the world of medical sciences and practices—the role of these reviews should not be underestimated. Besides its modest but increasing number of systematic reviews, the Campbell Collaboration sets the benchmark when it comes to scientific rigor and standards in social sciences, as well as determining what works in pertinent professional practice.

Sources of evidence tailored for professionals

Primary research results are traditionally published in scientific journals, books, reports, and online. As previously noted, there has been an explosion of publications, rendering access difficult or even impossible. Most professionals may not have the time, preparedness, and ability to read complicated scientific journal articles, doctoral dissertations, and other publications to keep up to date with evidence in their specialties. Recognizing this problem, the Cochrane and Campbell collaborations introduced plain-language summaries attached as introductory pages to systematic reviews, which are often written in technical language; these summaries also provide transparency for independent appraisals.

Parallel to primary research and systematic review formats, new and tailored methods of publishing research results have emerged. These new formats and sources include high-quality evidence-based clearinghouses, treatment manuals, and guidelines.

High-quality clearinghouses

A clearinghouse is an Internet-based information source. These days, the online world includes many scientific databases. Some of these databases are defined as clearinghouses. The word *clearinghouse* seems to have been imported to scientific evidence communities and their stakeholders from the world of finance, in which clearinghouse refers to an institution that ensures that a transaction between two entities is conducted properly and adheres to the rules of the game. In the context of scientific evidence, a clearinghouse is an institution that receives, reorganizes (tailors), and disseminates scientific information.

In the social sciences and professional practice, one of the first clearinghouses was *Preventing Crime: What Works, What Doesn't, What's Promising*, also known as the Maryland Report on Crime Prevention (Sherman et al., 1996), which was commissioned by the U.S. National Institute of Justice.

Interestingly, the Maryland Report was a written report and not an Internet-based information portal, but it featured the most important characteristics of what later came to be known as an evidence-based clearinghouse. The Maryland Report had a defined target group (the U.S. Congress); constructed one of the early scales for rating the quality of evidence (including ratings such as *works*, *doesn't work*, *promising*, and *don't know*); had a defined topic (crime prevention interventions); and was written in plain language. In our view, the most important contribution of this report was its development of one of the first scales for rating evidence in social, behavioral, and educational effectiveness studies.

In this book, we use the term *high-quality clearinghouse* to indicate a set of characteristics that differentiate high-quality evidence-based clearinghouses from many other information clearinghouses or databases. Soydan, Mullen, Alexandra, Rehnman, and Li (2010) listed the following characteristics as indicators of trustworthy evidence-based clearinghouses.

Target groups

A clearinghouse addresses the information needs of one or several target groups and tailors its content accordingly. Most clearinghouses are prepared for specific professional groups, such as social workers, child welfare administrators, mental health workers, and crime and justice professionals. Because of the multidisciplinary nature of many professional interventions, some high-quality clearinghouses may target more broadly defined groups and at times expand their reach to the general public.

Topic areas

Understandably, topic areas and target groups of clearinghouses go often hand in hand. A clearinghouse usually covers a primary topic area such as older adult care, child welfare, crime prevention, labor market programs, or primary education. Because of the interdisciplinary nature of most of the human services, clearinghouses often cover multiple topic areas.

Rating scales

Rating scales measure the strength of the research evidence that supports a given treatment or program. Rating scales are an indispensable component of modern clearinghouses and are constructed using scientific criteria indicating the rigor of studies in support of the treatments listed in the clearinghouse. Clearinghouses, while staying truthful to the fundamental values of scientific rigor, may adopt more rigorous or less rigorous rating scales depending on the understanding of the present state of the art within a specific topic area. In fields of practice in which there is a bounty of available evidence, scales are often more rigorous to exclude poor evidence and still retain strong evidence that supports the intervention being rated. In fields of practice in which there is a scarcity of evidence, rating scales tend to be less rigorous to avoid screening out the small amount of available evidence. Using scientific criteria pertinent to the quality and amount of intervention studies, rating scales place treatments in categories; for example, a scale might range from *well-supported* to *concerning* in reference to evidence supporting the practice. Some clearinghouses have developed additional scales to provide guidance to end users regarding the relevance of treatments in specific contexts, such as older adult care or cultural feasibility in a specific country.

Transparency

Providing transparency regarding internal procedures of a clearinghouse is a major quality indicator. Clearinghouses are expected to share with the public their procedures of data retrieval, inclusion and exclusion criteria for studies, ethical concerns, conflicts of interest, work procedures, and other relevant information. Transparency is the foundation of public trust and legitimacy. Furthermore, it is good practice to provide descriptive information to help users understand and adopt the interventions assessed and posted by the clearinghouse. Such information may include copyright issues, costs associated with implementation of the treatment, and training and mentoring available for successful implementation.

User-friendliness

Successful clearinghouses are user-friendly. The homepage of a clearinghouse must be easily recognizable and easy to find using common sense. A clearinghouse homepage hidden in some corner of a major institution's website that is difficult to locate is therefore less or not at all user-friendly. Clearinghouse websites must be technically appealing and have logical structures to ease navigation for less skilled users. Descriptive or audiovisual tutorials may help end users understand the information provided. Use of technical language may be necessary at times, but the use of plain language as much as possible will increase user-friendliness.

Cutting-edge information and updating

A high-quality clearinghouse needs to deliver up-to-date and cutting-edge information in a world in which scientific evidence is provisional. Methods, research designs, and theories of the scientific community are becoming increasingly sophisticated in an attempt to capture unexplored aspects of social reality. Human interaction and societal systems are constantly evolving and generating new problems. What is cutting-edge knowledge today may not be tomorrow. In terms of evidence regarding what works, what is promising, and what is potentially harmful in human services practice, we are becoming increasingly more sophisticated and focused. Subsequently, a high-quality clearinghouse needs to keep up with state-of-the-art evidence and revise its contents in an ongoing manner.

Sustainability

A high-quality clearinghouse needs to be sustainable. Not unexpectedly, it takes time to develop and maintain a functional infrastructure. It takes time to establish awareness of a clearinghouse among target populations and the public. Thus, a trustworthy clearinghouse is a sustainable clearinghouse that is able to serve target populations for a long time. Sustainability requires a high degree of commitment by the original funders of a high-quality clearinghouse.

An example of a high-quality clearinghouse is the California Evidence-Based Clearinghouse for Child Welfare (www.cebc4cw.org). In our view, this clearinghouse possesses all of the qualities described earlier. In addition to rating child welfare interventions, this clearinghouse provides screening and assessment tools for child welfare as well as a special section on implementation of evidence-based interventions.

Limitations of primary research

We would like to conclude this chapter with a few words of warning: "It is good science to recognize the limits of any gold standard, because a major problem in science is that it is impossible to know with 100% certainty what the truth is in any given research question" (Soydan, 2008b, p. 315).

As described in this chapter, research designs are tools employed by scientists to observe and organize the human experience and societal phenomena. Austrian–British scientist Karl Popper stated that the merit of any scientific research design is its ability to test the falsification of a hypothesis about a specific phenomenon. Popper first published *The Logic of Scientific Discovery* (or *Logik der Forschung* in German) in 1934, revolutionizing our understanding of the nature of growth in science. Popper (1972) wrote: "No matter how many instances of white swans we may have observed, this does not justify the conclusion that *all* swans are white" (p. 27). He continued:

> I shall certainly admit a system as empirical or scientific only if it is capable of being tested by experience. These considerations suggest

that not the *verifiability* but the *falsifiability* of a system is to be taken as a criterion of demarcation. In other words: I shall not require of a scientific system that it shall be capable of being singled out, once and for all, in a positive sense; but I shall require that its logical form shall be such that it can be singled out, by means of empirical tests, in a negative sense: it must *be possible for an empirical scientific system to be refuted by experience.*

(Popper, 1972, pp. 40–41)

Therefore, scientific theories are only hypotheses and may be falsified and replaced—their very existence is provisory.

In 2005, Greek–American epidemiologist John Ioannidis published a remarkable study with the provocative title of "Why Most Published Research Findings are False." He wrote:

There is increasing concern that most current published research findings are false. The probability that a research claim is true may depend on study power and bias, the number of other studies on the same question, and, importantly, the ratio of true to no relationships among the relationships probed in each scientific field. In this framework, a research finding is less likely to be true when the studies conducted in a field are smaller; when effect sizes are smaller; when there is a greater number and lesser preselection of tested relationships; where there is greater flexibility in designs, definitions, outcomes, and analytic modes; when there is greater financial and other interest and prejudice; and when more teams are involved in a scientific field in chase of statistical significance. Simulations show that for most study designs and settings, it is more likely for a research claim to be false than true. Moreover, for many current scientific fields, claimed research findings may often be simply accurate measures of the prevailing bias.

(Ioannidis, 2005, p. 696)

As a remedy to this dilemma, Ioannidis concluded that scientists should try to produce stronger evidence using large studies and less biased meta-analyses; they should be aware of the fact that it would be misleading to depend on the statistically significant findings of any single research team because what matters is the totality of available evidence; and instead of being obsessive about statistical significance, scientists should improve knowledge of the ratio of the number of *true relationships* to *no relationships* among those tested in the field.

Lessons learned: It is likely that we cannot attain the gold standard of evidence, and a conscientious social worker should act responsibly and cautiously to avoid harm.

4

SUPPORTING EVIDENCE-BASED PRACTICE

The adoption, implementation, and sustainment of evidence-based practice (EBP) require several conditions, including an external environment that creates a demand for such practice and a supply of resources to sustain it, practitioners who are committed to its use with fidelity, and clients or consumers who benefit from its application to addressing their personal needs. However, one of the most important components of EBP lies with the organization in which it is introduced, used, and sustained. EBP takes place in the context of human services organizations. The characteristics of these organizations may or may not facilitate the EBP process; as research and experience show, organizational factors may at times be barriers to successful EBP.

In this chapter, we explore the organizational context of EBP in social work, including the structure, culture, and climate of an organization; attitudes toward innovation in general and EBP in particular; support from leadership and practice champions; resource allocation; training and supervision; and size and structure of social networks. Using this examination of organizational context as a backdrop, we then elaborate on issues of evidence dissemination, translation, implementation, and sustainability—components without which EBP would be an empty promise. We conclude with an examination of strategies for preparing organizations to adopt a culture of EBP.

Models of research translation

Several different conceptual frameworks and models have been developed to identify the key components of the structure and process of translating research into evidence and the implementation of EBP and practices, treatments, and interventions (Damanpour, 1991; Fixsen, Naoom, Blase, Friedman, & Wallace, 2005; Frambach & Schillewaert, 2002; Greenhalgh, Robert, Macfarlane, Bate, & Kyriakidou, 2004; Klein & Sorra, 1996; Real & Poole, 2005; Rosenheck, 2001; Schoenwald, Kelleher, Weisz, & the Research Network on Youth Mental Health, 2008; Shortell et al., 2001; Simpson, 2002). Characteristic of most of these models are variables that describe the practice or intervention itself; the broader social and economic environment that creates demand for the practice and resources to sustain it; the individuals and organizations responsible for delivering services; and the processes involved in moving an intervention from its initial adoption by these individuals and organizations to its routine and continued use.

Reasons for adopting EBPs may be divided into characteristics that define the outer context and those that define the inner context. Among those in the former category are demands for improvements in the quality of services provided, either in terms of the anticipated outcomes (e.g., reduction of symptoms, client financial independence or autonomy, improved quality of life) or in terms of the manner in which services are delivered (e.g., reduction in cost, reduction in length of time necessary to achieve successful outcomes, number of personnel involved, burden on the client). These demands may be the result of government mandates, conditions for funding, or client familiarity with EBPs and preference for their use. In the inner context, the demand for EBPs may represent a top-down initiative from leaders who are familiar with EBPs or see their potential in improving the quality of service at reduced cost. The demands may also reflect a bottom-up initiative from line staff members who may have heard about specific practices from other members of their professional social networks or during a presentation at a professional meeting or workshop.

The Consolidated Framework for Implementation Research (Damschroder et al., 2009) offers an overarching typology of implementation research and features five major domains: (1) the intervention; (2) the inner and (3) outer settings in which the intervention is implemented; (4) the individuals involved in implementation; and (5) the process by which implementation is accomplished. This framework is based on an analysis of several existing models of innovation. An illustration of this framework and the components of each domain is provided in Figure 4.1.

A more recently developed model proposed by Aarons, Hurlburt, and Horwitz (2011) is particularly relevant to the field of social work because it was used to describe the structure and process of implementation of EBPs in child welfare and child mental health. Similar in structure to other models of innovation (Damschroder et al., 2009; Greenhalgh et al., 2004), this model identifies characteristics of the inner context (including intraorganizational and individual adopter characteristics) and outer context (including service and

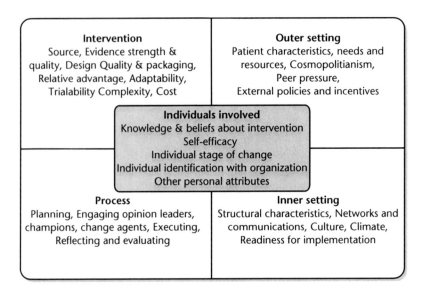

FIGURE 4.1 Consolidated framework for implementation research

interorganizational environment and consumer support or advocacy) that are likely to affect implementation of EBPs during four phases of implementation: exploration, preparation/and adoption, implementation, and sustainment. One of the characteristic features of this model is that it acknowledges that different elements of the inner and outer contexts may exert different influences at each stage of the implementation process, as described in Figure 4.2.

The organization as the locus of evidence-based practice

The extent to which the organization influences the practice of EBP and the use of specific EBPs is determined by characteristics of the organization (intraorganizational components) as well as characteristics of the relationships among organizations (interorganizational components). As Glisson and colleagues (2008) observed:

> Variations in organization-based social contexts may explain in part the gap between what we know about treatment efficacy and about how to best deliver effective treatments in the community. For this reason, a well-developed science of implementation effectiveness requires a better understanding of organizational social context and of methods for measuring and incorporating organizational social context into community-based effectiveness studies.
>
> *(p. 99)*

Exploration

OUTER CONTEXT
Sociopolitical Context
Legislation
Policies
Monitoring and review
Funding
    Service grants
    Research grants
    Foundation grants
    Continuity of funding
Client Advocacy
    Consumer organizations
Interorganizational networks
    Direct networking
    Indirect networking
    Professional organizations
    Clearing houses
    Technical assistance centers

INNER CONTEXT
Organizational characteristics
    Absorptive capacity
    Knowledge/skills
    Readiness for change
    Receptive context
    Culture
    Climate
    Leadership
Individual adopter characteristics
    Values
    Goals
    Social Networks
    Perceived need for change

Adoption Decision/ Preparation

OUTER CONTEXT
Sociopolitical
    Federal legislation
    Local enactment
    Definitions of "evidence"
Funding
    Support tied to federal and
    state policies
Client advocacy
    National advocacy
    Class action lawsuits
Interorganizational networks
    Organizational linkages
    Leadership ties
    Information transmission
        Formal
        Informal

INNER CONTEXT
Organizational characteristics
    Size
    Role specialization
    Knowledge/skills/expertise
    Values
    Leadership
    Culture embedding
    Championing adoption

Active Implementation

OUTER CONTEXT
Sociopolitical
    Legislative priorities
    Administrative costs
Funding
    Training
    Sustained fiscal support
    Contracting arrangements
    Community based organizations
Interorganizational networks
    Professional associations
    Cross-sector
    Contractor associations
    Information sharing
    Cross discipline translation
    Intervention developers
    Engagement in implementation
Leadership
    Cross level congruence
    Effective leadership practices

INNER CONTEXT
Organizational characteristics
    Structure
    Priorities/goals
    Readiness for change
    Receptive context
    Culture/climate
    Innovation-values fit
    EBP structural fit
    EBP ideological fit
Individual adopter characteristics
    Demographics
    Adaptability
    Attitudes toward EBP

Sustainment

OUTER CONTEXT
Sociopolitical
    Leadership
    Policies
        Federal initiatives
        States initiatives
        Local service system
        Consent decrees
Funding
    Fit with existing service funds
    Cost absorptive capacity
    Workforce stability impacts
    Public-academic collaboration
    Ongoing positive relationships
    Valuing multiple perspectives

INNER CONTEXT
Organizational characteristics
    Leadership
    Embedded EBP culture
    Critical mass of EBP provision
    Social network support
    Fidelity monitoring/support
    EBP Role clarity
    Fidelity support system
    Supportive coaching
Staffing
    Staff selection criteria
    Validated selection procedures

FIGURE 4.2 Conceptual model of implementation phases and factors affecting implementation in public service sectors

Reproduced from Aarons, Hurlburt, and Horwitz, 2011, with permission.

Several features of an organization can either support or inhibit the implementation of specific EBPs in particular or the EBP process in general. These include characteristics of an organization's structure, culture, and climate; attitudes of staff members toward innovation and change; leadership and the presence of an EBP advocate; resources and absorptive capacity for change; availability of training and support; and the nature and quality of social networks both within and between organizations.

Organizational structure

Alignment of an organization's structure with the requirements of an EBP is considered an essential element of the latter's successful implementation and sustainment. "In instances where structures are not initially aligned with an EBP and structural change cannot be fully realized, the EBP may not be appropriately implemented and fidelity to the model could suffer" (Zazzalli et al., 2008, p. 42). Characteristics of an organization that are likely to influence the adoption and routine use of an EBP include its size, age, and maturity (Damschroder et al., 2009). "Larger organizations may have greater resources to commit to evaluating and exploring the potential utility of different innovative practices" (Aarons et al., 2011, p. 11). A meta-analysis of structural determinants conducted by Damanpour (1991) found the ratio of managers to total employees to be positively associated with innovation whereas the concentration of decision-making autonomy was negatively associated with innovation. Private-sector organizations tend to have more organizational supports for the use of an EBP than their public-sector counterparts (Aarons, Sommerfeld, Hecht, Silovsky, & Chaffin, 2009). Likewise, organizations with formalized, centralized, and differentiated structures and a formal research infrastructure have greater success in implementing and sustaining innovative practices (Aarons et al., 2011; Frambach & Schillewaert, 2002; Greenhalgh et al., 2004; Mendel, Meredith, Schoenbaum, Sherbourne, & Wells, 2008; Simpson, 2002; Wisdom, Chor, Hoagwood, & Horwitz, 2013). "Organizational structure can also influence the fit between specific practices and the organization. Fit of a practice with the roles, structure, values, and authority of an organization may contribute to the likelihood that a particular practice is adopted or not" (Aarons et al., 2011, p. 11).

Organizational culture

In many respects, (e.g., emphasis on growth, concentration of decision making), an organization's structure is the visible product of its culture. Organizational culture can be defined as the implicit norms, values, shared behavioral expectations, and assumptions of a work unit that guide behaviors

(Cooke & Rousseau, 1988). As with cultural systems in general, the culture of social services organizations is composed of learned systems of meaning; is communicated by means of a language and other symbol systems; has representational, directive, and affective functions; and is capable of creating cultural entities and particular senses of reality (D'Andrade, 1984).

> [Cultural systems also represent] a moral process of interpretation and collective experience, composed of many voices, created by and, in turn, creator of social action, and located not in the minds of individuals, but between people, in the medium of intersubjective engagements that spread through the social world of families, work settings, networks, and whole communities.
>
> *(Lewis-Fernández & Kleinman, 1995, p. 434)*

Both the structure and process of organizational cultures are encapsulated in a set of shared understandings or value orientations. Value orientations are complex but definitely patterned, resulting from the traditional interplay of basic values (normative values), social values (prescriptive ethics), and their physical expression (artifacts). These values give order and direction to organizations. The cultural logic that articulates normative values explains why a social services organization does what it does (e.g., addresses the needs of vulnerable populations), whereas the social knowledge that is embedded in prescriptive ethics explains how it is done (e.g., by providing evidence-based treatment for depression or anxiety). The artifacts of normative and prescriptive values explain what is done, who does it, and when and where it is done (Hatch, 1993). These three elements are arranged in hierarchical fashion with normative truths that are taken for granted at the top, followed by values that operate at a more conscious level and represent the standards and goals for behavior, and artifacts at the bottom (H. T. O. Davies, Nutley, & Mannion, 2000; Palinkas, Allred, & Landsverk, 2005). The higher the element, the more resistant it is to change from the outside.

Organizational culture can affect how readily new EBPs are considered and adopted in practice (Aarons et al., 2011; Damschroder et al., 2009; Hemmelgarn, Glisson, & Dukes, 2001; Simpson, 2002; Wisdom et al., 2013). A culture that values learning, innovation, and change may be more interested in innovative practices and more adept at implementing them (Rosenheck, 2001). In human services, organizational cultures influence case manager attitudes, perceptions, and behaviors (Glisson & James, 2002). "The expectations (e.g., the extent to which clinicians are expected to be proficient in their work), perceptions (e.g., whether clinicians perceive a high level of personal engagement in their work with clients), and attitudes (e.g., clinicians commitment [*sic*] to the organization in which they work) are believed to either encourage or inhibit the adoption of best practices"

(Glisson et al., 2008, p. 99). Aarons and Sawitzky (2006) found that a constructive organizational culture of programs providing mental health services for youths and families was associated with positive attitudes of providers toward adoption of EBP. Glisson and colleagues (2008) found organizational culture to be a significant independent predictor of new program sustainability. Schoenwald and colleagues (2008) also found that for-profit organizations were more likely to implement new practices; however, organizational mission was of greater importance to public nonprofit organizations. In contrast, Manuel, Mullen, Fang, Bellamy, and Bledsoe (2009) found a lack of agency culture encouraging and supporting EBP implementation to be a significant barrier to implementing the Bringing Evidence to Social Work Training intervention. A study of a multifaceted implementation strategy to implement cognitive behavioral therapy for adolescents with depression in two publicly funded mental health centers found that productivity demands and recent changes in paperwork requirements had limited the ability of clinicians to engage in new learning (Kramer & Burns, 2008). A study of private- and public-sector service organizations by Aarons and colleagues (2009) found the latter possess cultures that are resistant to innovation and provide less support for EBP.

Organizational climate

Often confused and used interchangeably with organizational culture, organizational climate refers to employee perceptions and affective responses to the work environment (Joyce & Slocom, 1984; Sells & James, 1988). Climate includes characteristics of the job (e.g., autonomy, variety, feedback, role clarity) and work group (e.g., cooperation, warmth and intimacy: Glisson, 1989).

> Climate can be defined at two levels. At the individual level, *psychological* climate is the individual's perception of the psychological impact of the work environment on his or her own well-being (James & James, 1989). If employees in the same work unit share the same perceptions, their perceptions can be aggregated to describe the *organizational* climate of that unit (Jones & James, 1979; Joyce & Slocum, 1984).
>
> *(Glisson, Dukes, & Green, 2006, p. 858)*

Similar to organizational culture, organizational climate has been linked to the likelihood of successful EBP implementation and sustainment. Glisson and Hemmelgarn (1998) and Schoenwald, Sheidow, Letourneau, and Liao (2003) demonstrated that organizational climate significantly affected clinical outcomes for youths receiving publicly funded human services. Staff turnover, a consequence of poor organizational climate, has been identified by several studies as a barrier to innovation in general (Edmondson, Bohmer, & Pisano, 2001; Swain, Whitley, McHugo, & Drake, 2010; Woltmann et al., 2008) and adoption of specific EBPs in particular (Brunette et al., 2008). However, implementation of new practices may also improve staff morale and reduce the likelihood of turnover (Aarons et al., 2009).

A climate conducive of innovation is also important in understanding openness to change among human services organizations (Anderson & West, 1998; Klein & Sorra, 1996), and has been associated with provider attitudes toward adopting EBPs (Aarons & Sawitzky, 2006). Damschroder and colleagues (2009) identified six subconstructs as contributing to a positive implementation climate: (1) tension for change, or the degree to which stakeholders perceive the current situation as intolerable or needing change; (2) compatibility, or the degree of tangible fit between meaning and values attached to the intervention by involved individuals and existing workflows and systems; (3) relative priority, or shared perceptions of the importance of implementation within the organization; (4) organizational incentives and rewards; (5) goals and feedback; and (6) learning climate, or a climate in which leaders express their own fallibility and need for assistance and input from team members; team members feel they are essential, valued, and knowledgeable partners in the change process; individuals feel psychologically safe to try new methods; and there is sufficient time for reflective thinking and evaluation.

Attitudes toward organizational change

Combined with the social and demographic characteristics of an organization's staff and leaders (e.g., age, gender, education, professional status), organizational culture and climate influence the process of research translation by influencing attitudes towards EBP (Aarons, 2004). Efforts to introduce EBP in treatment settings are more successful when members of an organization are "ready to change" (B. D. Smith, 2013, p. 380). Provider resistance to change in general and EBPs in particular is often cited as a barrier to implementation (Proctor et al., 2007). "Favorable attitudes toward evidence-based practice can indicate that an organization is ready to change and that the implementation process will go more smoothly (Fixsen, Naoom, Blase, Friedman & Wallace, 2005; Simpson & Flynn, 2007)" (B. D. Smith, 2013, p. 380). A study of implementation of evidence-based supported employment by Marshall, Rapp, Becker, and Bond (2008) found that staff resistance to change was common across all study sites and that such resistance slowed the ability of sites to achieve full implementation of fidelity on specific elements of the model. "In general, agencies countered resistance by providing additional training, mandating procedural changes, or terminating or transferring the resistant employees" (Marshall et al., 2008, p. 891). Attitudes toward EBP have been shown to be more favorable in less bureaucratic organizations (Aarons, 2004), in private nonprofit organizations relative to publicly funded ones (Aarons, Cafri, Lugo, & Sawitzky, 2012), in organizations with more resources and those with a strong sense of practitioner solidarity and agency mission and purpose (Fuller et al., 2007), in research-oriented organizations (Lundgren, Krull, de Saxe Zerden, & McCarty, 2011), and in small organizations with fewer clients and organizations with higher levels of collective responsibility and a lesser focus on easily measured outcomes (B. D. Smith, 2013).

Leadership

Likewise, the attitudes and leadership styles of agency directors may influence the process of research translation. According to Zazzalli and colleagues (2008):

> Leaders may be responsible for selecting new programs or services, while in other instances they may serve as more of a facilitator in terms of supporting decisions to adopt EBPs that are made at other levels in the organization. Leaders can support the implementation of EBPs by allocating and/or obtaining the necessary resources, and coordinating and motivating the professionals to support these programs. Leaders may also influence the development of the culture of an organization, making the organization more receptive to new programs and ideas.
>
> *(p. 41)*

Numerous studies have found the involvement of agency leadership to be critical to the successful adoption of successful EBPs (Damschroder et al., 2009; Gioia & Dziadosz, 2008). Aarons (2006) found both transformational (charismatic or visionary) and transactional (based on exchanges between leader and follower) leadership to be positively associated with more positive attitudes toward adoption of EBP; transformational leadership was negatively associated with perceptions of a difference between current practice and EBP. Judge, Thoresen, Pucik, and Welbourne (1999) found two general characteristics of managers (i.e., risk tolerance and positive self-concept) to be most predictive of employee acceptance of major organizational transition. Brunette and colleagues (2008) found administrative leadership to be significantly associated with implementation of integrated dual disorders treatment in community mental health settings. "Leaders at successful (high fidelity) sites made implementation a priority among their myriad, competing responsibilities, and they took action by making administrative and policy changes to implement the new practice" (Brunette et al., 2008, p. 992). In contrast, leaders at low-fidelity sites were unable or unwilling to prioritize implementation and take facilitative action. Along with partnerships with universities, Proctor and colleagues (2007) found directorial leadership and support for providers to be important leverage points to implement evidence-based treatments in such settings. Marshall and colleagues (2008) reported that a multilevel commitment of agency leaders was associated with the implementation of high-fidelity supported-employment programs in the National Evidence-Based Practice Project. This commitment included formation of leadership teams to monitor implementation progress, administrative adjustments, and provision of moral support by attending planning meetings, participating in supported employment training, and building relationships with community partners. Backer, Liberman, and Kuehnel (1986) found that top-down leadership was negatively associated with the adoption of innovative practices.

EBP champion

In addition to being more likely to have supportive administrators, organizations that are successful in implementing and sustaining EBPs have designated champions or advocates for the EBP (Berta et al., 2005; Greenhalgh et al., 2004; Simpson, 2002; Valente, 1996). Aarons and colleagues (2011) noted that the presence of an internal organizational champion raises the probability that an EBP will move past the exploration and adoption phases and into the implementation phase.

Resources

Another organizational requirement for the successful implementation and sustainment of EBPs is the availability of necessary resources.

> Programs that are new to an organization, whether they are evidence-based or not, may require new sets of resources in order for them to be appropriately implemented. For example, organizations need space for seeing clients, the right kinds of clinicians and support staff with the appropriate skills and training, documentation, and record keeping systems, billing systems, etc. The degree to which an organization has the correct types of resources available in-house will greatly facilitate the implementation of a new EBP.
>
> (Zazzalli et al., 2008, p. 41)

One such resource, to be addressed in greater detail in the next chapter, is the ability to access, evaluate, and apply research evidence relating to an EBP. Limited access to research was identified by Proctor and colleagues (2007) as a barrier to implementation of EBP in community behavioral health, whereas a partnership with universities was identified as a leverage point. The capacity to monitor practice outcomes is another determinant of successful implementation. Marty, Rapp, McHugo, and Whitley (2008) found that the existence and ability of a management information system to collect outcomes relevant to an EBP and report it in a timely way distinguished high-achieving agencies from their low-achieving counterparts. The availability of trained and qualified staff with skills necessary to effectively use an EBP has been cited as another important resource requirement. Other resource barriers include staff shortages, burdensome workloads, time constraints, and limitations in computer access (Proctor et al., 2007; Proctor & Rosen, 2004).

Absorptive capacity for change

Other organizational characteristics that promote the implementation of EBPs include an organization's absorptive capacity (Frambach & Schillewaert, 2002; Greenhalgh et al., 2004; Horwitz, Chamberlain, Landsverk, & Mullican, 2010; Wisdom et al., 2013).

> Absorptive capacity refers to an organization's preexisting knowledge/ skills, ability to use new knowledge, specialization and mechanisms to support knowledge sharing. Organizations that start with good knowledge/skills, can incorporate new knowledge, are highly specialized, and have mechanisms in place to spread knowledge throughout the organization, are much more likely to explore EBPs and eventually initiate them (Damanpour 1991; Ferlie and Shortell 2001; Greenhalgh et al. 2004; Grol et al. 2007).
>
> *(Aarons et al., 2011, p. 8)*

In contrast, public-sector agencies such as child welfare systems are often characterized as employing inadequately trained staff with multiple responsibilities and few venues for knowledge sharing (Yoo, Brooks, & Patti, 2007).

Training

In the absence of practitioners already qualified to use a particular EBP, staff training is a paramount requirement for successful EBP implementation and sustainment (Backer et al., 1986; Frambach & Schillewaert, 2002;

Greenhalgh et al., 2004; Wisdom et al., 2013). Training costs were identified by Proctor et al. (2007) as a barrier to implementation. Merely having its staff attend a training workshop, however, is insufficient to prepare an organization to successfully implement an EBP. Ongoing supervision, monitoring of performance, and booster training sessions are also viewed as essential to preparing an organization and its staff to successfully and routinely use an EBP (Swain et al., 2010). Gioia and Dziadosz (2008) reported that constant supervision was crucial to the successful adoption of four EBPs in a community mental health center. In contrast, spending too much time in training (Gioia & Dziadosz, 2008) or experiencing a delay between training and first use of an EBP (Palinkas et al., 2008) has been found to be a barrier to implementation.

Social networks

Finally, although many factors influence the diffusion of EBPs, researchers have consistently found that interpersonal contacts within and between organizations and communities are important influences on the adoption of new behaviors (Aarons et al., 2011; Frambach & Schillewaert, 2002; Greenhalgh et al., 2004; Rogers, 2003; Valente, 1996). Based on diffusion of innovations theory (Rogers, 2003) and social learning theory (Bandura, 1986), Valente's (1995) social network thresholds model calls for identification and matching of champions within peer networks that manage organizational agenda setting, change, and evaluation of change (e.g., data collection, evaluation, and feedback). Studies and meta-analyses have shown that having trusted others in one's personal network and access and exposure to external information are important influences on rates of adoption of innovative practices (Valente, 2010). Palinkas and colleagues (2011) found that implementation of an EBP for at-risk youth in foster care at the 2-year follow-up of a randomized controlled trial was associated with the level of in-degree centrality (the extent to which individual members are sought out for information and advice) in collaborating networks.

Building an organizational culture of evidence-based practice

Earlier, we noted the existence of several models that identify the key components of successful EBP implementation. Other models offer prescriptions for facilitating the process of EBP implementation. Among the better-known models are the RE-AIM (which stands for reach, efficacy/effectiveness, adoption, implementation, and maintenance) model developed by Glasgow (2009); the Institute for Healthcare Improvement's (2004) Breakthrough

Series; the Department of Veterans Affairs' Quality Enhancement Research Initiative model (Demakis, McQueen, Kizer, & Feussner, 2000); and the Precede-Proceed model developed by L. W. Green and Kreuter (2005). In each of these models, organizations exert a major influence on the process and outcome of efforts to implement EBPs.

A model of particular relevance to social work is the Availability, Responsiveness and Continuity (ARC) model developed by Charles Glisson. ARC is a community- and organization-oriented model that emphasizes the role of the social context in implementation of evidence-based interventions (Glisson, 2002; Glisson et al., 2006; Glisson & Green, 2006; Glisson & Schoenwald, 2005). The model is intended to prepare organizations to deliver an evidence-based treatment effectively and with high quality to clients in a specific social and organizational environment. The model draws from theories of the diffusion of innovations (Rogers, 2003), the transfer of technology (Backer, David, & Saucy, 1995), interorganizational domain development (Trist, 1985), and organizational development (Porras & Robertson, 1992), as well as sociotechnical models of organizational effectiveness (Rousseau, 1977). The model is based on three fundamental assumptions: (1) the implementation of an evidence-based intervention is a social process; (2) social and mental health services are delivered in a complex context of organizations and social institutions including service providers, services organizations, family, and community; and (3) the effectiveness of service delivery is a function of how well an evidence-based intervention is mediated by the social environment in which it is delivered.

Typically, this model develops and supports an implementation strategy by studying, understanding, and operationalizing organizational and interorganizational factors in each given implementation context. It represents collaboration among the model developers, trained staff, and service systems leaders and staff. It is intended to foster the emergence of organizational cultures that value innovation and organizational climates that encourage learning, risk, and innovation. On an organizational level, the ARC model integrates characteristics of the organizational setting with evidence-based interventions.

Because service provider organizations operate in a larger social context of other organizations, community stakeholders, and other important local actors (Aarons et al., in press; Palinkas et al., 2014), the ARC model aims to integrate the context of the service provider organization with the broader context of interorganizational factors. This context may include local, state, or federal government agencies, community and business sectors, and important local opinion leaders such as school principals, judges, and ministers.

The components of the ARC model include a set of activities to spur the implementation process. These activities are listed in Table 4.1. These ten activities are introduced by the change agent in four phases (problem

TABLE 4.1 Availability, Responsiveness and Continuity intervention activities

1. Personal relationships with community leaders, stakeholders, and individual members of key community groups are cultivated by change agents to provide the foundation for communication, sharing information, and removing barriers to addressing the targeted problem
2. Network development to build relationships among service providers, community groups, and key opinion leaders
3. Team building to help community groups and service teams to address service and community support issues that affect the target population and problem
4. Information and data management strategies to evaluate the extent of the targeted problem and impact of existing treatment or service programs on criteria of interest to the respective groups
5. Feedback about service effectiveness and barriers to care
6. Participatory decision making to provide an opportunity for input from service providers and community opinion leaders into decisions about service implementation and community support
7. Conflict resolution to mediate differences in opinion or competing interests that threaten efforts to address the target problem
8. Continuous quality improvement to provide the means for changing institutional rules and policies to address the targeted problem
9. Job redesign efforts to involve service providers in eliminating barriers to service by changing job design characteristics that impede success
10. Self-regulation and stabilization of the implementation of the evidence-based intervention to make sure that the service provider organization is self-sustaining in terms of information, training, and tools to continue providing the evidence-based interventions once the implementation project is concluded

Reproduced from Glisson and Schoenwald (2005).

identification, direction setting, implementation, and stabilization) at three levels (community, organization, and individual). The first six activities are introduced in the first phase, activities 7 and 8 in the second phase, activity 9 in the third phase, and activity 10 in the fourth phase.

These strategies to facilitate the implementation process at all levels are supported by change agents who are trained by ARC project managers or their assigned coworkers. Change agents usually come from the ranks of doctoral or master's-level practitioners in clinical psychology, industrial organizational psychology, and counseling. Change agents work with attitudes, opinions, and decisions on individual, group, organizational, and community levels.

The effectiveness of the ARC model in facilitating implementation of EBPs and improving consumer outcomes has been demonstrated in two recent studies. In the first, Glisson and colleagues (2010) conducted a randomized controlled trial of multisystemic therapy (MST) and the ARC organizational intervention to test their effectiveness in reducing problem behavior youths with delinquent behaviors residing in 14 rural counties in Tennessee. The study featured a two-by-two design in which 615 adolescents between 9 and 17 years old were randomized into receiving MST or treatment as usual and counties were randomized into receiving or not receiving the ARC intervention. A multilevel mixed-effects regression analysis of 6-month treatment outcomes found that youth problem behavior in the MST plus ARC condition was at a nonclinical level and significantly lower than in other conditions, and that youths in the MST plus ARC condition entered out-of-home placements at a significantly lower rate (16%) compared to youths in the control condition (34%).

In the second study (Glisson, Hemmelgarn, Green, & Williams, 2013), 18 community mental health programs that served youths between the ages of 5 and 18 were randomly assigned to ARC or control conditions. Youth outcomes were significantly better in programs that completed the 18-month ARC intervention. Analyses also showed that youth outcomes were best in programs with the most improved organizational social contexts following the ARC intervention.

Conclusion

The successful implementation and sustainment of EBP are dependent upon several factors, including an outer context that features both demand for EBP and resources necessary to support and sustain it; individuals who are motivated and capable of using the EBP successfully; and characteristics of the EBP that enable users to explore, experiment, and learn. However, central to the inner context of EBP implementation and sustainment is the organization in which such practice occurs. Organizations most likely to implement and sustain EBP have the following characteristics: a formalized, centralized, and differentiated structure with a formal research infrastructure; a culture that values learning, innovation, and change; a climate that offers a sense of psychological safety and enables risk taking; leaders who are fully committed to innovation in general and the EBP in question in particular and are fully engaged in its implementation; a designated advocate or champion for the EBP; qualified clinicians and support staff with the appropriate skills and training, documentation, and record keeping and systems; preexisting knowledge and skills and the ability to use new knowledge, specializations, and mechanisms to support knowledge sharing (absorptive capacity); training and ongoing supervision of staff members responsible for implementation; and a supportive network of advisors and opinion leaders both within and among organizations involved in the implementation process. Assuming that each of these characteristics is not already present, strategies such as the ARC intervention are available to help develop an inner context that is supportive of EBP implementation and sustainment.

5

CHALLENGES OF USING EBP IN SOCIAL WORK PRACTICE

As we noted in Chapter 1, the evidence-based practice (EBP) movement originated in medicine and eventually moved into mental health services. Although there has been substantial pressure to adopt EBP in social work practice, the extent to which the profession is a suitable home for EBP as a method of practice or for individual EBPs has been the subject of much debate. This debate is examined in greater detail in Chapter 6. In this chapter, we identify and describe challenges of the profession as a backdrop to the emergence of EBP. The social work profession has historically defined its mission as operating in the service of individuals and communities, the underprivileged, the oppressed, and the neediest individuals. However, supporting, empowering, and treating clients is a professional activity that takes place in real-world conditions subject to limitations and constraints.

As in health services in general (Institute of Medicine, 2001), there remains a large gap between the development of interventions shown to be effective in the prevention and treatment of mental health and behavioral problems among vulnerable populations and their use in everyday social work practice. Although numerous EBPs, treatments, interventions, and policies exist, they are rarely used routinely by social workers; those that are used routinely have little evidence to suggest they are effective or achieve their objectives. For instance, Hoagwood and Olin (2002) estimated that only 10% of public agencies serving youths routinely use EBPs. A more recent study by Raghavan, Inoue, Ettner, Hamilton, and Landsverk (2010) found that 60% of youths in child welfare systems receive evidence-based services. Many in the field agree that more research is needed to identify factors that facilitate or impede EBP implementation in service sectors that cater to children and adolescents, including specialty mental health, schools, juvenile justice, primary care, and child welfare (Aarons & Palinkas, 2007; Fixsen, Naoom, Blase, Friedman, & Wallace, 2005; Garland, Kruse, & Aarons, 2003; Glisson, 2002; Hoagwood, Burns, Kiser, Ringeisen, & Schoenwald, 2001; Schoenwald & Hoagwood, 2001). This also applies to other areas of social work practice.

Several reasons have been advanced to account for the gap between research and practice in social work. For instance, as Rosen (2003) observed:

> Use of research-based knowledge in practice is influenced by complex factors that impinge on and interact to impede implementation of EBP. Such factors can be grouped into five general categories: (1) characteristics of the knowledge to be used, (2) characteristics of the practice situation and setting, (3) characteristics of the practitioner, (4) attributes of the medium through which knowledge is communicated, and (5) the social–cultural context in which utilization takes place (Rosen, 1983).
>
> *(p. 199)*

In this chapter, we focus on the complexity of social and behavioral problems addressed by social workers; the conceptual models that govern social work practice and their capacity to accommodate or challenge EBP; the limits of knowledge even under the best circumstances provided by more access to better scientific evidence; organizational constraints; and problems associated with evidence-to-action processes.

Complexity of client social and behavioral problems

One of the chief complaints of EBP is that, although individual practices are usually designed to address a specific problem and are typically evaluated for their effectiveness in doing so, the reality of social work practice is that clients usually present with a multitude of problems and symptoms (Weisz et al., 2012). An EBP designed to address depressive symptoms in a combat veteran may not be adequate to address comorbid conditions such as substance abuse and posttraumatic stress disorder. Similarly, using an EBP designed to address conduct problems in a young child may not be feasible due to constant interruption to deal with more immediate crises affecting the household. Furthermore, during the course of treatment, as some problems are resolved, new problems may emerge.

The complexity of problems faced by social work clients is often mirrored in the complexity of services offered to these clients. Both are perceived as barriers to successful EBP implementation and sustainment. Heiwe and colleagues

(2013) found that 78% of their sample of Swedish medical social workers identified the perception that EBP does not take into account the limitations of the clinical practice setting as a barrier to the use of EBP. Rosen (2003) argued that "factors inherent in practitioners and in the practice situation render much of EBP incompatible with its routine application in practice" (p. 197).

Conflict with conceptual models of social work practice

In addition to the practical challenges of implementing EBP in complex service delivery systems, EBP is seen as a manifestation of an antiquated positivist paradigm that has no role in social work (Karger, 1983). As Rosen (2003) noted:

> In the social sciences, and subsequently in social work, prevailing orientations to science and knowledge were challenged as being mechanistic, dehumanizing, disempowering, antifeminist, and generally insensitive to personal and cultural diversity. In social work, logical positivism and its kindred epistemological derivatives were challenged as inappropriate models for research and knowledge generation generally and in direct practice in particular (compare Davis, 1985; Gergen, 1985; Heineman, 1981; Karger, 1983; Kondrat, 1992; Peile, 1988; Rodwell, 1998; Witkin, 1991). The discrediting of the traditional scientific approach and methodologies—as positivist, deterministic, or quantitative—was perhaps exemplified by Tyson (1995) who, as part of advocating a "heuristic paradigm" of research, implied that social work's alleged use of positivist research methods was tantamount to social work's relinquishing its values of social justice.
>
> *(p. 200)*

Practitioner attitudes towards EBP are often framed by their exposure to EBP principles in school, with younger providers being more accepting of EBP adoption and older providers being more resistant to adoption (Aarons & Palinkas, 2007; Palinkas & Aarons, 2009; Palinkas et al., 2008). However, even those who have been exposed to EBP principles during their social work training express concerns that EBP will interfere with their therapeutic alliance with clients (Palinkas et al., 2013). Likewise, providers who view social work practice as more of an art than a science are reluctant to adopt EBP.

Limits of knowledge

There are two issues related to the limits of knowledge that guides EBP in social work. The first issue is limited access to this knowledge. Lack of access among social workers to research evidence has been identified by scholars (Atherton, 2002; Barratt, 2003; Gilgun, 2005; Proctor et al., 2007) as a barrier to successful EBP implementation and sustainment. Heiwe and colleagues (2013) found 46% of their sample of Swedish medical social workers identified lack of knowledge about relevant research as a barrier to the use of EBP. Barratt's (2003) examination of views of staff members in social services departments in the United Kingdom found a lack of consensus regarding what constitutes evidence and how it can be put to use. She also found that access to research and locally collected data is essential to inform and guide policy and practice, and emphasized the need for mechanisms to support access to evidence and understanding of its relevance.

The second issue is the nature of knowledge. R. M. Epstein (1999) argued that knowledge, skills, values and experience that "seasoned practitioners" bring to bear on clinical decision making is a "different kind of evidence" (p. 834). Rosen (2003) pointed to the inherent dilemma in the idiographic representations of normative generalizations, especially given that the latter is:

> fraught with uncertainty, even when obtained through optimal research designs. This uncertainty is related to the probabilistic nature of all scientific inferences and conclusions, which, although they may reduce the uncertainty in a given phenomenon, seldom if ever account for all its variability. Another source of uncertainty relates to the fact that research-based generalizations are always of circumscribed validity, relating to the populations and samples (that is, individuals, behaviors, or situations) that were actually studied. These factors are inherent to all research-based knowledge and rightly affect and qualify the extent to which empirical generalizations can be applicable to a particular client or circumstance (Rosen, 1983, 1996).
>
> *(pp. 200–201)*

Embedded in most models of EBP implementation is the transfer of research evidence from intervention developers to potential users of EBP (Golden-Biddle et al., 2003; Greenhalgh, Robert, Macfarlane, Bate, & Kyriakidou, 2004; Klein & Sorra, 1996; Rynes, Bartunek, & Daft, 2001; Schoenwald et al., 2008; Tunis, 2007). Some of these models focus explicitly on the use of research evidence (Honig & Coburn, 2008; Kennedy, 1984; Nutley, Walter, & Davies, 2007); in other models, the use of research evidence is embedded in broader processes of innovation, including the dissemination and implementation of EBPs (Fixsen et al., 2005; Greenhalgh et al., 2004). Many of these models represent typologies of research use. For instance, several researchers have distinguished between an instrumental model in which use of research consists of making a decision and research evidence is assumed to be instructive to the decision, and a conceptual model in which use refers to thinking about the evidence. Whereas the central feature of the instrumental model is the decision, the central feature of the conceptual model is the human information processor—a cognitive model to calculate how long it takes to perform a task. Hence, the instrumental model focuses on the outcome of using research evidence, whereas the conceptual model focuses on the process of evidence use (Kennedy, 1984). Nutley and colleagues (2007), for instance, identified four factors influencing the use of research evidence: (1) the nature of the research to be applied; (2) the personal characteristics of both researchers and potential research users; (3) the links between research and its users; and (4) the context in which the research will be used. Honig and Coburn (2008) emphasized the process (searching for evidence, incorporating or not incorporating it in decision making) and predictors (features of the evidence, working knowledge, social capital, organization, normative influence, political dynamics, and state and federal policies) of evidence use.

Each of these models contains elements that reflect distinct theoretical orientations (e.g., human information processing, distributed cognition, diffusion of innovations, decision-making theory) and organizational settings (e.g., health care, education); however, most, if not all, models acknowledge two essential considerations to understanding when and in what ways research will be used (Nutley et al., 2007). The first consideration is the context of research use. As noted by H. Davies, Nutley, and Walter (2008), "research use is a highly contingent process. Whether and how new information gets assimilated is contingent on local priorities, cultures and systems of meaning. What makes sense in one setting can make a different sense in another" (p. 190). The second consideration is that "interpersonal and social interactions are often seen as key to accessing and interpreting such research knowledge, whether among policy or practice colleagues, research intermediaries or more directly with researchers themselves" (H. Davies et al., 2008, p. 189).

Two key elements of the context of research use identified in many of the models described earlier are external conditions that regulate the supply and demand of research use and the culture and climate of organizations contemplating the implementation of an EBP. Successful, large-scale implementation of EBPs into existing social services systems is likely to involve multiple levels of constituents, in part because they affect multiple stakeholders in the funding, planning, coordinating, delivering, and receiving of services. This is similar to Shortell's (2004) four-level model for assessing organizational and managerial performance in health care delivery systems. Further, the successful implementation of many EBP models requires substantial interagency linkages. In a report on behalf of the Blueprints for Healthy Youth Development initiative, Mihalic, Fagan, Irwin, Ballard, and Elliott (2004) found these linkages to be crucial to whether programs had stable funding, a stable referral base, and coordinated case-planning activities, especially for clients involved in multiple systems. In addition to interagency coordination, these linkages often include system-level factors that affect the implementing organization's operation; are related to federal and state laws and regulations; and influence larger human resources decisions (e.g., colocation of staff from multiple agencies), access to funding streams, and contracting issues.

Several models point to the importance of the external environment in determining how evidence is used. The model developed by Honig and Coburn (2008), for instance, includes federal and state policies and programs that both provide funding and impose regulations. It also includes market forces such as reviews by the Administration on Children, Youth and Families. These policies, programs, and market forces can be conceptually divided into those that provide support for the implementation and sustainability of the EBP and those that exert constraints or limitations on these processes. Some support mechanisms affect the supply of resources for the development and maintenance of an EBP, whereas other mechanisms affect the demand for an EBP.

Supply characteristics that are likely to be associated with the extent of EBP implementation include the following: (1) whether there is a sufficient supply of revenues to cover the cost of implementation (e.g., as reflected in county poverty rates and population size); (2) whether there is sufficient support from external sources for implementation (e.g., state and federal mandates, private foundation initiatives); and (3) whether there is sufficient supply of staff and resources to support implementation (e.g., funding for a systems of care framework for children's mental health services). Demand characteristics that are likely to be associated with the extent of dissemination and implementation of an EBP include the following: (1) whether or not funding agencies and consumers perceive a genuine need for implementation; (2) whether there is sufficient demand from above (e.g., from regulatory agencies, government, Administration on Children, Youth and Families reviews); and (3) whether there is sufficient demand from below (e.g., from clients, consumer advocacy organizations: Schoenwald et al., 2008).

Conceptual models of evidence use acknowledge that the use of research evidence to make or support decisions is often a collective endeavor rather an activity performed by an individual decision maker (Spillane, Diamond, Walker, Halverson, & Jita, 2001). This collective endeavor involves the utilization of social capital (Honig & Coburn, 2008; Spillane et al., 2001), social networks (Valente, 1995; Valente, Hoffman, Rin-Olson, Lichtman, & Johnson, 2003); and the exchange of knowledge or information between researchers and practitioners and within networks of practitioners (Lomas, 2000; Mitton, Adair, McKenzie, Patten, & Waye Perry, 2007; Nutley et al., 2007).

Palinkas and colleagues (2013) conducted an investigation of the use of research evidence in the implementation of a widely used EBP by public agencies responsible for providing services to youths in California and Ohio. Specifically, they examined research evidence use by agency directors and senior administrators of county child welfare, mental health, and juvenile justice agencies. Their objectives were to understand and measure the use of research evidence by decision makers in public youth-serving agencies, identify factors that predict the use of research evidence, and determine whether consensus on use of research evidence is associated with stage of implementation of a specific EBP.

This study was part of a larger randomized controlled trial designed to assess the effectiveness of community development teams (CDTs: Sosna & Marsenich, 2006) in scaling up the implementation of multidimensional treatment foster care (MTFC), an EBP designed to reduce out-of-home placement in group and residential care, juvenile arrests, substance abuse, youth violence, pregnancy, and behavioral and emotional problems (Chamberlain et al., 2008; Wang, Saldana, Brown, & Chamberlain, 2010). Public youth-serving systems in 40 California counties and 11 Ohio counties that had not already implemented MTFC were invited to participate. The 40 California counties were matched based on background factors (e.g., population, rural vs urban, poverty, and early periodic screening, diagnosis, and treatment utilization rates) and divided into six equivalent clusters: two with six counties and four with seven counties. Each of these six comparable clusters was assigned randomly to one of three sequential cohorts in a wait-list design with staggered start-up times. Randomization of the 11 Ohio counties occurred following their acceptance of the invitation to participate to maintain a balanced randomized design. Within each cohort, counties were randomly assigned to CDT or standard implementation conditions. Progress toward implementation was assessed by means of a stage-of-implementation checklist (Chamberlain et al., 2008).

The use of research evidence study was conducted in two phases. In the first phase, semistructured interviews were conducted with ten juvenile justice system leaders and eight county mental health system leaders and a focus group was conducted with eight child welfare system leaders to collect information on how research evidence in general was acquired, evaluated, and applied in making decisions to adopt innovative programs, policies, and practices. Data from these interviews and the focus group were combined with data collected from 38 leaders in California child welfare, mental health, and juvenile justice systems during an earlier study (Palinkas et al., 2011, 2013). These data were used to construct two measures, one assessing patterns of use of research evidence (structured interview of evidence use) and one assessing the extent to which interactions between key stakeholder groups led to changes in their respective organizational cultures (cultural exchange inventory). These two instruments were then administrated via a web-based survey to 156 leaders of county child welfare, juvenile justice, and mental health systems participating in the study, ten leaders in other counties and states other than California and Ohio, and 37 state-level systems leaders participating in a study of the use of research evidence in implementing statewide programs for monitoring use of psychotropic medication by child welfare-involved youths.

The investigators learned three fundamental lessons from this project. First, in addition to research evidence, systems leaders use three other types of evidence when considering whether to seek and apply research evidence when making decisions: (1) evidence of resources necessary and available from the external environment for making use of research evidence (supply); (2) evidence of the need for research evidence, usually obtained from local conditions of client and service needs (demand); and (3) personalized evidence gained from experience (i.e., the congruence of research evidence with practice experience). These three types of evidence serve as the context of research evidence use.

The second lesson learned was that not all research evidence is created equal. Table 5.1 provides a list of 20 different sources of evidence reported by study participants. The top five sources are external to systems leaders and their county or state. This external evidence may be viewed as being global in nature because it is intended to apply across all settings. The next four sources are internal to the county or state, particularly data collected by each leader's own agency. In contrast to global evidence, this evidence is more local in nature. Three of those four sources involve some form of inter-personal networks. Systems leaders were more likely to rely on published materials or experts than on their networks ($p < 0.001$). Academic journals, in which research evidence is most likely to appear soon after it is generated, were not given highest priority but instead ranked tenth on that list.

A description of how systems leaders evaluated research evidence is provided in Table 5.2. Systems leaders relied on outcomes and whether the intervention had been tested in the field to determine validity. They assessed reliability of evidence based on whether strengths and weaknesses had been identified and how the evidence was structured. Highest priority, however, was given to assessing the relevance of the evidence to each leader's jurisdiction. Two of the indicators of relevance were related to similarity between the study population and the leader's own population (i.e., *compare own needs with that of research population* and *jurisdictions have similar demographics*), and two indicators were related to local constraints on implementation (i.e., *cost and time to train staff*). Systems leaders were more likely to conduct self-assessments of validity, reliability, and relevance of research evidence than to rely on the assessments of people they know ($p < 0.001$).

TABLE 5.1 Source of research evidence: Input

Rank	Source	M	SD
1	Internet	3.92	0.84
2	Someone who has implemented it	3.37	0.94
3	Conferences or workshops	3.35	0.72
4	Training manuals/book/curricula	3.30	0.91
5	Professional association meetings	3.10	1.10
6	Data collected by my own agency	3.03	1.07
7	Regular staff meetings	3.03	0.99
8	Regular meetings with professionals in my county	3.01	0.98
9	Staff members from my agency	2.87	1.09
10	Academic journals	2.81	0.99
11	Someone I heard at a conference	2.81	0.95
12	People who developed the program	2.75	1.00
13	Web-based clearinghouses	2.74	1.22
14	California Institute for Mental Health/Center for Innovative Practice	2.71	1.35
15	Local college or university expert	2.47	1.05
16	Federal or state government agencies	2.44	0.91
17	Nonprofit organizations/foundations	2.29	0.89
18	Administrator in another agency	2.29	0.96
19	A consultant	2.19	1.02
20	My clients or their parents	2.07	1.00

Finally, a description of how research evidence was applied by study participants is provided in Table 5.3. The most common application of research evidence was for supporting a decision that had already been made. Research evidence was also used for the purpose of quality improvement, such as using evidence to determine if a program could hurt clients, to determine how much adaptation is needed to meet needs of clients, or to eliminate ineffective programs. Systems leaders will not implement an intervention if it is not supported by evidence; however, they will also ignore evidence if it fails to align with local conditions (e.g., the program cannot be adapted, it is not feasible for one's own jurisdiction, there are no resources to implement it even if it can be adapted or is feasible, or it does not match the skill level of the organization's staff). Nevertheless, systems leaders were more likely to use evidence than to ignore it ($p < 0.001$).

Analyses of the predictors of research evidence indicated that evidence use was influenced by roles within the organization. Program managers were most likely and clinical supervisors least likely to access and evaluate evidence.

TABLE 5.2 Evaluation of research evidence: Process

Rank	Source	M	SD
Validity			
1	Outcomes	4.34	0.64
2	Tested in the field	4.01	0.79
3	Subject matter experts	3.80	0.78
4	Experience of other counties	3.75	0.78
5	Clinicians using the program	3.74	0.73
6	Credibility of program developers	3.61	0.90
7	Based on theory	3.50	0.93
8	Reliance on people I know and trust	3.45	0.92
9	Reliance on organizations like California Institute for Mental Health	3.25	1.22
10	Only after it is implemented in my county	2.75	1.16
Reliability			
1	Strengths and weaknesses listed	4.05	0.74
2	How evidence is structured	3.98	0.81
3	Information comes from more than one source	3.85	0.85
4	Methods clearly described	3.79	0.90
5	Reliance on people I know and trust	3.46	0.93
Relevance			
1	How much it costs to implement	4.18	0.90
2	Compare own needs with that of research population	4.11	0.73
3	Time required to train staff	4.01	0.80
4	Jurisdictions have similar demographics	3.94	0.81
5	Reliance on peers to determine relevance	3.35	0.92

Directors were most likely to use research evidence and not ignore it when making decisions. Second, use of research evidence was inversely associated with level of education after controlling for specific agency role. Less educated leaders may be under greater pressure to access evidence, whereas more educated leaders may devote more effort to evaluating and applying evidence. Third, evidence use was influenced by characteristics of the clients served and the communities in which they live. Leaders devoted more effort to use of evidence when they served a greater proportion of clients with minority racial and ethnic backgrounds. In this instance, research was evaluated for its relevance to these clients. However, the same leaders devoted less effort to evidence use when more of the residents in their county were living in poverty, perhaps because there were fewer resources to support use

TABLE 5.3 Application of research evidence: Output

Rank	Source	M	SD
Adoption			
1	Use evidence to support a decision on adopting a program	3.96	0.80
2	Use evidence to determine if program could harm clients	3.91	0.89
3	Consider information from experts and community members	3.84	0.74
4	Use evidence to determine how much adaptation is required to meet needs	3.77	0.93
5	Use evidence to find a program that meets needs of population	3.76	0.83
6	Use evidence to eliminate ineffective programs	3.65	0.86
7	Review evidence as a team with partner agencies	3.57	0.87
8	Use evidence to compare multiple programs' strengths and weaknesses	3.27	0.89
9	Will find money to implement if evidence is strong enough	3.24	0.87
10	Will not introduce an intervention not supported by evidence	3.17	1.09
11	Give greater weight to outcomes from my own county	3.02	0.99
12	Would rather implement intervention adopted by colleagues	2.98	0.93
13	Visit counties that have implemented	2.93	0.97
14	Rely on strategies that have proven effectiveness	2.77	0.89
15	Defer to decisions of people I work for	2.72	0.93
Ignore the evidence			
1	Ignore evidence if program is not feasible for my state/county	2.22	0.68
2	Ignore evidence if program too rigid (cannot be adapted)	2.18	0.72
3	Ignore evidence if program doesn't match staff skill level	2.13	0.67
4	Ignore evidence if no resources to implement the program	2.09	0.74
5	Ignore evidence if not convinced the program will work	2.01	0.73

of research evidence and because there may have been less of a need to use research evidence if there were no funds to support new programs. Fourth, improvements in culture and climate over time were associated with greater effort devoted to evaluating and using evidence. Finally, changes in evidence use were associated with perceived increases in cultural exchanges and the effects of those exchanges on the organization.

The third lesson from this project related to the use of research evidence and EBP implementation. Using data from 33 clusters (counties with three or more study participants), investigators tested two specific hypotheses: (1) use of research evidence would be significantly associated with stage of implementation; and (2) consensus regarding use of research evidence would be significantly associated with state of implementation. With respect to the first hypothesis, stage of implementation was significantly associated with the extent to which leaders engaged in evaluating research evidence for validity, reliability, and relevance ($r = 0.42$, $p = 0.015$), the extent to which they used research evidence in their decisions ($r = 0.47$, $p = 0.006$), and their overall use of research evidence ($r = 0.40$, $p = 0.022$). With respect to the second hypothesis, the effect of considering what kinds of evidence to access and use and how to prioritize evidence access and use on implementation of an EBP was significantly associated with the level of consensus regarding research evidence use among systems leaders involved in the implementation decision ($p < 0.05$). In other words, the greater the consensus among systems leaders regarding type of evidence and the means of evaluating and applying it, the greater the likelihood of implementation of an EBP. In particular, stage of implementation was significantly associated with an increased effort to access and evaluate research evidence, as well as overall use of research evidence.

Finally, investigators examined whether research evidence use was greater in clusters that participated in CDTs, and whether consensus regarding use of research evidence was greater in clusters that participated in CDTs. With respect to the first hypothesis, clusters participating in CDTs were found to be more engaged in evaluating research evidence for validity, reliability, and validity ($p < 0.05$). With respect to the second hypothesis, consensus as measured by variance scores was significantly greater in CDT clusters than in control clusters ($p < 0.001$). These finding confirm the role of CDTs in supporting EBP implementation by presenting research evidence supporting the EBP on one hand and building social networks that provide access to research evidence to network members on the other hand. Social networks, in turn, were found in earlier research (Palinkas et al., 2011) to be a significant independent predictor of stage of implementation.

All three lessons learned involve decisions to use local and global evidence. Global evidence is external in that it originates outside of agency or jurisdiction; it is based on standards of scientific rigor (e.g., randomized controlled trials) and it places emphasis on the generalizability or transferability of findings from one state or county to another. In contrast, local evidence is internal—it originates within an agency or jurisdiction, may include administrative data, is based on personal experience (either involvement in data collection and analysis or familiarity with population studied), and places emphasis on uniqueness of population and its needs (specificity). Research evidence use is rarely entirely local or global. Although some forms of evidence use are dominated by global or local evidence (perhaps even exclusively so), most forms are mixed. This observation is significant because local evidence is generally not considered to be research evidence in the same sense as global evidence (Stoesz, 2010); yet it plays an important role in decision making and EBP implementation among systems leaders (I. Epstein,

2011; Haight, 2010). Understanding that role will enable us to better align what is viewed as global evidence to local needs and preferences.

Organizational constraints

In the preceding chapter, we identified certain characteristics of social services organizations associated with successful implementation and sustainment of EBP. These include a formalized, centralized, and differentiated structure with a formal research infrastructure; a culture that values learning, innovation, and change; a climate that offers a sense of psychological safety and enables risk taking; leaders who are fully committed to innovation and particular EBPs and their implementation; a designated advocate or champion of EBP; qualified clinicians and support staff with the appropriate skills and training, documentation, and record keeping and systems; absorptive capacity; training and ongoing supervision of staff responsible for implementation; and a supportive network of advisors and opinion leaders both within and among organizations involved in the implementation process. Presumably, organizations lacking these characteristics are less likely to implement and sustain EBP.

Limited time and resources of practitioners have often been cited as a barrier to use of EBP across all sectors of health and social services (Glasgow, Lichtenstein, & Marcus, 2003). Heiwe and colleagues (2013) found that 78% of their sample of Swedish medical social workers identified lack of time as a barrier to the use of EBP. Systems leaders noted that giving staff time to acquire training in EBP may result in lost revenues to the agency (Palinkas & Aarons, 2009). Another frequently cited barrier is the lack of feedback and incentives for use of EBPs. From an agency perspective, more efficient treatment may result in a loss of revenue as the cost per client diminishes. From a provider perspective, lack of feedback regarding performance and incentives for the additional time and effort required to learn an EBP and use it with fidelity is often cited as a barrier to EBP implementation. Insurance may not cover more than a limited number of sessions or may exclude parent training (Palinkas et al., 2008). In contrast, the acquisition of new skills by staff and the availability of additional clinical supervision have been reported to facilitate EBP implementation (Palinkas & Aarons, 2009).

Along with these other characteristics, the organizational culture of a social services system may account for the lack of use of EBP. The literature suggests that agency leaders must proactively cultivate a research-attuned culture in which evidence is valued and reinforced (Huberman, 1994; Lavis et al., 2003; Roos & Shapiro, 1999). Barratt (2003) distinguishes between social services organizational cultures that are oral and those that are knowledge-based; the former is more likely to value direct practice experience over, and often to the exclusion of, other forms of learning.

Problems associated with evidence-to-action processes

A final challenge to the successful implementation and sustainment of EBP is embedded in the process by which evidence is generated and applied to practice. This process is both translational and transactional in nature. The translational element involves the design of efficacy, effectiveness, and implementation research trials. According to Ruth and Matusitz (2013):

> An explicit assumption of EBP is that research can be placed into hierarchical order according to quality of methodology and, implicitly, clinical utility (Magill, 2006). This system is unsuitable to the needs of social work because of its alignment with the principles of the physical sciences (Smith, 2002).
>
> *(p. 288)*

They further noted:

> The EBP rankings prioritize those that meet current standards for establishing internal validity such as randomization, experimental control, treatment manualization, and sufficient follow-up (Reynolds, 2000). These characteristics of rankings ignite objections from practitioners because they are inherently subjective to a controlled research environment and not the actual day-to-day uncontrolled settings.
>
> *(Ruth & Matusitz, 2013, p. 288)*

Thus, although it ensures internal validity, the randomized controlled trial may suffer from limited external validity because findings are specific to the population studied and not necessary to the population encountered by the average social worker (Landsverk et al., 2012; Palinkas & Soydan, 2012). Furthermore, "the quest for knowledge development through the withholding of service or random assignment of service to client is ethically abhorrent" (I. Epstein, 2009, p. 218), contributing to the reluctance of many social work practitioners and the communities they serve to participate in such studies.

The transactional aspect of research translation involves the interactions between researchers or knowledge generators and practitioners or knowledge consumers. Relationships between knowledge producers and consumers are highly variable, ranging from long-term associations perceived to be mutually beneficial to both parties to more exploitative episodes in which practitioners are used to recruit study participants, provide data, or both with very little in return (Begun, Berger, Otto-Salaj, & Rose, 2010; Palinkas et al., 2012). Researchers are often viewed by practitioners as being insensitive to their needs and preferences, whereas practitioners are often viewed by researchers as uninterested, provincial, and irrational (I. Epstein, 2011; Stoesz, 2010). However, these generalizations tend to devalue the numerous instances in which researchers and practitioners have worked together to forge collaborations that have resulted in knowledge of high scientific value and practical application. Examples of such collaborations include the Communities That Care intervention (Hawkins & Catalano, 2002) and the Collaborative HIV Prevention and Adolescent Mental Health Project (Madison, McKay, Paikoff, & Bell, 2000). It is these positive experiences of research-to-practice transactions that offer clues to the development of a culture of EBP in social work.

Conclusion

The barriers to successful EBP implementation and sustainment identified in this chapter are certainly not unique to social work practice. They may be found in other fields of health care and social services (Glasgow et al., 2003). However, awareness of these barriers provides an understanding of both the potential and the limits of EBP in social work. The limits are well known and involve the nature of the interventions produced by EBP and the knowledge that supports such interventions; the external environment that creates the supply and demand of EBP; and the inner setting of organizations that deliver EBPs as well as other services to vulnerable populations. The potential for EBP in social work lies in the construction and nurturing of a culture that is a model both of and for EBP. In the last chapter, we outline a model for the development of a culture supportive of EBP. However, organizations must first address the challenges outlined in this chapter, for unless they are able to do so, any efforts to construct such a culture and impose it from the top down will be rendered meaningless.

6

CONTROVERSIES

It has been several decades since some of the original ideas of evidence-based practice (EBP) first emerged in evidence-based medicine (EBM) as a response to the shortcomings of medical practice. Since then—and especially after the importation of some ideas from EBM to EBP pertinent to social and behavioral professions such as social work, criminal justice, and education—objections have been raised against the EBP model and its proponents, as well as challenges to its worth and merit. This chapter provides an account of the most frequent objections and elaborates on points made by opponents of EBP. These include a shortage of coherent and consistent scientific evidence, difficulty applying evidence to the care of individual patients and clients, and barriers to the practice of high-quality medicine and social work, as well as factors unique to EBP such as the need to develop new skills, limited time and resources, and a paucity of evidence that EBP works. There are also misperceptions that EBP denigrates clinical expertise, ignores patient values and preferences, promotes a cookbook approach to practice, is a cost-cutting tool or an ivory-tower concept, is limited to clinical research, and leads to therapeutic nihilism in the absence of evidence from randomized trials. In this chapter we take the position that scientific controversies are a mostly healthy component in the process of scientific advancement and should be welcomed when serious in nature and based on facts rather than ideological standpoints.

Physicist and philosopher of science John Ziman (2000) wrote that the "history of science is a chronicle of bitter intellectual controversies between strongly partisan groups" (p. 29). When a comprehensive history of EBP is written in the future, historical controversies will undoubtedly fill a fair amount of space. Scientific controversies are not an exception specific to EBP.

In fact, many scientific achievements and progress of scientific knowledge have been surrounded by controversies prior to the settlement of arguments for and against a specific achievement (Machamer, Pera, & Baltas, 2000).

By definition, scientific controversies are disagreements based on evidence and its interpretation, rather than values, ideologies, ethics, personal preferences, and even misconceptions. A scientific controversy can be defined as a transparent, public debate on the significance of evidence for or against an assertion over a sustained period of time. Its very rationale is based on the understanding that, in scientific processes, achievements and errors are subject to systematic critique and science will benefit from transparent scrutiny. Once a settlement is agreed upon, the result is in all likelihood a scientific achievement that advances scientific knowledge. In the real world, however, controversies concerning scientific issues extend easily beyond the sphere of scientific evidence and are contaminated by values, ideologies, and personal preferences. Some controversies originate on the basis of, and are fought in the name of, ethical considerations.

One common ground for most controversies is the limits and uncertainty of scientific knowledge. In Chapter 3, we observe that it is impossible to know with 100% certainty the truth of any scientific outcome. Scientific knowledge is always an estimate of or hypothesis about a real-world phenomenon that is subject to perpetual change and therefore will manifest differently in time and place. Further, real-world phenomena are complex, especially in social and behavioral contexts.

Uncertainty of knowledge, possibility of change, and exposure to complexities force us to operate with estimates, make assumptions, and interpret scientific outcomes. Because outcomes often can be interpreted in varied ways, controversies may emerge. In a worst-case scenario, controversies are affected by nonscientific arguments and poison a sane public debate.

Fortunately, the scientific community makes continuous efforts to correct deficits of its methods of investigation in the pursuit of reducing uncertainty. For example, as noted earlier in this book, the probability that a research outcome is true or an estimate has a high degree of precision may depend on study power and bias, the number of other high-quality studies on the same question, and the ratio of significant to nonsignificant relationships among the issues probed in a scientific field. In the long run, EBP is dependent on evidence accumulation. Evidence should be based on many observations made with increasingly sophisticated methods of data collection and analysis.

Critique of the epistemological basis of evidence-based practice

We begin this overview of the realm of philosophy of science and epistemology by acknowledging the risk of getting stuck on unsolvable issues. Issues in philosophy of science are often unsolved and end with all parties agreeing to disagree. This occurs because perspectives in the philosophy of science are based on fundamental assumptions—that do not render themselves to empirical testing—about the nature of human beings, society, and the relationship between human action and society. By definition, such assumptions are the foundation on which theoretical and empirical research is based. Nevertheless, approaching these issues provides a useful perspective on the relative importance of real-world problems that have particular salience for individuals and communities and require real solutions.

In 1972, in reaction to opinion-based medicine, or rather, ignorance-based medicine, Archie Cochrane (as discussed in Chapter 2) suggested that the randomized controlled trial was the best known method of assessing the effectiveness of an intervention X for condition Y. His book on effectiveness and efficiency was perhaps the starting point of modern EBM and later EBP. Especially during the early stages of its development, proponents adhered to a narrow understanding of EBM as involving an assertion that is empirically based, thus degrading professional judgment to lower echelons of the evidence hierarchy. This view established grounds for accusing EBM, and later EBP, of simple positivism, a scientific paradigm that is grounded in observable facts as perceived by human observers, often with quantitative research designs; employs determinism and mechanical rationality; and confuses empirical observations with reality itself, although at times opposing EBP on less evident epistemological premises (Egger, Davey Smith, & Altman, 2001; Hammersley, 2003; Nevo & Slonim-Nevo, 2011; Pawson, 2002, 2006; Webb, 2001). This issue still haunts EBP today.

From a practitioner perspective, it is obvious that epistemological issues and theoretical arguments for and against an evidence-based intervention are not of primary value. What counts for practitioners is what works in real-world situations, in social work agencies, community development projects, and in the context of large-scale policy making. Similarly, not many clients are interested in epistemological issues of the treatment they receive; they and their families are more interested in whether the intervention will help. Successful results can be achieved and costly, less effective, and harmful interventions can be avoided without solving or even acknowledging epistemological issues that are often given prominence in the ivory tower of academia. Epistemological discourses take place and generate tension perhaps in an effort to influence attitudes toward EBP in a certain direction, favorable or antagonistic. In a recent article, Kelly and Moore (2012) returned to the epistemological perspective, seeking solutions to ease some of the tensions between proponents and opponents of EBP. They suggested introducing to EBP some of the conceptual distinctions that were made three centuries ago by David Hume in Scotland and Immanuel Kant in Prussia.

Both Hume and Kant argued that there is a distinction between the observation and the object being observed. Our process of observation is a mental representation of material and immaterial phenomena and stimuli that are integrated through our senses, the scientific tools we employ, or both. As such, all observations are partial and subject to interpretation. Further, Hume suggested that experience and observation are imperfect and fallible maps of the real world; consequently, observations are subject to distortion. To characterize this distinction, Kant used the terms *phenomenon* to refer to an object or event as it appears based on our mental perceptions and observations and *noumenon* to refer to an item that is real.

Kelly and Moore (2012) observed:

> This fundamental position is simultaneously central to EBM and ignored by it. It is central because EBM acknowledges that single observations are potentially unreliable and that the best (but not necessarily final) account of the relationship between the drug and the outcome is obtained by multiple observations. This is firmly in the Humian/Kantian tradition. However, EBM seldom goes to the stage further and questions the reality of the evidence itself. It tends to treat the evidence not as a proxy for reality, but as if it were reality. This is to confuse empirical observation with reality itself in what appears to be a crude form of positivism.
>
> *(pp. 8–9)*

To demonstrate how nonpositivist EBM needs to be, and how its components clearly go beyond simplistic assumptions of positivism, Kelly and Moore (2012) used a conceptual trichotomy originated by Hume, further developed by Kant, and later expanded by John Stuart Mills. The trichotomy consists of three types of judgment we use to interpret sensory data or scientific evidence: (1) analytic a priori judgments, which are based on logical and rational thinking before the observation or fact; (2) synthetic a posteriori judgments, which are made after the fact and based on observational data; and (3) synthetic a priori judgments, which are percepts (as in mathematics and natural science) that cannot be determined on the basis of experience alone. For each of these judgment types, Kelly and Moore (2012) gave examples of core components in EBM, arguing that these concepts provide a better understanding of the epistemological soundness of EBM and, we argue, of EBP.

Analytic a priori judgments

Analytic a priori judgments are true by definition and denying them would be self-contradictory, as would be the case for one of the most central components of EBP, the hierarchy of evidence. This component of EBP is based on the judgment that there are real relationships among phenomena, and confounding factors or biases blur those relationships. The hierarchy of evidence ranks the ability of confounding factors to mask the relationships among specific phenomena of interest. Our methods of data collection are designed to more or less control bias.

Other analytic a priori tools follow this principle, including judgments that randomized controlled trials control for extraneous or confounding factors during an assessment of an intervention; confidence intervals help distinguish between true and random effects; and summing results in meta-analyses produces a truer result than a single observation. The hierarchy of evidence does not suggest the possibility of elimination of bias, but rather how much bias can be diminished to reveal a pure relationship uncluttered by other factors (Kelly & Moore, 2012).

Synthetic a posteriori judgments

Synthetic a posteriori judgments include the core activity of EBP: establishing estimates of causal relationships among independent and dependent variables as observed entities. These judgments are purely empirical in nature and can be observed only after an event has taken place. For example, randomized controlled studies attempt to establish the relative effectiveness of a social work intervention as compared to another social work intervention in the context of a specific mental disorder by computing the difference in effect size. During this process, three observations have taken place: what one intervention does, what the other intervention does, and the difference between them.

Synthetic a priori judgments

In the Kantian framework, synthetic a priori judgments connect the domains of analytic a priori and synthetic a posteriori judgments. Kelly and Moore (2012) stated that without synthetic a priori judgments, EBM would be impossible. This is typically the case because induction is a process involving judgment and interpretation to make sense of empirical data. The EBP model is very much dependent on synthetic a priori judgments to bridge the empirical findings of synthetic a posteriori evidence of effectiveness and the rational analytic a priori concept of the hierarchy of evidence. Two examples of synthetic a priori judgments in EBP are discussed here.

As described in Chapter 3, external validity, a central component that makes EBP especially useful, is dependent on probabilistic judgments about the applicability (transportability) of the scientific outcomes of

ome of the issues raised by Kelly and Moore (2012) but not
ctive, Webb's criticism is based on a historical controversy in
sophy of science regarding the primacy of subjectivism versus
m. Such disagreements are based on basic assumptions about
ture, the nature of society, and the relationship between human
d society, and constitute a philosophical foundation to scientific
s (paradigms). By their nature they are incommensurable, that is,
conclude which is more accurate with the tools available to us.
cal analysis of paradigmatic positions in social sciences and social
Soydan (2010a).

is no doubt that the EBP process model implies social better-
d on action informed by the best available and effective evidence.
t prescribes that whenever possible, gold-standard evidence and
distilled by meta-analysis should be used for scientific guidance. Its
al approach is the cautious and judicious implementation of the
ble evidence. However, as noted several times in this book, the
el fully recognizes factors such as client values and preferences as
cial worker judgments, common sense, and discretion when the
EBP is constrained by imperfect scientific evidence. EBP recog-
client values and preferences and other nonscientific factors may
acy in client action despite the existence of high-quality evidence
prescribe otherwise.

istorical issues: critique and counterarguments

out the years, a rich collection of criticism has been published on
comings (real or alleged) of EBM and later of EBP. Criticism has
sed on various levels, including practical, methodological, theoret-
al, and ideological. Further, some criticism has been generated by
information or simple ignorance of what constitutes EBP. Perhaps
ost influential review of different types of criticism was developed
and McAlister (2000) with reference to EBM. Later, social work-
d and adapted the framework suggested by Straus and McAlister to
rk and EBP (Gibbs & Gambrill, 2002; Mullen, Shlonsky, Bledsoe,
ny, 2005; Mullen & Streiner, 2004). Meritoriously, Straus and
r organized objections into two main categories: limitations and
ptions of EBM. In their typology, the limitations of EBM include
niversal to the practice of medicine such as a shortage of coherent
stent scientific evidence, difficulties applying evidence to the care
dual patients, and barriers to the practice of high-quality medicine,
s factors unique to EBM such as the need to develop new skills,
me and resources, and a paucity of evidence that EBM works

an intervention study in a context and un
the intervention has not been tested. Asses
sophisticated theoretical thinking to bridge
from multiple contexts.

A second example of synthetic a priori ju
diagnostics. To solve a problem, social work
ing the observation of problems in the real
these empirical descriptions to a taxonomy
described in EBP as a process model; diagn
conceptualized client problem framework ar
tion to prompt change (healing). Taxonomi
lems and do not fully map a specific client
situation. This occurs because taxonomies ar
ent problems change based on time and plac
in EBP, synthetic a priori judgments are u
construct and empirical observations.

In sum, there is little doubt epistemologi
troversies will continue with regard to EBF
tradition of progress throughout the history
concepts developed by Hume and Kant, Ke
productive framework that may help the m
opponents of EBP reconsider their objectio

Evidence-based practice model vers

In recent years, Stephen A. Webb authored
the validity of EBP in social work. Webb (2

Evidence-based practice is derived
behavior in a planned and systematic
concentrating on 'epistemic processes
chological inference it is claimed tha
the determinants of decision making
model suggests that decision making i:
optimal at best and based on a limited
workers engage in a reflexive underst
certainty based decision-making proc
Complex phenomena such as decisior
mined or subject to 'control'. . . . [T]
into 'facts' and 'values' implicit in ev
mines professional judgment and disc

Akir
as cc
the
obje
hum
bein
appr
we c
For a
work

T
ment
Furth
evide
profe
best a
EBP
well
proce.
nizes
have
that n

Othe

Throu
the sh
been f
ical, et
a lack
the for
by Str
ers ado
social
& Bel
McAli
misper
factors
and co
of indi
as well
limited

(Straus & McAlister, 2000). Misperceptions include arguments that EBM denigrates clinical expertise, ignores patient values and preferences, promotes a cookbook approach to medicine, is a cost-cutting tool, is an ivory-tower concept, is limited to clinical research, and leads to therapeutic nihilism in the absence of evidence from randomized trials. In the following section, we summarize some of the most contested arguments and counterarguments pertaining to social work.

Shortage of evidence

One of the first authors to point out the challenge of shortage of evidence in medical practice with reference to EBM was Canadian physician C. David Naylor, who in a *Lancet* article stated: "In a recent attack on evidence-based medicine, a philosopher urged doctors to defend clinical reasoning based on experience and pathophysiological mechanisms and criticised the effects of clinical epidemiology and health services research on practice," adding later, "evidence-based medicine offers little help in the many grey zones of practice where the evidence about risk-benefit ratios of competing clinical options is incomplete or contradictory" (Naylor, 1995, p. 840).

What Naylor pointed out is a serious challenge to all professions with foundations in scientific evidence. Although evidence is accumulative in one sense and our collective knowledge gradually becomes broader, deeper, and more comprehensive, it also is ever changing and advancing. Many scientific truths of yesterday are not today's scientific truth. Most scientific truth of today won't survive tomorrow. Further, the amount and quality of accumulated and collective knowledge vary in time in every discipline, professional field, and subspecialty. For instance, there may be more high-quality evidence regarding interventions for crime prevention than elderly care. Perhaps we know more about the treatment of cardiovascular diseases than we know about certain types of cancer. The state of the art in each discipline and subdiscipline varies. Even when evidence is available, it can be inconclusive, contradictory, imperfect, incomplete, and irrelevant to real-life conditions. Furthermore, for reasons we discuss in Chapter 3, there are fundamental limits to our ability to know with certainty; our knowledge is nothing but estimates of the truth. Therefore, regardless of the presence of an EBP model, any professional practice with a base in science is contingent on the amount and quality of evidence.

The most straightforward response to the argument regarding a shortage of evidence is that the EBP model represents a systematic way of dealing with this challenge. In moments of uncertainty caused by shortage of coherent and consistent evidence, the EBP model invites practitioners to use extra caution and transparency and emphasizes follow-up in the implementation of this very evidence.

In our view, although an element of uncertainty will apply to many, if not to all, professional interventions, there is also cause for optimism. Mullen and colleagues (2005) referred to studies indicating that many professional decisions across several professional practices are still made without satisfactory high-quality evidence, and Soydan (2009) pointed out that too many interventions are used without accurate evidence, even though such evidence exists. Yet there are also studies that show increasing awareness and use of evidence for prevention, diagnostics, and treatment among professionals, including social workers. In addition, the amount of high-quality evidence has been increasing, especially after the inception of the Cochrane and Campbell collaborations, development of high-quality clearinghouses, and creation of guidelines based on the best available evidence, now more than a decade after Straus and McAlister (2000) published their article (Mosteller & Boruch, 2002; Socialstyrelsen, 2011; Soydan, 2008a). In particular, the number of systematic research reviews with high scientific standards has been substantially increasing. For instance, since its inception 20 years ago, the Cochrane Collaboration has increased the number of its reviews from near zero to around 5,000 currently in the Cochrane Library. Evidence is supplied further by the Campbell Collaboration and many high-quality clearinghouses, as well as by qualified guidelines for professionals. This optimism was expressed by Mullen and his colleagues (2005) nearly a decade ago:

> We think these several aspects of the shortage of evidence challenge can be addressed in a number of ways. First, evidence-based social workers must remember that, when they make decisions for which little or no evidence exists, they should exercise caution and perhaps be even more vigilant in monitoring outcomes. Second, shortages of evidence can be addressed and corrected over time. When a knowledge gap is identified, this should point the way to needed research. Fields of practice wherein little research evidence exists should be prioritised. Methodological corrections should be instituted to deal with the inflation of evidence issue. Where interventions are found to have small and transient effects of limited importance, this should be acknowledged and addressed. The under-utilisation of existing valid and relevant assessment instruments should be corrected by enhanced training, improved dissemination of information, and increased funding to purchase such tools. In short, we think that much can be done through research and education to address the shortage of evidence challenge.
>
> *(pp. 74–75)*

Difficulties applying generalized estimates to individual clients

As described in previous chapters, evidence obtained through experimental studies (and other quantitative research designs) represents average estimates of outcomes for individuals in a sample. By nature and due to societal dynamics, there are always biological and sociobehavioral variations in the reception and response of individuals to interventions. A close examination of experimental study results shows that there are always individuals in the experimental group who do not positively respond to the intervention, and at times have worse outcomes than some subjects in the control group. Similarly, there are always individuals in the control group who do better than those in the experiment group. This type of variation has misled some scholars to reject EBP (Charlton, 1997) and emphasize the role of professional wisdom and experience instead (Garfield, 1998).

However, it can be legitimately argued that variations in social behavior generate a complexity that affects all scientific inquiry and human professions, not only EBP. Thus, making this challenge a basis for rejecting only EBP and no other sciences and professions does not seem logically consistent.

Two further arguments were developed by Mullen and Streiner (2004):

> The alternative to using evidence based interventions—with their known rate of failure—is to use unproven procedures, based only on the hope that they may work, but without any real knowledge of how often they do or do not, except our recall of successful cases. However, memory is a slippery thing. We do very well in recalling our successes, but very poorly in remembering our failures—what has been called the "denominator problem."
>
> . . . EBP does not mean only applying the results of large randomized trials conducted by others. Practitioners can and should view each person as an "$N = 1$" study (Barlow & Hersen, 1984). That is, EBP also involves using techniques such as interrupted time series, multiple baseline assessments, before-after designs, and the like, combined with objective measures of functioning, with every person seen (Lueger et al., 2001; Streiner, 1998).
>
> (pp. 115–116)

Finally, we would like to mention a method designed to compute the probability that an individual will respond positively to treatment; this method is called *number needed to treat* and indicates the number of individuals that need to be treated to obtain an additional positive response to a treatment (Mullen

& Streiner, 2004; Straus & McAlister, 2000). For example, a comparison of screened and unscreened women in a randomized study in Sweden showed that 1,592 women between 50 and 74 years of age had to receive a mammogram to prevent one death from breast cancer 7 years after the screening was established as a routine (Tabár et al., 1985). Although this method is helpful, it also has limitations (Laupacis, Sackett, & Roberts, 1988) and does not automatically compensate for the shortcomings of the scientific method of generating estimates of intervention effectiveness.

Barriers to the practice of high-quality social work

This objection was originally directed toward EBM, arguing that the gap between growing demand for health services and ever-increasing health care costs and shrinking resources paralyzes the application of high-quality evidence in medicine in general and EBM in particular (Straus & McAlister, 2000). The pressure generated at the intersection of demand and resources is assumed to impair the ability of physicians to make use of evidence in patient care. The idea of barriers to adequate evidence use in social services was later directed toward EBP and is perhaps most known as EBP's cost-cutting role. Strong tendencies toward integrated social, mental health, and health services; demographic shifts; and further advancement of medical equipment throughout the world might further accentuate this traditional gap between needs and resources. In particular, with the growth of externally managed care, many have assumed that governments will use EBP as a tool to reduce costs, thus limiting the use of high-quality evidence and endangering the quality of care (Mullen & Streiner, 2004). Based on this argument, the concept of managerialism, referred to as neoliberalism in some countries such as the United Kingdom and as total quality management in countries such as the United States (Davies, 2003), has been applied to EBP and carries a negative connotation (Webb, 2001). What started as an empirical observation of the gap between demand and resources in EBM became an ideological argument against EBP. Gibbs and Gambrill (2002) described this argument as resulting from "ignorance of EBP" (p. 458), and Straus and McAlister (2000) classified it among various "misperceptions of evidence-based medicine" (p. 838).

Proponents of EBP have objected to arguments regarding barriers and cost-cutting policies (Gibbs & Gambrill, 2002; Mullen & Streiner, 2004; Straus & McAlister, 2000). Straus and McAlister (2000) stated:

> Indeed, increased attention to the principles of evidence-based medicine among policy-makers and purchasers should lead to the preservation of funding for proven efficacious therapies and the elimination only of interventions that have been shown to be harmful or ineffective.
>
> *(p. 838)*

Regarding cost-cutting policies, Mullen & Streiner (2004) argued:

> This would be a gross distortion of the way EBP should be used, for two reasons. First, as mentioned previously, the choice between or among competing procedures is dictated not only by their respective effectiveness, but also by taking into consideration the practitioner's expertise and the client's wishes. Second, cost is only half of what should be examined; the other half is benefit, or effectiveness. That is, a proper criterion (although, as we have said, never the sole criterion) should be the cost-benefit or cost-effectiveness of the intervention (for a discussion of the differences, see Drummond & Mooney, 1981; Torrance, Stoddart, Drummond, & Gafni, 1981); how much of the outcome does $1 buy? A given procedure may be relatively inexpensive to deliver, but if its results are limited, its cost/benefit ratio may actually be higher than a more expensive but much more effective procedure.
>
> *(pp. 117–118)*

Limited time and resources, and need for training

In Chapter 2, we describe a generic model of EBP as conceived by its originators (Sackett, Richardson, Rosenberg, & Haynes, 1997); this model is a multistep process that involves formulating an answerable question based on client problems, finding evidence of an adequate response to the problem, critically appraising the quality of the evidence, matching the evidence with the client, and following up on outcomes. Originators of the EBP process model viewed these steps as an interactive process involving: (1) the patient's preferences, traditions, and actions; (2) the clinical environment and circumstances, including organizational frames; and (3) the research evidence. This model has a reputation of being complicated, time consuming, high maintenance, and simply unrealistic to implement in real-life conditions.

Without doubt, this is a complex process that requires skills, resources, and adequate time to apply. The question is, however, whether there is a more rational and effective alternative to EBP if the process means clients and patients will be treated ethically, professionally, respectfully, and with transparency and that available resources will be used cost efficiently. Arguments have been developed regarding why it is wiser to use EBP compared to intervening in human lives and communities without any evidence to support such actions. We briefly summarize those arguments. Further, as described in Chapter 4 and elsewhere (Palinkas & Soydan, 2012), implementation of evidence-based interventions and application of an EBP process model is no longer the domain of lone workers but rather an organizational matter with all support components that come with such an approach.

Mullen and Streiner (2004) pointed out several useful tools that support the work of individual workers and teams. These tools include cutting-edge evidence sources such as the Cochrane and Campbell libraries, evidence-based clearinghouses, guidelines, and desktop references. Most sources are available online, which reduces the time needed to find and retrieve evidence. An increasing number of schools of social work and other institutions educate and train their students to understand and appraise the quality of evidence. Even a decade ago, Mullen and Streiner (2004) provided accounts of successful training with students in psychology, nursing, social work, health care administration, special education, and other fields. Today, many continuing education programs for professionals are offered by universities, colleges, and human services agencies.

In terms of finding time to employ the EBP model, we acknowledge difficulties and agree with Mullen and Streiner (2004). They observed:

> For the practitioner rushing from one person to the next, sometimes finding even 5 minutes to do a search may not always be feasible. Time spent doing a search may save many hours later, because effort is not spent on a procedure that hasn't been shown to be effective, but we recognize that though this may seem reasonable in the abstract, it may not be practicable in reality. We would argue, however, that it may be worthwhile in these circumstances to save questions about the effectiveness of an intervention or the utility of an assessment procedure to the end of the day, and to spend 15 or 30 minutes reviewing the evidence.
>
> *(p. 116)*

Although this recommendation might seem unrealistic to many practitioners, what Mullen and Streiner foresaw regarding organizations is indeed accurate, and this brings us to the next criticism of EBP.

Inadequate infrastructure and systems organization to support translation

Typically, objections against the EBP process model on the basis of limited time and resources and a need for training are related to inadequate infrastructure and systems organization. When attributed to the organizational context, the core problem expands beyond these issues of limited time, resources, and training. In a systematic literature review, Greenhalgh, Robert, Macfarlane, Bate, and Kyriakidou (2004) distilled factors promoting or impeding successful translation and implementation of EBPs in organizational settings. Organizational shortcomings in translating and implementing EBPs have been noted by various researchers who tested implementation models in organizational settings; for a comprehensive account of such efforts, see Palinkas and Soydan (2012). Many of these efforts relate to rec-ommendations such as the following:

> Organizations will need to consider how such information can be distributed best in their particular contexts. For larger organizations this may mean expanded responsibilities for a centralized informatics department. For smaller organizations one or more individuals may need to be designated as information experts. In nearly all cases the process can benefit from teamwork and collaborative sharing.
>
> *(Mullen & Streiner, 2004, pp. 116–117)*

In Chapter 4 of this book, we describe the crucial role played by organizations as the loci of EBP implementation. Organizations provide the structural and cultural framework that influences the success or failure of EBP implementation. Due to an increased emphasis on translational and implementation research during the last 10 years or so, successful application of EBP has become better understood. Rather than primarily an individual activity, EBP is increasingly becoming an institutional effort. Implementation of evidence-based interventions requires an organizational culture that supports everyone's efforts to serve clients; we believe this is a very promising perspective. Research on the translation and implementation of EBPs in organizational contexts has largely focused on four distinct levels of service delivery: (1) the larger service system or environment; (2) the implementing organization; (3) groups or teams of individuals delivering the practice; and (4) the individual service providers and consumers (Palinkas & Soydan, 2012). With more evidence of how organizations function as the setting of social work practice and increased awareness among decision makers and other actors in and associated with those organizations, many hindrances to successful EBP implementation will decrease.

Misconceptions

As noted in the beginning of this chapter, scientific controversies are disagreements based on evidence. However, intentional or unintentional misconceptions about scientific data and models often generate or prolong controversies. EBP has its fair share of misconceptions that have generated controversy. In this section, we briefly review some of the most serious controversies that proponents of EBP assess as misconceptions.

EBP ignores client values and preferences and undermines professional expertise

Webb (2001) triggered criticism that later became common among opponents of EBP in his critique of the now-defunct Centre for Evidence-Based

Social Care in Exeter, United Kingdom, an institution that was one of the very early opponents of opinion-based social work and proponents of EBP in social work. Webb wrote:

> [A statement by the center] indicates a preference to change professional practice from decisions based on opinion to those made on the basis of evidence. Explicit in this statement, although they shift their ground in the very next paragraph, is the view that opinion-based judgment is inferior to evidence-based decision making, and the extraneous influences such as resource constraints and professional values should not contaminate the evaluative process. According to this view, social work decisions should rest solely on evidence leading to effective outcomes.
>
> *(p. 62)*

In the same article, Webb (2001) suggested the idea of EBP as a cookbook approach that ignores professional skills and thus undermines professional expertise and wisdom.

This package of criticism suggesting that EBP ignores client values and valuable professional judgment is perhaps one of the most puzzling objections to EBP. It is puzzling because the EBP model, as explicitly stated by its originators (Sackett et al., 1997; Sackett, Rosenberg, Muir Gray, Haynes, & Richardson, 1996), involves the integration of research evidence; client values, preferences, and actions; and clinical circumstances, including professional judgment. Importantly, the EBP model recommends a great degree of deference to client desires, especially when there is a scarcity or lack of evidence about outcomes or disagreement regarding the comparative effectiveness, costs, and potential harm of available interventions.

Only research results of randomized controlled studies should be used in EBP

Another common misperception is the assumption that the evidence-based process model favors randomized controlled trials as the gold standard and denigrates other methods of measuring the effectiveness of interventions. This misconception has also been directed toward the Cochrane and Campbell collaborations, and perhaps the EBP model has indirectly inherited this view. However, both the policies of the Cochrane and Campbell collaborations and the guidelines of the EBP model are explicit on this issue. The Cochrane and Campbell collaborations have established themselves as forums of high-quality evidence on what works, what is promising, and what is potentially harmful in health, mental health, and social and behavioral interventions. They are dedicated to randomized controlled research designs to maximize control of biases in all levels of the research process and to deliver the best estimates of the effectiveness of interventions. However, they also recognize the merit and value of nonrandomized studies, and have developed tools and strategies to use nonrandomized results in the absence or scarcity of randomized controlled trials. By making use of these tools and strategies, the collaborations provide transparency, allowing anyone to assess the quality and deficits of estimates of the effectiveness of interventions.

The EBP model was designed by its originators to make use of any good-quality scientific evidence. Sackett and colleagues (1997) explicitly stated: "Evidence-based medicine is not restricted to randomized trials and meta-analysis. It involves tracking down the best external evidence (from systematic reviews when they exist; otherwise from primary studies)" (p. 4). This specific understanding of the EBP model's scientific foundations is emphasized constantly.

Evidence-based practice brings nihilism to professional practice

The concept of nihilism has a strong negative connotation; by definition, it is an extreme form of skepticism and denial. Proponents of EBP are said to deny all scientific evidence in absence of the perfect gold standard, thus preventing professionals from taking any reasonable course of action. This is a strong statement.

As emphasized by proponents of EBP (e.g., Soydan, 2008b), all scientific knowledge has limitations. This is due to our imperfect methods of observation and analysis and the complexity and dynamic nature of human behavior and societal structures in real-life situations. Capturing a causal relationship in a real-world situation only refers to generating an estimate of this causal relationship. Although the more we can control bias, the better estimates we can generate, we will never be perfect. This leaves us with the fact that caution in professional action and intervention is always imperative.

Mullen and Streiner (2004) use the terms "limitations" and "fatal flaws" (p. 118) with reference to the imperfect nature of our estimates. Limitations will always exist, with or without EBP. However, practitioners need to be aware of fatal flaws in evidence because serious deficits (heavily biased results) can jeopardize evidence and threaten or undermine professional action. As described earlier, one of the steps of the EBP process model is the critical appraisal of evidence. This skill must be taught by educators and learned and embraced by practitioners and professionals.

Conclusion

This chapter summarized the most common and serious objections to EBP, as well as refutations of those objections. As noted, scientific controversies are transparent and open public debates on the significance of evidence for or against an assertion during a sustained period of time. Controversies about the deficits and merits of EBP should be viewed in this historical perspective and accepted as sound expressions of serious debate that should ultimately benefit the advancement of EBP as a new professional culture for social work and other human services professions. However, controversies based on factors such as misconceptions, ideological standpoints, and other nonscientific arguments confuse the profession, to the detriment of those we are dedicated to serve.

7

GLOBALIZATION OF EVIDENCE-BASED PRACTICE

This chapter examines globalization of evidence from the perspective of transportability. One of the ultimate ambitions of scientific knowledge production is to generalize knowledge across boundaries, be they geographical, national, social, cultural, ethnic, or socioeconomic. Although evidence may not always be transportable or may be transportable to a limited degree depending on various circumstances, generalizability remains a significant goal for the scientific community. There is no doubt that some scientific evidence is valid for a long time and in multiple places and contexts, whereas other evidence and knowledge is less temporally or contextually valid. Ultimately, any knowledge may become invalid if real-life circumstances change or a paradigm shift occurs.

Internationalization of evidence in this book refers to cross-national movement of evidence from one country to other countries. Most technical innovations originating in the natural and medical sciences become diffused internationally, especially in the contemporary world due to advanced communication tools available to large populations. However, the question remains: What are the circumstances in which evidence in the human services may or may not spread across borders to be implemented successfully?

In this chapter, we emphasize globalization of evidence rather than internationalization of evidence, which in our view fails to capture the complexity of factors and circumstances that may facilitate or impede implementation of evidence across boundaries. Globalization of scientific evidence, especially in terms of evidence pertaining to social and behavioral interventions, is contingent upon factors that facilitate or impede uptake and integration of innovations. Nations, cultures, and individuals share common elements despite diversity. Although cultural differences may impede uptake of innovations, cultural similarities may have the inverse effect, thus facilitating uptake. In this chapter, we elaborate on the effect of globalization of values, lifestyles, and other factors that may increasingly stimulate globalization of evidence-based interventions (EBIs).

As described in Chapter 4, social and behavioral interventions take place in organizational settings. Although organizations develop their own internal cultural cores, they also are affected by external cultural factors, must adapt themselves to such factors, and may become increasingly similar to one another on a global level. This chapter also elaborates on the relationship between globalization of evidence and service organizations that adopt globally recognized work cultures.

In the field of social, behavioral, and health practices, the Cochrane Collaboration and later the Campbell Collaboration pioneered the globalization of evidence. The efforts of these collaborations seem to have triggered interest in research on globalization of evidence and related issues. This chapter describes some of those efforts and their effect, as well as similar efforts such as evidence-based clearinghouses that capitalize on the foundations of the two collaborations.

External validity and generalizability

The concept of generalizing knowledge from one setting to another is a highly contested issue in the history of social and behavioral sciences. The topic has been a matter of discourse in the philosophy of science for centuries, but it received significant attention during the Enlightenment and subsequent decades from sociologists such as Auguste Comte, who ardently argued the merits of generalizability. Others such as Max Weber and Georg Simmel countered by pointing out the uniqueness of knowledge as historically embedded in a specific context, therefore rejecting generalizability between settings as a goal of social sciences (Soydan, 1999). The discourse on the possibility of and need for generalization of evidence continues to this day, fomenting a divide in the social sciences.

One aspect of this scientific strand is the question of hypothesis testing versus hypothesis generating. In 1997, William J. McGuire published a seminal article emphasizing the need for psychology to engage in hypothesis generating, which had been neglected by a primary focus on hypothesis testing. McGuire (1997) presented a typology of heuristic approaches to help the scientific community educate students and mentors with regard to hypothesis generating. Underlying McGuire's typology was the assumption that existing theory and empirical evidence should be used to hypothesize reasonable generalizations to other settings, where they can and should be tested. This assumption is a practical tool and acknowledges real-life circumstances; for example, practitioners may consider implementing a crime prevention program that works among majority youths with a certain group of minority youths. Similarly, decision makers in one country may consider implementing a successful program that was developed in another country, as is the case with the evidence-based program *Oportunidades*, which was developed and tested in Mexico and successfully implemented in several other low- and middle-income countries around the world (Nigenda & González-Robledo, 2005). Successful implementation of EBIs in diverse contexts necessitates a focus on the generalizability or external validity of those interventions.

As noted in Chapter 3, Donald T. Campbell differentiated between internal and external validity, characterizing external validity as the representativeness or generalizability of evidence from one setting to another. He raised the question, "To what populations, settings, and variables can this effect be generalized?" (Campbell, 1957, p. 297). As argued by Cronbach (1982), most external validity and generalization issues are in the context of treatments, units, settings, and outcomes that were not studied during the experiment in question, although external validity at times may involve variations in treatments, units, settings, and outcomes that were part of the experiment. Elaborating on threats to external validity in a detailed review that extends beyond the purposes of this book, Shadish, Cook, and Campbell (2002) emphasized that understanding external validity involves identifying ways in which a causal relationship might or might not change across units, settings, treatments, and outcomes. This position is very similar to the concept of an incremental approach to generating hypotheses described by McGuire (1997). In sum, the question of generalizability boils down to crafting plausible hypotheses based on previous studies, theories, and empirical evidence that can be tested.

Current thinking about the transportability or globalization of evidence is akin to the classic notion of generalizability and recognizes the value and necessity of multisite (or cross-boundary) testing of evidence via replication studies as the ultimate gateway to successful global transportation of evidence. However, the notion of global transportability goes beyond the notion of generalizability by actively searching for cultural, social, and organizational factors that may facilitate or impede uptake of evidence given the absence or scarcity of evidence in the new context in question. As noted in the next section, given the complications of replication studies (which may vary depending on the domain, such as treatment or prevention), deficits of contemporary methods, and controversies associated with those issues, we hold that there is reason to explore other complementary means of assessing the global cross-boundary transportability of evidence.

Replication studies

Replication studies constitute the classic backbone of generalizability, and therefore validity, of evidence across boundaries. By repeating the same experiment in a new context, researchers attempt to gain insight about whether or not the experiment or intervention remains valid. However, a debate triggered by a recent study prepared by a group of researchers from the Society for Prevention Research (Valentine et al., 2011a, 2011b) revealed that the concept of replication studies remains contested (Aos et al., 2011; Hansen, 2011).

The classic question is: "Does study Y replicate study X?" This question underscores the concept of reproducibility and generalizability in the foundation of all scientific endeavors. Reproducibility assumes that details of the design and implementation of study X are reported accurately so that independent researchers can repeat the same experiment (study Y), and that results of the experiments are equivalent. However, what seems reasonable as an assumption becomes very difficult to realize in real-world conditions.

Commenting on the Valentine et al. (2011a) article, Hansen (2011) cited a truism coined by Herodotus, an ancient Greek historian who lived from 484 to 425 BC, that one cannot step into the same stream twice because both the stream and the individual are ever changing, suggesting that replication may not be possible. Hansen (2011) argued that, although poor intervention design may be one of the causes of failed replication studies because interventions are very complex processes, additional factors may also challenge replication studies.

Failure to implement with fidelity is one such factor. Fidelity in implementation refers to how well an intervention is applied in terms of adherence to the original evidence-based version of the intervention, including dosage, duration, and frequency with which it is delivered. Maintaining fidelity in a strict sense is very difficult and challenging in practice. Furthermore, there is a specific form of deviation from fidelity necessitated by the need to adapt the original EBI in a new environment, such as when it is offered to culturally diverse populations. This type of deviation, although intentional, conflicts with the underlying concept of fidelity. In sum, implementation with fidelity is a highly contested factor that remains a topic of investigation by researchers.

Another challenge to implementing interventions successfully is adapting EBIs to the setting of implementation. Adaptation of some degree is almost always a necessary component of successful implementation, increased impact, or both. Therefore, adaptation should always be considered when practitioners implement EBIs in clinical settings or when researchers implement interventions for experimental research purposes. However, when adaption blurs the core and active elements of the intervention, it may be neutralized to produce no effect or even become harmful (Hansen, 2011). The current state of knowledge does not offer much guidance in terms of the adaptation process and its consequences, thus making replications imperfect and limited.

Mediators are variables that "describe the process by which the intervention achieves its effects" (MacKinnon, 2011, p. 675), given that the purpose of interventions is to change characteristics of participants or alternatively to change the social and physical environments of participants to generate behavioral change. As Hansen (2011) pointed out, "not all mediators are created equal" (p. 119); some mediators have strong bonds with behaviors and are thus in a better position to affect behaviors as intended, whereas others have weak relationships with behaviors and are in a poor position to prompt behavioral change in the right direction. Failure to change mediators is a major cause of implementation failure, thus constituting an impediment to successful replication.

Finally, referring specifically to the field of prevention, Hansen (2011) pointed out deficits in terms of the lack or absence of insight and motivation among implementers. He argued that, in prevention science, implementers of EBIs typically recruit only inexperienced candidates.

> Indeed, in practice, prevention research methods eschew the recruitment of highly motivated or insightful teachers for two reasons. First, we require control groups to fail. Should motivated and skilled teacher [*sic*] be assigned to the control condition, their enthusiasm might dampen hoped for effects. Second, if they are assigned to the treatment condition, their insight and motivation would be confounded with program content. Yet, insight and motivation may be key elements of intervention success in the dissemination environment. Replications that continue to involve only novice implementers limit our understanding of how insight and motivation can affect outcomes.
>
> *(Hansen, 2011, p. 119)*

These and other arguments (Aos et al., 2011) constitute significant challenges to the idea of replication studies, which were historically conceptualized as the backbone of scientific generalizability and external validity. Nevertheless, the scientific community continues to conduct replication studies while at times remaining cognizant of their pitfalls.

Implementation in culturally diverse societies

One specific case of the transportability of interventions pertains to implementation of interventions among diverse populations of a single country in which all populations share a common set of national cultural characteristics.

In research on dissemination and use of evidence-based practices (EBPs) and EBIs across diverse populations, one major step forward was triggered by controversies regarding whether or not EBPs, EBIs, and service delivery systems should be tailored to diverse ethnic groups to more effectively respond to their specific problems.

Ethnic diversity in particular has been a major challenge to social work practice in Western countries, in which most EBPs and EBIs are developed and tested for mainstream populations. Growing concern and awareness during the 1970s and 1980s about the needs and rights of ethnically diverse populations served as a backdrop to these controversies. Especially in light of the lack of empirical support for either approach, the issue of tailored versus mainstream interventions became ideologically biased and unproductive from professional and client perspectives. It is obvious that, when clients of different ethnic groups are assumed to have different needs or responses to services, the social services delivered to those client groups become a matter of debate and controversy.

In the United States (Soydan, Jergeby, Olsson, & Harms-Ringdahl, 1999) and later with growing migration in Europe (Williams, Soydan, & Johnson, 1998), the necessity of tailoring social work practice to meet the special needs of ethnically diverse populations has received increased attention. The literature in the United States on this topic is especially extensive, including books such as *Cultural Awareness in the Human Services* (J. W. Green, 1995), *Ethnic-Sensitive Social Work Practice* (Devore & Schlesinger, 1996), and *Social Work Practice & People of Color* (Lum, 1996).

The debate on tailored versus mainstream interventions culminated with the publication of *Controversial Issues in Multiculturalism*, edited by Diane de Anda (1997). De Anda and contributors to the volume raised issues such as: Should programs and service delivery systems be culturally specific in their design? Has the emphasis on multicultural practice resulted in more effective and appropriate services for ethnic minority clients? Can ethnic agencies serve ethnic communities more effectively than mainstream agencies? Is the therapeutic process more effective if the client and the helping professional are of the same ethnic or cultural group? In an exchange between two participants of the debate regarding whether an emphasis on multicultural practice has resulted in more effective and appropriate services for ethnic minority clients, John Longres wrote of his colleague Sherlon Brown:

> Dr. Brown argues that multicultural practice has brought about more effective and appropriate services. I argue that it has not. . . . In the first place, Dr. Brown is largely talking about appropriateness, not effectiveness. She offers anecdotal evidence to demonstrate that her students, her colleagues, and apparently their clients seem to be satisfied with the counseling they are receiving. This anecdotal evidence hardly stands up

to rigorous evaluation and so has to be taken for what it is, the opinion of an educator. Even if her evidence were more rigorously represented, Dr. Brown supplies no evidence of effectiveness: the clients and their helping professionals may feel good, but do the clients behave differently, and have their lives been changed for the better? The evidence suggests that as a collective, people of color are treading water; their lives have not been improved by the growth of a new multicultural sensitivity, however more appropriate it may appear to be.

(de Anda, 1997, pp. 18–19)

As indicated by Longres' remarks, the controversy of tailored versus mainstream interventions for ethic minority groups has seldom been based on well-founded empirical knowledge. When conceptualizing a meta-analysis on this issue, Wilson, Lipsey, and Soydan (2003) observed that there were indicators suggesting that reality could be more complicated. For example, empirical research related to a foster care intervention showed that differences in outcomes among ethnic groups, if they existed at all, did not necessarily favor majority groups (Burkas, 2008). In another study, Barth and Blackwell (1998) demonstrated that Hispanic and White children in foster care have higher mortality rates than their counterparts in the general population, but the mortality rates of African American foster children are comparable to those of African American children in the general population. However, in another study, Jonson-Reid and Barth (2000) found that the risk of incarceration after exiting foster care was greater for African American youths than for Hispanic or White youths, even when age at first placement, gender, and characteristics of placement history were controlled.

In a pioneering systematic research review, Wilson et al. (2003) conducted a major meta-analysis of 305 effectiveness studies to synthesize outcomes of mainstream interventions for minority juvenile delinquents compared to White youths. The meta-analysis aimed to answer the question of whether "mainstream interventions that are not culturally tailored for minority youth have positive outcomes on their subsequent antisocial behavior, academic performance, peer relations, behavior problems, and other outcomes" (Wilson et al., 2003, p. 3). Results were stunning for both proponents and critics of culturally tailored interventions:

The results showed positive overall intervention effects with ethnic minority respondents on their delinquent behavior, school participation, peer relations, academic achievement, behavior problems, psychological adjustment, and attitudes. Overall, service programs were equally effective for minority and White delinquents. Although there were slight differences in effectiveness for different service types between minority and majority youth, none of these differences was statistically significant.

(Wilson et al., 2003, p. 3)

Furthermore, the researchers concluded:

> We believe the most defensible interpretation of the available research is that mainstream treatments for juvenile delinquents are generally effective and no less effective for ethnic minority youth than White youth. We must emphasize, however, that this does not mean that issues of cultural sensitivity are unimportant to such programs when minority youth are served. It could well be that the effects of programs with cultural tailoring would be larger than those of programs without even though those without do not have differential effects for minority and White youth. The evidence reviewed here only shows that cultural tailoring is not necessary for the programs to have positive outcomes and that the absence of such tailoring does not diminish the effects for minorities relative to Whites.
>
> *(p. 24)*

This meta-analysis was an early indicator of the usefulness of mainstream intervention programs for populations that were not initially targeted by the specific program. In the following years, the results of Wilson et al.'s (2003) study were matched by additional meta-analysis studies in other intervention fields, including diverse problems in treatment-as-usual settings (Weisz, Jensen-Doss, & Hawley, 2006), anxiety disorders (Silverman, Pina, & Viswesvaran, 2008), and attention-deficit hyperactivity disorder (ADHD: Fabiano et al., 2009). In other words, EBIs may be transportable and quite useful across ethnic and cultural boundaries.

In the area of mental health and psychosocial interventions, Miranda and her colleagues (2005) published a well-crafted comparative review that in its own way pointed in the same direction. In this study, the researchers selected efficacy and effectiveness results of randomized controlled studies measuring outcomes of issues such as bipolar disorder, schizophrenia, depression, and ADHD among youths and adults. The studies were selected from a pool of studies reported in *Mental Health: Culture, Race and Ethnicity*, published by the U.S. Department of Health and Human Services in 2001. Only outcome studies with ethnically diverse samples that had enough statistical power to allow subgroup comparisons were included. The results were encouraging.

The most powerful and rigorously conducted outcome studies available clearly showed that EBIs for depression improved outcomes among African American and Hispanic clients; interestingly, results were equal or greater than for White Americans. Although fewer studies were available for Asian client populations, researchers were able to conclude that well-tested EBIs may also be effective for these client groups. Furthermore, researchers found outcome studies for preventive interventions that included samples of American Indian and Alaskan Native populations. Native youths were mostly involved in mainstream (not tailored), school-based preventive programs. Such programs were found to lower depressive symptoms and suicidal ideation. Miranda and colleagues (2005) concluded:

> We believe that existent literature suggests that evidence-based parent management training and ADHD care for children and depression treatments for adults do generalize to African American and Latino populations. In fact, the literature to date would suggest that evidence-based care is likely to generalize to both American and Latino populations. Although the evidence is very sparse for Asian Americans, initial studies appear positive.
>
> *(p. 133)*

Furthermore, the researchers also confirmed that, although culturally adapted interventions were shown to be effective, evidence regarding the comparative effectiveness of tailored versus mainstream interventions was missing.

In recent years, several comparative studies have been undertaken. In a review study, Huey and Polo (2008) found efficacious evidence-based treatments for minority youth with anxiety disorders, ADHD, trauma-related syndromes, and other clinical problems. In a randomized clinical trial, McCabe and Yeh (2009) studied the effectiveness of a culturally adapted version of parent–child interaction therapy (PCIT), titled *Guiando a Niños Activos* (GANA), compared to the effectiveness of standard PCIT and treatment as usual for young Mexican American children with behavioral problems. The researchers found that GANA outcomes were significantly superior to treatment as usual across a wide variety of both parental reports and observational indexes. GANA and PCIT did not differ significantly from each other, whereas PCIT was superior to usual care on two of the parental report indexes and almost all of the observational indexes. Another randomized pilot study conducted by Pan, Huey, and Hernandez (2011) compared outcomes of standard one-session treatment (OST-S) and culturally adapted OST (OST-CA) with phobic Asian Americans. A main outcome measured at 1-week and 6-month follow-ups demonstrated that both OST-S and OST-CA were effective in terms of reducing phobic symptoms compared with self-help control. Moreover, OST-CA was superior to OST-S for several outcomes. For general fear and catastrophic thinking, moderator analyses indicated that less acculturated Asian Americans benefited more from OST-CA than OST-S. Both treatments were equally effective for more acculturated participants.

In a review of the latest evidence regarding the effectiveness of culturally tailored versus standard mainstream EBIs, Huey and Polo (2010) established strong evidence that mainstream EBIs are effective with African American and Latino youths, the two largest minority youth populations in the United States.

> Many gaps remain, however, and much more work is needed to address critical questions concerning what treatments are efficacious for which minority youth, what mechanisms account for clinical change for ethnic minority youth in treatment, and which factors enhance or impede treatment efficacy for these youth. Of special concern is whether these "minority" EBTs can be transported effectively to real-world clinical practice, particularly because ethnic minorities with mental health needs are less likely than European Americans to receive evidence-based care.
>
> *(Huey & Polo, 2010, p. 462)*

In sum, research on the transportability of EBIs among diverse groups in one country in which the national population shares common values and traditions is still in its initial stages. Preliminary results indicate that empirical research has significant potential to map which standard interventions work under which circumstances and with which subgroups of the population.

Globalization, translation, and transportability

Translation and transportability of evidence across national boundaries are not dissimilar to implementation of EBIs and EBPs across diverse populations in an intervention's country of origin. In the previous section, we presented an account of efforts made by researchers and practitioners to determine transportability of EBIs and EBPs across ethnically and culturally diverse populations within a country. The purpose of this section is to examine various aspects of translating and transporting EBIs and programs across national boundaries and cultures. Both of these activities are mediated or moderated by cultural structures and processes at various levels.

The question of translation and transportability, a longstanding historical challenge for social and behavioral sciences, has come into focus during the last two decades with the development of systematic research reviews as products of evidence for global dissemination by the Cochrane and Campbell collaborations. As reviewed in Chapter 3, the principles of the collaborations include the working assumptions of promoting access to evidence through dissemination of Cochrane reviews and other products worldwide in collaboration with other networks and in user-friendly formats, as well as enabling wide international participation in the exchange of evidence by encouraging diverse participation, providing support, and maintaining a global presence.

In principle, all reviews are global in the sense that data searches of published and gray literature, which should be exhaustive, are conducted using global databases and all studies that meet inclusion criteria are included in the review regardless of the country of origin or language. The universality of these databases is only limited by language bias, because publications published in English primarily populate these databases. However, the Cochrane and Campbell collaborations attempt to compensate for language bias via several methods, including the development of national and regional centers or branches, inclusion of texts in many other languages and translated by contributors to the collaborations, and advanced global communication networks. In fact, the organization of these two trendsetting and benchmarking collaborations is global and their reviews are globally accessible syntheses of the global production of scientific evidence. Therefore, the challenge of translation and transportability has global immediacy.

Translation and transport of EBIs and EBPs take place in cultural, social, economic, political, legal, and organizational settings. A broad definition of culture may include all those dimensions. Therefore, what is culture?

The all-inclusive nature of culture was emphasized by early students of the concept. For example, Edward Burnett Tylor, in his 1871 book *Primitive Culture*, included dimensions such as knowledge, art, beliefs, laws, customs, morals, and mores in a complex model of human societies. To some extent, this perspective persists today. For several decades following the publication of Tylor's (1871) book, many definitions of culture were proposed. In a comprehensive book, Kroeber and Kluckhohn (1952) were able to identify close to 200 definitions.

A shared dimension of these early definitions was a view of culture as a static and contained system. A static system is a closed system that immunizes itself to external influence and change. However, this perspective has been challenged in the globalizing world and was replaced to a great extent by a perspective of culture as an open, dynamic, and perpetually changing concept (Barth, 1969, 1984; Hannerz, 1992, 2000).

In his milestone book *Cultural Complexity: Studies in the Social Organization of Meaning*, Hannerz (1992) defined culture as follows:

> To study culture is to study ideas, experiences, feelings, as well as the external forms that such internalities take as they are made public, available to the senses and thus truly social. For culture, in the anthropological view, is the meanings which people create, and which create people, as members of societies. Culture is in some way collective.
>
> *(p. 3)*

Although culture has some degree of permanency and continuity, it is also constantly subject to interpretation and reinterpretation, thus changing its nature. Hannerz (1992) perceived this specific nature of culture as a paradox, and tried to capture it with the concept of *cultural flow*. He wrote:

> When you see a river from afar, it may look like a blue (or green, or brown) line across a landscape; something of awesome permanence. But at the same time, "you cannot step into the same river twice," for it is always moving, and only in this way does it achieve its durability. The same way with culture—even as you perceive structure, it is entirely dependent on ongoing process.
>
> *(p. 4)*

In this perspective, the idea of a cultural mosaic—or on a global level, national and cultural boundaries—with well-defined forms, edges, and boundaries becomes less viable as a result of cultural "interconnectedness" (Hannerz, 1992, p. 218) or the increasingly "hyper-connected world" (Friedman & Mandelbaum, 2011, p. 69). Some of the consequences of interconnected, constantly changing, and fluid cultural systems include the fact that cultural autonomy and boundedness is a matter of degree; global cultural flow is internally diverse; not all cultures are local in the sense that they are not bound to national or other territories; and "it is hardly self-evident that the end result of the cultural processes connected to transnational center/ periphery relationships must be a global homogenization of culture" (Hannerz, 1992, p. 262).

What are the implications for evidence translation and transport within a framework in which cultures with a national locus are seen as flowing, constantly evolving settings that only temporarily sustain their permanence and characteristics? Evolving cultures are open systems that by definition are influenced by and have an influence on other cultures. Empirically, this is what is seen in the process of globalization—not only the global exchange of capital, labor, goods, and services, but also culture. Looking for unique and uniform characteristics of diverse cultures (Sztompka, 1990) might be a key to understanding capacity and opportunities to translate and transport evidence between cultures.

In an earlier work (Palinkas & Soydan, 2012), we elaborated on the distinction between phase 1 and phase 2 translation. Phase 1 refers to translating research into practice through the development and evaluation of effective EBIs. Phase 2 translation refers to translating EBP developed in one nation to another nation through strategies of dissemination and implementation. Both of these processes take place in cultural settings. In flowing and constantly evolving cultural settings, identification and use of culturally unique and uniform characteristics might be the gateway to successful translation and transportation of EBIs.

Figure 7.1 is a visualization of our model of cultural influence on evidence translation and transportation. Introduction, dissemination, implementation, and sustainability of effective interventions in a new country are contingent on the cultural preparedness for and openness of the country to innovative interventions. There are at least four distinctive levels in which translation occurs (Palinkas & Soydan, 2012). These levels are: (1) larger system and macroenvironmental circumstances, which determine cultural dimensions of supply and demand for services; (2) the organization level, at which goals and procedures for accomplishing those goals are shaped; (3) the group or team level, at which diverse patterns of interaction take place, priorities are set, and tasks are allocated; and (4) the individual level, or the locus at which client–practitioner interaction takes place and expectations, values, and preferences determine client adherence to an intervention. Furthermore, several national and cultural aspects are pertinent to successful translation of EBIs, including the relevance of EBIs to the population in general; the willingness of social work agencies and implementers to accept innovation and deliver EBIs; meanings attributed to the intervention by clients, their families, and social workers; and the value and benefit of outcomes for participants and implementers.

Country prototypes

The concept of *country prototypes* is an attempt to categorize countries (or nation-based core cultures) into groups with the purpose of understanding possibilities and limits of transporting EBIs between countries belonging to a specific country prototype.

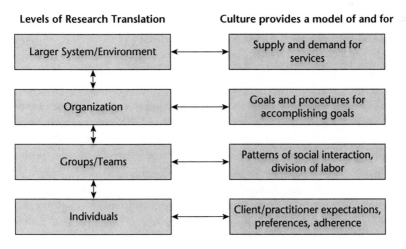

FIGURE 7.1   Cultural influences on phase 2 translation

Although the assumption of "you cannot step into the same river twice" discourages construction of country prototypes, the framework of unique and uniform cultural characteristics invites such efforts to categorize countries and cultures by prototype. Transportability of innovations such as EBIs and EBPs would be more feasible among cultures that are classified in the same prototype category. Although not undisputed, there is a longstanding tradition of categorizing cultures based on cultural prototypes. Sussman, Unger, and Palinkas (2008) referred to studies that described efforts to construct country prototypes. Geographical characteristics, language, religion, and historically shared events may constitute cultural prescriptions that make residents of a country react similarly to innovations. Hofstede (1991), a classic scholar in this field, identified four characteristics that distinguish national cultures: (1) power distance among members of hierarchies; (2) cultural emphasis on collectivism versus individualism; (3) differentiation of gender roles; and (4) degree of uncertainty avoidance. Other important dimensions may include the degree of formality or explicitness of agreement in cultures and a culture's openness to physical contact between individuals when addressing each other (contact versus noncontact cultures). Based on these and other similarities and dissimilarities, countries or national cultures may be grouped in country prototypes that may be useful in assessing the feasibility of transporting innovations across national boundaries.

On the other hand, there are challenges to the idea of country prototypes. In a previous section, we noted that considerable effort has been invested in testing mainstream interventions among nonmainstream populations on the assumption that understanding cultural differences in a single country is important for successful implementation. In some instances, intracountry differences may be considerable and even more pronounced than cultural differences between countries (e.g., when controlling for class). Intracountry cultural heterogeneity is a serious factor that challenges the idea of country prototypes. Sussman and colleagues (2008) warned against developing country-level stereotypes that are based on false attributions to a culture. Cultural stereotypes may be either positive or negative but nevertheless false. For example, four comparable and consecutive studies of attitudes toward other cultures conducted in Sweden between 1960 and 1993 consistently showed that judgments about other cultures are often based on stereotypes (Soydan, 2010b). The Personality Profiles of Cultures Project studied the perceptions of approximately 4,000 participants about themselves and others across 50 cultures and found that Australians saw themselves as extraverts, Canadians described themselves as agreeable, and German Swiss believed that they are characterized by conscientiousness. This research project also found that European and American cultures differ from Asian and African cultures by featuring higher levels of extraversion and openness to experience and lower levels of agreeableness (Sussman et al., 2008). Furthermore, others concluded that this data "seems to point in the direction of the psychic unity of human-kind, at least that which concerns underlying personality dispositions. . . . It is likely that cultural unity is based, partly at least, on the psychic unity of all people" (Allik, 2005, p. 226).

These and other factors contribute to the complexity of exploring and establishing unique and uniform cultural characteristics, and leads us to seri-ously consider the concept that "you cannot step into the same river twice." Nevertheless, for pragmatic reasons, we agree with Sussman and colleagues (2008):

> In summary, there are many complexities contained in trying to make any inferences about country characteristics and their likelihood of using programming that is likely to work with them. Cultural differ-ences across countries can be observed at a macrolevel, but of course, cultures do not begin and end at the political boundaries between countries. Most countries consist of numerous cultures and subcultures (Triandis, 1995). One may conjecture that although the differences are not well measured and are not nearly as important as the commonality of individuals across cultures and the diversity of individuals within cultures (Au, 1997), there still are subtle nuances in language, behav-ior, and beliefs that differentiate countries. At minimum, there are pieces of information that researchers have found essential to permit their programs to work better and more widely within countries that may be unique to those countries and not others.
>
> *(p. 116)*

Perhaps one factor that mediates transferability of EBIs is the general process of globalization that continuously takes place on different levels of societies. Globalization includes increasing movement of capital, goods, and human labor across national borders; increasing similarities of consumption patterns and lifestyles promoted by transnational companies such as IKEA (which had a presence in almost 50 countries across five continents in 2013, making home decoration similar in millions of households across the world); increas-ing uniformity of cultural characteristics promoted by television, media, movies, and higher education; and an increasing sense of transparence and political voice promoted by media and facilitated by the Internet. These and other phenomena generate shared values and cultures across boundaries, thus increasing the possibility of transferring evidence-based innovations. However, let's not forget that, although shared values and cultures across boundaries are becoming increasingly influential, the complexity of cultures is also increasing. Consequently, capturing essential factors of innovation transfer becomes more complex, requiring empirical evidence and sophisticated decisions in each case. A list of factors (Table 7.1) that might be considered when planning to transfer evidence-based social, behavioral, and health innovations across boundaries is illustrative of the complexity in question.

TABLE 7.1 Factors critical to transportation of evidence

Political variables	Sense of nationalism, patriotism, devotion to government, structure of government, degree of centralization of government, degree or type of government control over elections and media, attitudes toward corruption in government, degree of contact with other countries and for what purposes, and degree of governmental involvement in the health care system
Social, educational, and historical variables	Behavioral elements (degree of personal space, acceptability of establishing eye contact, degree of smiling considered appropriate, appropriateness of stating opinions that may diverge from a group), holidays, festivals (civil and religious), common customs, traditions and crafts, popular foods (names and ingredients), popular clothes and where manufactured, average age of marriage, average number of children, popular stories, popular proverbs, popular child toys, objects aspired to by adults (cars, radios), emphasis on individual rights versus the collective, immigration and emigration statistics (who and what percentage of population), school system tracking (to academic versus vocational orientations), average education level achieved, literacy percentage, languages spoken (average number per person and which ones are popularly spoken in the country), primary ethnic groups and percentages, and brief history of country
Geo-economic variables	The level of disparities between high- and low-status jobs (salary, prestige, and power), work week and hours, average salary in country, gross national product, buying power of salary (what are expensive goods), key imports and exports, degree of industrialization, economic changes, and geographical size (number of time zones)
Health and illness status variables	Average lifespan achieved (males, females, ethnicities, as a function of social class), main causes of premature death, main explanations for extended quality of life and longevity, current state of health research and practice, how much and what type of health research is occurring, and what types of practices are popular in mental health, physical health, prevention, and cessation

Adapted from Sussman, Unger, and Palinkas (2008).

What experts consider when transporting evidence

It is worth repeating that the best evidence of transportability across national borders is the testing of an EBI in real-life conditions in the recipient culture. However, this is not always possible or feasible, neither in the short term nor from a longer-term perspective. Yet EBIs, particularly in the field of health but also increasingly in social work and mental health, are transported across boundaries for careful implementation, including client monitoring and follow-up. Frequently, in the absence of solid evidence, transportation of EBIs across boundaries is based on expert assessments. In this section, we illustrate some of the considerations made when transporting EBIs from the West to China (Soydan et al., 2010).

Case study: Transport of Healthy Families America

Healthy Families America (HFA) is a home-based prevention and intervention program designed for overburdened families at risk of child abuse and neglect and other adverse childhood experiences. In this program, families are assessed using a standardized test to determine eligibility. Home visit services are initiated by well-trained paraprofessionals either prenatally or within 3 months after the birth of an infant and are delivered for at least 3 years. The structured HFA program is designed to promote positive parent–child interaction, child development skills, and healthy and safe family practices. Several studies (Galano & Huntington, 2004; Klagholz & Associates, 2005; McFarlane et al., 2013) have documented the postintervention effects of HFA, although not all outcome variables were statistically significant in some studies.

An expert assessment of HFR for implementation in China stated the following:

> *The cultural relevance and sensitivity of the standardized assessment:* The parent survey is conducted to identify the presence of factors that could contribute to increased risk of child maltreatment or other poor childhood outcomes before families are determined eligible for home visit services. The parent survey needs to be tested for its reliability, validity, and cultural sensitivity based on a Chinese sample to establish an appropriate norm for screening.
>
> *Different norms of parenting:* Some Chinese parents might have very different ideas of parenting from those of Western parents. For example, many Chinese believe in very strict parenting, just like "tiger moms." Also, many parents do not believe in "positive" parent–child

interaction. Many Chinese children are taught to simply obey their parents without any interaction or negotiation. Therefore, the services providers might need to make extra efforts to discuss and come to agreement about parenting issues.

Human resources: Although it seems beneficial to provide home visit services within 3 months after the birth of the baby and lasting for at least 3 years, some agencies (including public and private units) simply do not have the needed resources to implement the program. Most helping professionals in Chinese societies are engaged in tertiary prevention work and do not have capacity for primary or secondary prevention work. The agency could recruit and train some volunteers to implement this program.

(April Chiung-Tao Shen, personal
communication, April 9, 2012)

HFA is an example of an EBI that may not be very successful in a Chinese context unless some preparatory measures are taken and special attention is given to some degree of cultural adaptation. Furthermore, a scientific follow-up of the implementation process may be critical.

Cultural adaptation

As noted, EBIs are becoming increasingly globalized and effectiveness research on the cultural adaptation of EBIs is becoming increasingly important (Ferrer-Wreder, Adamson, Kumpfer, & Eichas, 2012). One component of the implementation of EBIs across national and cultural borders is the cultural adaptation of those interventions. Expert assessments such as the example featured in the previous section provide guidance for implementers to culturally adapt EBIs.

Research on cultural adaptation of EBIs is in its infancy; there are no clear-cut guidelines for how adaption should be conducted and to what extent fidelity to the original EBI should be maintained (Bernal, Jiménez-Chafey, & Domenech Rodríguez, 2009; Latham et al., 2010). Some researchers have differentiated between the *surface* and *deep* structure of an intervention (McKleroy et al., 2006; Resnicow, Soler, Braithwaite, Ahluwalia, & Butler, 2000). Deep structure refers to an intervention's core components and core theory of change, whereas surface structure refers to any component that does not play a decisive role in the effectiveness of the intervention. In most instances, cultural adaptation of EBIs excludes alteration of deep structures, considered a serious threat to the fidelity. In cases of deep-structure adaptation, empirical testing of the implementation becomes a necessary procedure. Ferrer-Wreder, Sundell, and Mansoory (2012) identified nine models of cultural adaptation. They found that variations among the models reflect ambiguities of the fidelity-versus-adaptation discourse. Disagreements among researchers and differences among models pertain most often to alteration of deep structures, whereas most researchers agree on the feasibility of adapting surface structures of an intervention.

Fidelity during the implementation of an intervention normally pertains to delivery of an intervention with strict adherence to its original core components (Berkel, Mauricio, Schoenfelder, & Sandler, 2011). Adaptation of an intervention refers to changes made to the intervention to better fit the circumstances in which the intervention is to be delivered. There is no universal recipe for developing the right balance between fidelity and adaptation. A reasonable balance results in the successful implementation of an intervention that works as intended, and this is an empirical problem rather than a theoretical issue.

When possible, empirical testing of EBIs is conducted to validate them in the new context of implementation. For example, a Swedish study (National Board of Health and Welfare, 2011) showed that, of 134 Swedish outcome studies of social and behavioral interventions conducted between 1995 and mid-2010, 41% tested interventions that originated in other countries. A group of researchers (Sundell, Ferrer-Wreder, & Fraser, 2013) reported that, in many countries, transported family-based interventions have been tested and results have been mixed, indicating that transportation of EBIs is a challenging process. These results are aligned with the challenges discussed earlier in this chapter in the context of replication studies. It seems that some degree of adaptation of interventions is needed in cross-cultural implementation of EBIs, both nationally and globally. However, intervention adaptation is still in its early stages and we can expect more attention to be given to understanding the adaptation process.

Conclusion

Generalizability of knowledge has been a challenge for most sciences and remains a major aim for evidence production and dissemination of EBIs in social work. In this chapter, we summarized major challenges to globalization of evidence. We also presented an account of efforts to cross-culturally (nationally or globally) transport and implement EBIs. Although faced with considerable challenges, translational and implementation science is making progress. An increasing level of globalization across cultures provides a favorable backdrop to the transportation of EBIs.

8

CREATING A PROFESSIONAL CULTURE FOR EVIDENCE-BASED PRACTICE

Regardless of its merits or liabilities, it is clear that the field of social work has yet to develop a clear consensus concerning the value and application of evidence-based practice (EBP). Although the teaching of EBP has now become a standard feature of social work education and social workers are increasingly called upon by the agencies that employ them and the institutions that fund these agencies to embrace EBP, the controversies surrounding its use and the challenges involved in implementing and sustaining EBPs in real-world practice settings continue to confound educators, practitioners, and EBP researchers and developers.

The solution to this lack of consensus is to create a professional culture that both values EBP as an approach to delivering the highest-quality services available to our clients and offers a set of guidelines or instructions that clearly explain how EBP can be practiced and how specific EBPs can be implemented and sustained. To achieve that goal, we must first explain what is meant by the term *professional culture*. Broadly defined, culture is a set of shared understandings that serves as a model of and for behavior. As a model of behavior, a professional culture is based on experience, both positive and negative. As a model for behavior, it establishes a set of normative (how and why things should be done) and pragmatic roles for behavior. These understandings are arranged in hierarchical fashion, with normative rules at the top governing what should be done and pragmatic rules at the bottom that dictate how to accomplish those goals (Bailey, 1973). Promoting social justice, enhancing human well-being, and helping to meet the basic human needs of all people, with particular attention to the needs and empowerment of people who are vulnerable, oppressed, and living in poverty, are examples of the normative elements of the professional culture of social work. Adapting cognitive behavioral therapy for Spanish-speaking clients who do not wish to be stigmatized for being treated for depression is an example of pragmatic rules for professional behavior. Professional cultures are transmitted to members of the society of social workers through our educational systems and in our practice settings. They reside in the organizations we work for and the services we provide to our clients. The professional culture of social work is tied to the organizational culture of social workers and the two cultures of research and practice that define our profession.

"Kitson et al. (1998) suggest that the successful integration of evidence into practice may require action on three levels: the nature of the evidence, the organizational context, and the process of the facilitation" (Barratt, 2003, p. 144). In this chapter, we discuss how a professional culture of EBP in social work might be established by acting at each of these three levels.

The nature of the evidence

Throughout this book, we point to the lack of consensus regarding what constitutes necessary and sufficient evidence to support decisions about how to deliver services of the highest quality to clients in need. On the one hand, some argue that all evidence should be assessed with reference to a gold standard, the randomized controlled trial (RCT), and conducted with the utmost rigor to ensure validity and reliability. On the other hand, there are those who assert that such standards tend to devalue other forms of evidence, especially evidence generated by qualitative methods, even if such methods adhere to similar standards of rigor, validity, and reliability, as well as evidence generated by personal experience.

A professional culture of EBP must begin with the acknowledgment that there are multiple forms of evidence, each containing certain strengths and limitations. In Chapter 5, we describe two general categories of evidence inherent in EBP, one that is global and one that is local. Global evidence is external in that it originates outside of an agency or jurisdiction; it is based on standards for scientific rigor (e.g., RCTs) and it places emphasis on the generalizability or transferability of findings from one state or county to another. In contrast, local evidence is internal; it originates within an agency or jurisdiction, may include administrative data, is based on personal experience (either involvement in data collection and analysis or familiarity with population studied), and places emphasis on the uniqueness of a population and its needs (specificity). Research evidence use is never entirely one type or the other. Social work practitioners may be more inclined to make decisions based on local evidence because it is more intimate and familiar, even if it does not always adhere to the same standards of rigor and is certainly lacking in terms of external validity. It also represents a measure of individual control over the decision-making process rather than surrendering control to researchers, who are often perceived as being outsiders with little understanding of the local context. However, global evidence may also be lacking in terms of external validity, as described in Chapter 5.

The use of both types of evidence in building a professional culture of social work EBP must begin with an acknowledgment of the strengths and limitations of each. Although the strength of evidence has traditionally been arranged in hierarchical fashion, even evidence acquired through rigorous adherence to scientific standards and the use of RCT designs are not without shortcomings, including limited external validity and constraints imposed on participant selection, data collection, and data analysis. Similarly, local evidence may be constrained by limited internal validity and reliability and may lack the same rigor with respect to participant selection, data collection, and data analysis. Despite these shortcomings, there is something to be learned from each type of evidence.

We would further argue that both qualitative and quantitative methods can and should be used to fulfill specific roles in that process. Again, traditional hierarchical arrangements of research evidence usually place quantitative experimental studies at the top and qualitative descriptive studies at the bottom (McNeece & Thyer, 2004; Otto & Ziegler, 2008). However, the path to EBP can be viewed as moving across a series of steps that begins with identification and proceeds to description, explanation generation, explanation testing, and prescription or control. Identification first occurs through reports or studies that point to the existence of a previously unknown or unrecognized phenomenon. Description of the phenomenon may involve qualitative (narratives, case studies) or quantitative (frequencies, percentages) data or both. Both methodological approaches may be employed in the next step, which is the identification of associations between variables and the generation of hypotheses to be tested to explain why the variables are associated with one another. The next step is then to test the hypotheses and the validity of the presumed explanation. This step usually requires the use of prospective longitudinal designs and quantitative methods. The final step is the construction of experimental conditions that enable the investigator to control for the possibility of alternate explanations for the observed association between one variable, presumed to be the cause, and the other variable or variables, presumed to be the effect. This step usually requires the use of the RCT design and quantitative methods (Palinkas, in press). Qualitative methods are especially important in the early exploratory stages of scientific inquiry and for providing in-depth understanding of the causal chain and the context in which it exists. Quantitative methods are especially important in the later confirmatory stages of scientific inquiry and for generalizing findings to other populations in other settings. Both methods are fundamental to a professional culture of EBP in social work.

The integrated use of quantitative and qualitative methods is certainly not a novel concept. Haight (2010), for instance, called for the integration of postpositivist perspectives of critical realism, with an emphasis on quantitative methods and research designs, and interpretative perspectives, with an emphasis on qualitative or mixed research designs and methods. Although "postpositivist research using quantitative methods can help to identify generally effective interventions and eliminate the use of harmful or ineffective interventions . . . interpretist research using qualitative methods can enhance understanding of the ways in which cultural context interact with [cause] interventions, resulting in diverse outcomes [effects]" (Haight, 2010, p. 102). I. Epstein's (2009) model of evidence-informed practice calls for the integrated use of EBP, with its emphasis on standardized quantitative measures and RCT designs, and reflective practice, with its emphasis on qualitative observation. What is novel here is that the process of making causal inferences is not limited to quantitative methods or RCT designs.

Perhaps the greatest challenge we face in creating a professional culture of EBP in social work is being faithful to the principles of scientific inquiry while simultaneously being responsive to the needs, activities, traditions, and multiple perspectives of our discipline. The diversity of these needs, activities, traditions, and perspectives reflects the complexity of the problems we seek to solve and the underlying factors that are responsible for those problems. This complexity makes it difficult to identify single or specific causes of single or specific effects. Although this complexity may be viewed as an obstacle to the creation of a science of social work, it also represents a unique opportunity to create a science that acknowledges the importance of qualitative as well as quantitative methods, of practice-based evidence as well as EBP, and explanation grounded in social constructivism as well as logical positivism.

The organizational context of EBP

In Chapter 2, we note that EBP as a process was first formulated as EBM by Sackett and his colleagues in the mid-1990s as a method to help medical professionals make more informed, conscientious, explicit, and judicious decisions. Originally, the EBP process was conceptualized as a communicative relationship between the medical professional and the client. This individual-level aspect of the EBP process is predominant in almost all literature on EBP. It is only with the emergence of translational research and new, advanced approaches to implementation of evidence-based interventions in social work that the organizational context of EBP has come into focus. In this sense, there has been a major perspective shift from individual-level application of evidence-based interventions to a complementary organizational-level application.

In Chapter 4, we describe the importance of the organizational or inner context of successful EBP implementation and sustainment. We argue that organizations most likely to implement and sustain EBP have the following characteristics: a formalized, centralized, and differentiated structure with a formal research infrastructure; a culture that values learning, innovation and change; a climate that offers a sense of psychological safety and enables individuals to take risks; leadership that is fully committed to innovation in general and an EBP in particular and fully engaged in its implementation; a designated advocate or champion for EBP; qualified clinicians and support staff with the appropriate skills and training, documentation, and record keeping and systems; absorptive capacity; training and ongoing supervision for staff responsible for implementation; and a supportive network of advisors and opinion leaders both within and among organizations involved in the implementation process. Many of these characteristics can be nurtured and supported through the use of evidence-based strategies like the Availability, Responsiveness and Continuity intervention developed by Charles Glisson or through promising strategies such as community development teams (Sosna & Marsenich, 2006) or learning collaboratives (Nadeem, Olin, Hill, Hoagwood, & Horwitz, 2013). Other efforts underway involve the development of strategies to build leadership and interorganizational collaborations that are supportive of EBP implementation and sustainment.

Facilitating EBP

The process of EBP occurs through a series of interactions between professionals, clients, and other stakeholders, such as clients' families. The core of the professional culture of social work is the social worker's ability to identify client system deficits, access and assess the best research evidence, and use this evidence to eliminate deficits in the specific context of client values, culture, and preferences, in addition to identifying the opportunities and constraints generated by the context of human services organizations.

If we are to create a professional culture of social work that both values EBP and outlines the normative and pragmatic steps for conducting EBP, we must first begin with a search for common ground to highlight both knowledge and experiences that are understood and shared. This includes establishing common ground between those who adhere to a more positivist tradition of social work as a science with rules for practice that can be transferred from one setting to another, and those who adhere to a more social constructivist tradition that values the individuality of each client or community and eschews positivism as a prescription for power, domination, and discrimination. It includes establishing common ground between those who believe fervently in the need to implement EBPs with fidelity if they are to produce effective outcomes regardless of the client or clients and the settings in which they live and seek help, and those who believe in the need to deviate from fidelity for the purpose of adapting or tailoring EBPs for clients or groups of clients with specific needs or characteristics that must be taken into consideration when delivering services. It includes establishing common ground between researchers who generate evidence by application of rigorous procedures of scientific inquiry, disseminate that evidence through publication in scholarly journals or presentations at professional conferences, and are rewarded for their efforts through tenure and promotion, and practitioners whose consumption of such evidence is dictated primarily by the need and desire to serve their clients and communities and who are rewarded for doing so by means other than employment security. Finally, it includes establishing common ground between EBP and practice-based evidence.

A second, related component of establishing a professional culture is through the development and sustainment of academic–community or research–practice partnerships. "Research to inform practice relies on close communication and partnerships between researchers and community-based social service agencies and professionals" (Haight, 2010, p. 102). Barratt (2003) argued that one of the barriers to EBP implementation is the "poor links between those who carry out research and those who provide services" (p. 143). This barrier is echoed by Ruth and Matusitz (2013), who observed:

> EBP still places high value on RCT knowledge gathering results while creating a hierarchical knowledge structure. The evidence is coming from the top down. Social scientists conduct statistically-based [sic] experiments and create mandates from the results for the local social worker. In social work, the practitioner is the receiver of the knowledge (evidence) rather than a partner in the sharing of information. This gap between research and practice is a result of a lack of collaboration. The local actors in the field of social work are overlooked and forced to use a generalized best practice.
>
> *(p. 288)*

One of the challenges to developing such partnerships is overcoming the perception held by some that "practitioner disparagement appears to be both the raison d'être and the sine qua non of EBP rhetoric" (I. Epstein, 2011, p. 284). One solution to overcoming this challenge is to acknowledge that a truly pluralist evidence-based or evidence-informed practice would treat practitioners as producers as well as consumers of research evidence.

This is certainly not a new idea. There is a well-established tradition of community-based participatory research (CBPR: Israel, Eng, Schulz, & Parker, 2005; Minkler & Wallerstein, 2003) and its variants (e.g., participatory action research, community-partnered participatory research: Wells, Staunton, Norris, & the CHIC Council, 2006). We define research–practice partnerships in social work as long-term, mutual collaborations between practitioners and researchers that are intentionally organized to investigate problems of practice and solutions for improving the health and well-being of vulnerable communities.

CPBR is a "collaborative approach to research that equitably involves all partners in the research process and recognizes the unique strengths that each brings" (Minkler & Wallerstein, 2003, p. 4). Israel and colleagues (2005) identified four fundamental assumptions that govern the conduct of CBPR: (1) genuine partnerships require a willingness of all stakeholders to learn from one another; (2) in addition to conducting research, there must be commitment to training community members in research; (3) the knowledge and other products gained from research activities should benefit all partners; and (4) a long-term commitment is required of researchers to the community and the community to the goal of improving the health and well-being of its members. What is significant about this approach is that it requires an ability to communicate and compromise as much as it requires a willingness to collaborate. Collaborators communicate with one another for the purpose of generating and sharing knowledge to improve the functioning of community organizations and the health and well-being of community members (Currie et al., 2005). Participatory research is defined by a constant need to "negotiate a balance between developing valid generalisable knowledge and benefiting the community that is being researched" (Macaulay et al., 1999, p. 774).

For the most part, research–practice partnerships exist along a continuum of models with investigator-initiated research and minimal community input at one end and joint decision making on all aspects of research with active community direction and interpretation of the results at the other end (Baker, Homan, Schonhoff, & Kreuter, 1999; Hatch, Moss, Saran, Presley-Cantrell, & Mallory, 1993). At either end of this continuum is research initiated by the investigator or research initiated by the community; within the continuum is research initiated by investigator and community with the researcher or the community exercising the lead role.

Role definition, or determining who does what, is one of the first and foremost challenges to be addressed in developing a research–practice partnership. Lack of clarity in assignment of roles and responsibilities can lead to assignments not being completed, tasks not being performed, uncertainty, confusion, and conflict. The obvious solution to addressing this challenge is to assign roles based on skills and resources. Thus, academic partners may assume responsibility for research design, ensuring quality control of data collection, data analysis, training and supervision, and fidelity monitoring, whereas practitioner partners may assume responsibility for service delivery, including staffing, scheduling, and financing. However, roles may be assigned based on other considerations. For instance, leadership of the partnership may be assigned to systems leaders, agency directors, or intermediaries who can gain the support of both researchers and practitioners. Partners may also assume different roles at different stages of the partnership to support different goals (e.g., different phases of EBP implementation: Wells, Miranda, Bruce, Alegria, & Wallerstein, 2004). Protocols that document these roles and functions are highly recommended (Begun, Berger, Otto-Salaj, & Rose, 2010; Hawkins & Catalano, 2002; Madison, McKay, Paikoff, & Bell, 2000; Reid & Vianna, 2001).

Although perhaps not as immediate a challenge as role definition, the greatest challenge to be addressed in developing a research practice partnership is overcoming mistrust. As noted earlier in this chapter as well as in Chapter 5, researchers and practitioners often possess negative stereotypes of each other. These perceptions are often grounded in differences in organizational culture and previous experiences. Organizational cultures identify values, priorities, and normative and pragmatic rules for behavior. Although there is considerable overlap in the organizational cultures of researchers and practitioners, there are also important differences. Researchers, who are usually focused on tenure and promotion, give priority to scholarship with its demands for scientific rigor, slow and methodical progress, and publication of results in peer-reviewed journals. Conversely, practitioners are usually focused on meeting the needs of their clients and thus give priority to expediency, efficiency, and client satisfaction. Although the issue of one versus two cultures remains the subject of debate, a continued focus on these differences can lead to the perception that they are irreconcilable and thus not worth the effort. In addition, many of these stereotypes are based on actual experiences. Practitioners, for instance, are often quick to provide examples of interactions with researchers who *helicopter* into an agency or community for the purpose of recruiting study participants or gaining access to client data, and then helicopter out, never to be seen or heard from again (Begun et al., 2010; Sperber et al., 2008).

Avoiding such mistrust requires openness and honesty in all interactions (Begun et al., 2010) and a willingness to learn about other members of the partnership (Allen-Meares, Hudgins, Engberg, & Lessnau, 2005). Most importantly, it requires a willingness to make a long-term commitment to the partnership. De Geest and colleagues (2013) reported that academic–service partnerships usually last an average of 6 years. Palinkas and colleagues

(2013) found that continued affiliation with a university-based research center was an important incentive for community clinics to continue using EBTs for treatment of depression, anxiety, and behavioral problems among youths after the completion of an effectiveness trial.

Another key point of contention in the development of EBP research–practice partnerships is the extent to which scientific rigor is exercised in both generating evidence supporting a particular practice and applying the practice with fidelity. As noted earlier, there are several concerns related to the rigor of conducting RCTs and in the generation of global evidence or knowledge. RCTs are expensive and difficult to conduct in community-based settings. There are ethical concerns related to not providing timely or equal access to what is believed to be the most effective treatment, even if that belief has yet to be confirmed. There are also concerns about the external validity of such studies. To address these concerns, there have been efforts to seek alternatives to the classic RCT design. For instance, there are randomized designs that are considerably more complex than traditional RCTs but also more sensitive to issues of external validity. These include the randomized encouragement trial, which randomizes consumers to encouragement strategies for the targeted treatment and facilitates their preferences and choices under naturalistic clinical practice settings (West et al., 2008); the sequential multiple assignment randomized trial, a clinical trial design that experimentally examines strategy choices, accommodates patient and provider preferences for treatment while using adaptive randomization strategies, and allows multiple comparison options (Murphy, Lynch, Oslin, McKay, & Ten Have, 2007; Ten Have, Coyne, Salzer, & Katz, 2003; Ten Have, Joffe, & Cary, 2003); the optimal design trial (Duan, Bhaumik, Palinkas, & Hoagwood, in press); and the randomized fractional factorial design, which screens more efficiently and tests multiple treatment components with less cost (Collins, Murphy, Nair, & Strecher, 2005).

Similarly, quasi-experimental designs may be useful in addressing the limitations of the classic RCT design. These designs include the *controlled clinical trial*, in which participants (or other units) are definitely prospectively assigned to one or two (or more) alternative forms of intervention using a quasi-random allocation method (e.g., alternation, date of birth, patient identifier), or possibly prospectively assigned prospectively to one or two (or more) alternative forms of intervention using a process of random or quasi-random allocation; the *controlled before and after study*, in which intervention and control groups are defined other than by random process and a baseline period of assessment of main outcomes is included; and the *interrupted time series*, in which a change in trend is attributable to the intervention (Cochrane Effective Practice and Organisation of Care Review Group, 2002). These designs may also include models generated by mathematical constructions or reconstructions.

Alternative quasi-experimental designs are used for various reasons, including ethical concerns, unwillingness to use randomized controlled studies, practical problems of application of an RCT design, and budget and time restrictions. Yet we are aware that the worth of quasi-experimental designs as alternative to RCTs remains a contested issue. Throughout history, researchers have tried to understand relative levels of bias produced with quasi-experimental designs as compared to RTCs. Methods of between-study and within-study comparisons have been used.

As we have noted earlier in between-study comparisons of experimental and nonexperimental designs, researchers examine multiple studies conducted with different research designs. The bias in outcome estimates of these two types of designs is calculated by studying the relationship between the design and the estimates of effect. While within-study comparisons use design replication and study an intervention program's effect by using a randomized control group and one or several nonrandomized comparison groups, design replication method is a reestimation of the effect by using one or several comparison groups. In a major study Glazerman, Levy, and Myers (2003) concluded that "although the empirical evidence from this literature can be used in the context of training and welfare programs to *improve* [non-experimental] research designs, it cannot on its own justify the use of such designs" (Glazerman et al., 2003, p. 63). Likewise, there are concerns related to the rigor exercised in generating local evidence or knowledge. These include concerns about internal validity and reliability, quality control, and selection of appropriate methods for data collection and analysis. To address these concerns, there have been efforts to identify and disseminate more systematic and rigorous efforts to generate such knowledge. These include I. Epstein's (2011) proposal for clinical data mining.

An EBP research–practice partnership must also involve agreement with respect to the rigor involved in applying the evidence. As discussed in Chapter 6, several observers have noted the tension between the relative value of research-based fidelity versus input and program adaptations offered by practitioners (Bierman, 2006; Biglan, Mrazek, Carnine, & Flay, 2003). On the one hand, researchers are often portrayed as advocating for strict fidelity in the belief that any deviation from the original protocol found to be effective will invalidate the practice as being evidence-based because it will essentially be a different practice with unknown effectiveness. On the other hand, practitioners are often portrayed as wishing to adapt EBPs as a rule to accommodate their own preferences as well as the needs of their clients. However, between these two extremes there is certainly room for collaboration and compromise. For instance, the Modular Approach to Therapy for Children protocol (Chorpita, Daleiden, & Weisz, 2005) gives providers more flexibility in the use of EBPs than exists in traditional manualized approaches to EBT. This modular approach to treatment has found to be effective in reducing symptoms of depression, anxiety, and behavioral problems among youths in community-based treatment (Chorpita et al., 2013; Weisz et al., 2012). It has also been found to be acceptable to therapists because it is consistent with their approach to treatment and meets the needs of their clients (Palinkas et al., 2013).

The Dynamic Adaptation Process (DAP: Aarons et al., 2012) is another example of the potential for collaboration and compromise. Designed to allow for EBP, system, and organizational adaptation in a planned and considered rather than ad hoc way, the DAP involves identifying core elements and adaptable characteristics of an EBP, then supporting implementation with specific training on allowable adaptations to the model, fidelity monitoring and support, and the need for, and solutions to, system and organizational adaptations. The DAP is conducted by an implementation resource team composed of academic researchers, intervention developers, trainers and coaches, administrators, clinicians, and clients or patients.

Engaging in ethical conduct is another challenge to be addressed in developing and maintaining research–practice partnerships. We mentioned the practitioner concern for the ethics of randomizing clients into different groups in which one group receives a treatment that is believed to be more effective, or in the case of a wait-list design, receives the treatment sooner than later. In contrast, researchers point to the ethics of ignoring evidence-based treatments in favor of practices or treatments that have little or no evidence of effectiveness. Both practitioners and researchers face the challenges of all forms of research, practice, and policy involving human lives, including avoiding harm, achieving an acceptable balance between risk and benefit, respecting individual clients and their autonomy, insuring fairness and justice, promoting fidelity to agreements, and exercising precaution (Beauchamp & Childress, 2013).

A professional culture of social work EBP builds upon the existing organizational cultures of social work research and practice. However, it is not merely an aggregation of these cultures but rather the product of their transformation resulting from the exchange of understandings, values, attitudes, and rules for engaging in EBP that occur between researchers and practitioners (Palinkas & Soydan, 2012). This exchange occurs through a process of debate and compromise (Bailey, 1973). It requires identification of points or areas of convergence and divergence and a willingness to either eliminate or accommodate the latter. One might refer to this as "mutual self-interests" (Kellam, 2012, p. 318). It also requires an ability to communicate using a common language and a willingness to collaborate and compromise (Palinkas & Soydan, 2012).

There are three primary elements of a professional culture of social work EBP related to the practice of cultural exchange. The first is the establishment of a set of core principles. At a minimum, these principles should relate to the goals of social work practice, the needs of the clients and communities served by social workers, and rules for interactions between researchers and practitioners that establish boundaries that define interactions as ethical or moral (normative) and feasible (pragmatic).

The second element of a professional culture of social work EBP related to cultural exchange is the recognition that not all understandings, attitudes, and rules for behaviors must be shared by all members or stakeholders of the partnership. Our understanding of cultural systems has evolved to an acknowledgment that they are composed of distributed understandings (D'Andrade, 1984) such that some members of an organization possess specialized knowledge or understanding that is not possessed by all members but is nevertheless important to the functioning of the organization. Thus, not every employee of a social services agency possesses the knowledge, skills, or responsibility for treating depression in clients or helping clients obtain public welfare benefits. In their respective organizational cultures, researchers do not necessarily deliver services and practitioners do not necessarily conduct research. However, in a professional culture of social work EBP, practitioners may be engaged in the generation of local knowledge that complements and contributes to the global knowledge generated by researchers. The point here is that researchers and practitioners will continue to possess different areas of responsibility and expertise with respect to conducting social work, but they can contribute to or enhance the expertise of each other.

The third element of a professional culture of social work EBP related to cultural exchange is a focus on innovation and experimentation. Contributions resulting from an exchange of understandings, attitudes, and rules for behavior ultimately lead to innovations in both research and practice. However, such innovations are not possible unless there is a common understanding that innovation is both feasible and desirable. This means that everyone believes there will always be better ways to conduct social work research and practice. However, efforts to innovate are not always successful; an understanding of the need to experiment and risk failure is equally important.

Conclusion

The path to developing a professional culture of social work is likely to possess numerous obstacles or potholes, not the least of which is the absence of a universal agreement that EBP is a necessary or useful feature of social work practice. There will be those who continue to dismiss EBP as a neoimperialist, hegemonic, top-down, cookbook approach to delivering services, as well as those who continue to dismiss social work practice as devoid of intellectual rigor and relying more on intuition than on science. It is our conviction, however, that the vast majority of social workers lie within these two extreme versions of research and practice. For the most part, they are caught within the gap between research and practice as they struggle to achieve a common goal—to deliver the best-quality service to those most in need. Helping both researchers and practitioners extricate themselves from this gap is the aim of a professional culture of evidence-based social work practice. Such a culture should be founded on a mutual respect for the EBP of researchers and the practice-based evidence of social work practitioners. It should be founded on an organizational context that possesses the structure, culture, climate, leadership, and resources necessary to support and sustain EBP. Last but not least, it should be founded on a partnership between researchers and practitioners that is based on mutual trust and respect, clear definition of roles, ethical conduct, an appropriate distribution of resources, scientific rigor, and a willingness to engage in cultural exchange.

REFERENCES

Aarons, G. A. (2004). Mental health provider attitudes toward adoption of evidence-based practice: The Evidence-Based Practice Attitude Scale (EBPAS). *Mental Health Services Research, 6,* 61–74. doi:10.1023/B:MHSR.0000024351.12294.65

Aarons, G. A. (2006). Transformational and transactional leadership: Association with attitudes toward evidence-based practice. *Psychiatric Services, 57,* 1162–1169. doi:10.1176/appi.ps.57.8.1162

Aarons, G. A., Cafri, G., Lugo, L., & Sawitzky, A. (2012). Expanding the domains of attitudes towards evidence-based practice: The Evidence-Based Practice Attitude Scale-50. *Administration and Policy in Mental Health and Mental Health Services Research, 39,* 331–340. doi:10.1007/s10488-010-0302-3

Aarons, G. A., Green, A. E., Palinkas, L. A., Self-Brown, S., Whitaker, D. J., Lutzker, J. R., . . . Chaffin, M. J. (2012). Dynamic adaptation process to implement an evidence-based child maltreatment intervention. *Implementation Science, 7,* 32. doi:10.1186/1748-5908-7-32

Aarons, G. A., Hurlburt, M., Fettes, D., Willging, C., Gunderson, L., Chaffin M., & Palinkas, L. A. (in press). Collaboration, negotiation, and coalescence for interagency-collaborative teams to scale-up evidence-based practice. *Journal of Clinical Child & Adolescent Psychology.*

Aarons, G. A., Hurlburt, M., & Horwitz, S. M. (2011). Advancing a conceptual model of evidence-based practice implementation in public service sectors. *Administration and Policy in Mental Health and Mental Health Services Research, 38,* 4–23. doi:10.1007/s10488-010-0327-7

Aarons, G. A., & Palinkas, L. A. (2007). Implementation of evidence-based practice in child welfare: Service provider perspectives. *Administration and Policy in Mental Health and Mental Health Services Research, 34,* 411–419. doi:10.1007/s10488-007-0121-3

Aarons, G. A., & Sawitzky, A. C. (2006). Organizational culture and climate and mental health provider attitudes toward evidence-based practice. *Psychological Services, 3,* 61–72. doi:10.1037/1541-1559.3.1.61

Aarons, G. A., Sommerfeld, D. H., Hecht, D. B., Silovsky, J. F., & Chaffin, M. J. (2009). The impact of evidence-based practice implementation and fidelity monitoring on staff turnover: Evidence for a protective effect. *Journal of Consulting and Clinical Psychology, 77*, 270–280. doi:10.1037/a0013223

Allen-Meares, P., Hudgins, C. A., Engberg, M. E., & Lessnau, B. (2005). Using a collaboratory model to translate social work research into practice and policy. *Research on Social Work Practice, 15*, 29–40. doi:10.1177/1049731504272345

Allik, J. (2005). Personality dimensions across cultures. *Journal of Personality Disorders, 19*, 212–232. doi:10.1521/pedi.2005.19.3.212

American Educational Research Association. (2006). Standards for reporting on empirical social science research in AERA publications. *Educational Researcher, 35*(6), 33–40. doi:10.3102/0013189X035006033

Anderson, N. R., & West, M. A. (1998). Measuring climate for work group innovation: Development and validation of the Team Climate Inventory. *Journal of Organizational Behavior, 19*, 235–258. doi:10.1002/(SICI)1099-1379(199805)19:3<235::AID-JOB837>3.0.CO;2-C

Antman, E. M., Lau, J., Kupelnick, B., Mosteller, F., & Chalmers, T. C. (1992). A comparison of results of meta-analyses of randomized control trials and recommendations of clinical experts: Treatments for myocardial infarction. *Journal of the American Medical Association, 268*, 240–248. doi:10.1001/jama.1992.03490020088036

Aos, S., Cook, T. D., Elliott, D. S., Gottfredson, D. C., Hawkins, J. D., Lipsey, M. W., & Tolan, P. (2011). Commentary on Valentine, Jeffrey, et al.: Replication in prevention science. *Prevention Science, 12*, 121–122. doi:10.1007/s11121-011-0219-4

Arnd-Caddigan, M. (2011). Toward a broader definition of evidence-informed practice: Intersubjective evidence. *Families in Society, 92*, 372–376. doi:10.1606/1044-3894.4160

Atherton, C. (2002). Changing culture not structure: Five years of research in practice in child care. *Journal of Integrated Care, 10*(1), 17–21. doi:10.1108/14769018200200005

Backer, T. E., David, S. L., & Saucy, G. (1995). Introduction. In T. E. Backer, S. L. David, & G. Saucy (Eds.), *Reviewing the behavioral science knowledge base on technology transfer* (pp. 1–20). Rockville, MD: U.S. Department of Health and Human Services.

Backer, T. E., Liberman, R. P., & Kuehnel, T. G. (1986). Dissemination and adoption of innovative psychosocial interventions. *Journal of Consulting and Clinical Psychology, 54*, 111–118. doi:10.1037/0022-006X.54.1.111

Bailey, F. G. (1973). Promethian fire: Right and wrong. In F. G. Bailey (Ed.), *Debate and compromise: The politics of innovation* (pp. 1–15). Totowa, NJ: Rowman & Littlefield.

Baker, E. A., Homan, S., Schonhoff, R., & Kreuter, M. (1999). Principles of practice for academic/practice/community research partnerships. *American Journal of Preventive Medicine, 16*, 86–93. doi:10.1016/S0749-3797(98)00149-4

Bandura, A. (1986). *Social foundations of thought and action: A social cognitive theory.* Englewood Cliffs, NJ: Prentice Hall.

Barratt, M. (2003). Organizational support for evidence-based practice within child and family social work: A collaborative study. *Child & Family Social Work, 8*, 143–150. doi:10.1046/j.1365-2206.2003.00276.x

Barth, F. (1969). Introduction. In F. Barth (Ed.), *Ethnic groups and boundaries: The social organization of culture difference* (pp. 9–38). Oslo, Norway: Universitetsforlaget.

Barth, F. (1984). Problems in conceptualizing cultural pluralism, with illustrations from Somar, Oman. In S. Plattner & D. Maybury-Lewis (Eds.), *The prospects for plural societies: 1982 proceedings of the American Ethnological Society* (pp. 77–87). Washington, DC: American Ethnological Society.

Barth, R. P., & Blackwell, D. L. (1998). Death rates among California's foster care and former foster care populations. *Children and Youth Services Review, 20*, 577–604. doi:10.1016/S0190-7409(98)00027-9

Beauchamp, T. L., & Childress, J. F. (2013). *Principles of biomedical ethics* (7th ed.). New York, NY: Oxford University Press.

Begun, A. L., Berger, L. K., Otto-Salaj, L. L., & Rose, S. J. (2010). Developing effective social work university–community research collaborations. *Social Work, 55*, 54–62. doi:10.1093/sw/55.1.54

Berkel, C., Mauricio, A. M., Schoenfelder, E., & Sandler, I. N. (2011). Putting the pieces together: An integrated model of program implementation. *Prevention Science, 12*, 23–33. doi:10.1007/s11121-010-0186-1

Bernal, G., Jiménez-Chafey, M. I., & Domenech Rodríguez, M. M. (2009). Cultural adaptation of treatments: A resource for considering culture in evidence-based practice. *Professional Psychology: Research and Practice, 40*, 361–368. doi:10.1037/a0016401

Berta, W., Teare, G. F., Gilbart, E., Ginsburg, L. S., Lemieux-Charles, L., Davis, D., & Rappolt, S. (2005). The contingencies of organizational learning in long-term care: Factors that affect innovation adoption. *Health Care Management Review, 30*, 282–292. doi:10.1097/00004010-200510000-00002

Bierman, K. L. (2006). Commentary on the pitfalls and pratfalls of evaluation research with intervention and prevention programs. *New Directions for Evaluation, 110*, 87–96. doi:10.1002/ev.189

Biglan, A., Mrazek, P. J., Carnine, D., & Flay, B. R. (2003). The integration of research and practice in the prevention of youth problem behaviors. *American Psychologist, 58*, 433–440. doi:10.1037/0003-066X.58.6-7.433

Björk, B.-C., Roos, A., & Lauri, M. (2009). Scientific journal publishing: Yearly volume and open access availability. *Information Research, 14*(1). Retrieved from http://informationr.net/ir/14-1/paper391.html

Boruch, R. (2007). Encouraging the flight of error: Ethical standards, evidence standards, and randomized trials. *New Directions for Evaluation, 2007*(113), 55–73. doi:10.1002/ev.215

Boruch, R., Soydan, H., de Moya, D., & the Campbell Collaboration Steering Committee. (2004). The Campbell Collaboration. *Brief Treatment and Crisis Intervention, 4*, 277–287. doi:10.1093/brief-treatment/mhh024

Bowen, S., & Zwi, A. B. (2005). Pathways to "evidence-informed" policy and practice: A framework for action. *PlOS Medicine, 2*(7), e166. doi:10.1371/journal.pmed.0020166

British Association of Social Workers. (2012). *The code of ethics for social work: Statement of principles.* Retrieved from http://cdn.basw.co.uk/upload/basw_112315-7.pdf

Brunette, M. F., Asher, D., Whitley, R., Lutz, W. J., Wieder, B. L., Jones, A. M., & McHugo, G. J. (2008). Implementation of integrated dual disorders treatment:

A qualitative analysis of facilitators and barriers. *Psychiatric Services, 59*, 989–995. doi:10.1176/appi.ps.59.9.989

Bull, J. P. (1959). The historical development of clinical therapeutic trials. *Journal of Chronic Diseases, 10*, 218–248. doi:10.1016/0021-9681(59)90004-9

Burkas, D. (2008). Children in foster care: A vulnerable population at risk. *Journal of Child and Adolescent Psychiatric Nursing, 21*, 70–77. doi:10.1111/j.1744-6171.2008.00134.x

Campbell, D. T. (1957). Factors relevant to the validity of experiments in social settings. *Psychological Bulletin, 54*, 297–312. doi:10.1037/h0040950

Campbell, D. T. (1988). The experimenting society. In E. S. Overman (Ed.), *Methodology and epistemology for social science: Selected papers* (pp. 290–314). Chicago, IL: University of Chicago Press.

Campbell, D. T., & Russo, M. J. (1999). *Social experimentation.* Thousand Oaks, CA: Sage.

Campbell, D. T., & Stanley, J. C. (1963). *Experimental and quasi-experimental designs for research.* Chicago, IL: Rand McNally.

Campbell Collaboration. (n.d.). *About us.* Retrieved from http://www.campbellcol laboration.org/about_us/index.php

Chalmers, I. (2005). If evidence-informed policy works in practice, does it matter if it doesn't work in theory? *Evidence & Policy, 1*, 227–242. doi:110.1332/1744264053730806

Chamberlain, P., Brown, C. H., Saldana, L., Reid, J., Wang, W., Marsenich, L., . . . & Bouwman, G. (2008). Engaging and recruiting counties in an experiment on implementing evidence-based practice in California. *Administration and Policy in Mental Health and Mental Health Services Research, 35*, 250–260. doi:10.1007/s10488-008-0167-x

Charlton, B. G. (1997). Restoring the balance: Evidence-based medicine put in its place. *Journal of Evaluation in Clinical Practice, 3*, 87–98. doi:10.1046/j.1365-2753.1997.00097.x

Chorpita, B. F., Daleiden, E. L., & Weisz, J. R. (2005). Modularity in the design and application of therapeutic interventions. *Applied and Preventive Psychology, 11*, 141–156. doi:10.1016/j.appsy.2005.05.002

Chorpita, B. F., Weisz, J. R., Daleiden, E. L., Schoenwald, S. K., Palinkas, L. A., Miranda, J., . . . the Research Network on Youth Mental Health. (2013). Long-term outcomes for the Child STEPs randomized effectiveness trial: A comparison of modular and standard treatment designs with usual care. *Journal of Consulting and Clinical Psychology, 81*, 999–1009. doi:10.1037/a0034200

Christakis, N. A. (2012). *A new kind of social science for the 21st century.* Retrieved from http://edge.org/conversation/a-21st-century-change-to-social-science

Claridge, J. A., & Fabian, T. C. (2005). History and development of evidence-based medicine. *World Journal of Surgery, 29*, 547–553. doi:10.1007/s00268-005-7910-1

Cochrane, A. L. (1972). *Effectiveness & efficiency: Random reflections on health services.* London, United Kingdom: Nuffield Provincial Hospitals Trust.

Cochrane, A. L. (1979). 1931–1971: A critical review with particular reference to the medical profession. In G. Feeling-Smith & N. Wells (Eds.), *Medicines for the year 2000* (pp. 1–11). London, United Kingdom: Office of Health Economics.

Cochrane Collaboration. (2014). *Our principles.* Retrieved from http://www.cochrane.org/about-us/our-principles

Cochrane Effective Practice and Organisation of Care Review Group. (2002). *Data collection checklist*. Retrieved from http://epoc.cochrane.org/sites/epoc.cochrane.org/files/uploads/datacollectionchecklist.pdf

Cohen, I. B. (Ed.). (1980). *The life and scientific and medical career of Benjamin Waterhouse: With some account of the introduction of vaccination in America*. New York, NY: Arno Press.

Collins, L. M., Murphy, S. A., Nair, V. N., & Strecher, V. J. (2005). A strategy for optimizing and evaluating behavioral interventions. *Annals of Behavioral Medicine*, *30*, 65–73. doi:10.1207/s15324796abm3001_8

Cook, T. D., & Campbell, D. T. (1979). *Quasi-experimentation: Design & analysis issues for field settings*. Chicago, IL: Rand McNally.

Cooke, R. A., & Rousseau, D. M. (1988). Behavioral norms and expectations: A quantitative approach to the assessment of organizational culture. *Group & Organization Management*, *13*, 245–273. doi:10.1177/105960118801300302

Cooper, H., & Hedges, L. V. (Eds.). (1994). *The handbook of research synthesis*. New York, NY: Russell Sage Foundation.

Cronbach, L. J. (1982). *Designing evaluations of educational and social programs*. San Francisco, CA: Jossey-Bass.

Currie, M., King, G., Rosenbaum, P., Law, M., Kertoy, M., & Specht, J. (2005). A model of impacts of research partnerships in health and social services. *Evaluation and Program Planning*, *28*, 400–412. doi:10.1016/j.evalprogplan.2005.07.004

Damanpour, F. (1991). Organizational innovation: A meta-analysis of effects of determinants and moderators. *Academy of Management Journal*, *34*, 555–590. doi:10.2307/256406

Damschroder, L. J., Aron, D. C., Keith, R. E., Kirsh, S. R., Alexander, J. A., & Lowery, J. C. (2009). Fostering implementation of health services research findings into practice: A consolidated framework for advancing implementation science. *Implementation Science*, *4*, 50. doi:10.1186/1748-5908-4-50

D'Andrade, R. G. (1984). Cultural meaning systems. In: R. A. Shweder & R. A. LeVine (Eds.), *Culture theory: Essays on mind, self, and emotion* (pp. 88–122). Cambridge, United Kingdom: Cambridge University Press.

Davies, B. (2003). Death to critique and dissent? The policies and practices of new managerialism and of 'evidence-based practice.' *Gender and Education*, *15*, 91–103. doi:10.1080/0954025032000042167

Davies, H. T. O., Nutley, S. M., & Mannion, R. (2000). Organisational culture and quality of health care. *Quality in Health Care*, *9*, 111–119. doi:10.1136/qhc.9.2.111

Davies, H., Nutley, S., & Walter, I. (2008). Why 'knowledge transfer' is misconceived for applied social research. *Journal of Health Services Research & Policy*, *13*, 188–190. doi:10.1258/jhsrp.2008.008055

de Anda, D. (Ed.). (1997). *Controversial issues in multiculturalism*. Boston, MA: Allyn and Bacon.

De Geest, S., Dobbels, F., Schönfeld, S., Duerinckx, N., Sveinbjarnardottir, E. K., & Denhaerynck, K. (2013). Academic service partnerships: What do we learn from around the globe? A systematic literature review. Nursing Outlook, *61*, 447–457. doi:10.1016/j.outlook.2013.02.001

Demakis, J. G., McQueen, L., Kizer, K. W., & Feussner, J. R. (2000). Quality Enhancement Research Initiative (QUERI): A collaboration between research and clinical practice. *Medical Care*, *38*(Suppl. I), I17–I25. doi:10.1097/00005650-200006001-00003

Denzin, N. K., & Lincoln, Y. S. (Eds.). (1994). *Handbook of qualitative research.* Thousand Oaks, CA: Sage.

Des Jarlais, D. C., Lyles, C., & Crepaz, N. (2004). Improving the reporting quality of nonrandomized evaluations of behavioral and public health interventions: The TREND statement. *American Journal of Public Health, 94*, 361–366. doi:10.2105/AJPH.94.3.361

Devore, W., & Schlesinger, E. G. (1996). *Ethnic-sensitive social work practice* (4th ed.). Boston, MA: Allyn and Bacon.

Diaz, M., & Neuhauser, D. (2004). Lessons from using randomization to assess gold treatment for tuberculosis. *JLL Bulletin: Commentaries on the History of Treatment Evaluation.* Retrieved from James Lind Library website: www.jameslindlibrary.org

Dodd, S.-J., & Epstein, I. (2012). *Practice-based research in social work: A guide for reluctant researchers.* Abingdon, United Kingdom: Routledge.

Duan, N., Bhaumik, D. K., Palinkas, L. A., & Hoagwood, K. (in press). Optimal design and purposeful sampling: Twin methodologies for implementation research. *Administration and Policy in Mental Health and Mental Health Services Research.*

Edmondson, A. C., Bohmer, R. M., & Pisano, G. P. (2001). Disrupted routines: Team learning and new technology implementation in hospitals. *Administrative Science Quarterly, 46*, 685–716. doi:10.2307/3094828

Egger, M., Davey Smith, G., & Altman, B. G. (Eds.). (2001). *Systematic reviews in health care: Meta-analysis in context* (2nd ed.). London, United Kingdom: BMJ.

Epstein, I. (1996). In quest of a research-based model for clinical practice: Or, why can't a social worker be more like a researcher? *Social Work Research, 20*, 97–100. doi:10.1093/swr/20.2.97

Epstein, I. (2001). Using available clinical information in practice-based research: Mining for silver while dreaming of gold. In I. Epstein & S. Blumenfield (Eds.), *Clinical data-mining in practice-based research: Social work in hospital settings* (pp. 15–32). Binghamton, NY: Haworth Press.

Epstein, I. (2009). Promoting harmony where there is commonly conflict: Evidence-informed practice as an integrative strategy. *Social Work in Health Care, 48*, 216–231. doi:10.1080/00981380802589845

Epstein, I. (2011). Reconciling evidence-based practice, evidence-informed practice, and practice-based research: The role of clinical data-mining. *Social Work, 56*, 284–288. doi:10.1093/sw/56.3.284

Epstein, R. M. (1999). Mindful practice. *Journal of the American Medical Association, 282*, 833–839. doi:10.1001/jama.282.9.833

Fabiano, G. A., Pelham, W. E., Jr., Coles, E. K., Gnagy, E. M., Chronis-Tuscano, A., & O'Connor, B. C. (2009). A meta-analysis of behavioral treatments for attention-deficit/hyperactivity disorder. *Clinical Psychology Review, 29*, 129–140. doi:10.1016/j.cpr.2008.11.001

Ferrer-Wreder, L., Adamson, L., Kumpfer, K. L., & Eichas, K. (2012). Advancing intervention science through effectiveness research: A global perspective. *Child & Youth Care Forum, 41*, 109–117. doi:10.1007/s10566-012-9173-y

Ferrer-Wreder, L., Sundell, K., & Mansoory, S. (2012). Tinkering with perfection: Theory development in the intervention cultural adaptation field. *Child & Youth Care Forum, 41*, 149–171. doi:10.1007/s10566-011-9162-6

Fixsen, D. L., Naoom, S. F., Blase, K. A., Friedman, R. M., & Wallace, F. (2005). *Implementation research: A synthesis of the literature* (FMHI Publication No. 231). Tampa, FL: National Implementation Research Network, Louis de la Parte Florida Mental Health Institute, University of South Florida.

Frambach, R. T., & Schillewaert, N. (2002). Organizational innovation adoption: A multi-level framework of determinants and opportunities for future research. *Journal of Business Research, 55,* 163–176. doi:10.1016/S0148-2963(00)00152-1

Friedman, T. L., & Mandelbaum, M. (2011). *That used to be us: How America fell behind in the world it invented and how we can come back.* New York, NY: Picador.

Fuller, B. E., Rieckmann, T., Nunes, E. V., Miller, M., Arfken, C., Edmundson, E., & McCarty, D. (2007). Organizational readiness for change and opinions toward treatment innovations. *Journal of Substance Abuse Treatment, 33,* 183–192. doi:10.1016/j.jsat.2006.12.026

Galano, J., & Huntington, L. (2004). *Healthy Families Virginia FY 2000-2004: Executive summary: Statewide evaluation report.* Retrieved from Healthy Families America website: http://www.healthyfamiliesamerica.org/downloads/eval_hfva_2004.pdf

Gambrill, E. (1999). Evidence-based practice: An alternative to authority-based practice. *Families in Society, 80,* 341–350. doi:10.1606/1044-3894.1214

Gambrill, E. (2001). Social work: An authority-based profession. *Research on Social Work Practice, 11,* 166–175. doi:10.1177/104973150101100203

Gambrill, E. (2006). Evidence-based practice and policy: Choices ahead. *Research on Social Work Practice, 16,* 338–357. doi:10.1177/1049731505284205

Gambrill, E. (2008). Evidence-based (informed) macro practice: Process and philosophy. *Journal of Evidence-Based Social Work, 5,* 423–452. doi:10.1080/15433710802083971

Garfield, S. L. (1998). Some comments on empirically supported treatment. *Journal of Consulting and Clinical Psychology, 66,* 121–125. doi:10.1037/0022-006X.66.1.121

Garland, A. F., Kruse, M., & Aarons, G. A. (2003). Clinicians and outcome measurement: What's the use? *Journal of Behavioral Health Services & Research, 30,* 393–405. doi:10.1007/BF02287427

Gibbs, L. E. (2003). *Evidence-based practice for helping professions: A practical guide with integrated multimedia.* Pacific Grove, CA: Brooks/Cole–Thompson Learning.

Gibbs, L. E., & Gambrill, E. (2002). Evidence-based practice: Counterarguments to objections. *Research on Social Work Practice, 12,* 452–476. doi:10.1177/1049731502012003007

Gilgun, J. F. (2005). The four cornerstones of evidence-based practice in social work. *Research on Social Work Practice, 15,* 52–61. doi:10.1177/1049731504269581

Gioia, D., & Dziadosz, G. (2008). Adoption of evidence-based practices in community mental health: A mixed-method study of practitioner experience. *Community Mental Health Journal, 44,* 347–357. doi:10.1007/s10597-008-9136-9

Glasgow, R. E. (2009). Critical measurement issues in translational research. *Research on Social Work Practice, 19,* 560–568. doi:10.1177/1049731509335497

Glasgow, R. E., Lichtenstein, E., & Marcus, A. C. (2003). Why don't we see more translation of health promotion research to practice? Rethinking the efficacy-to-effectiveness transition. *American Journal of Public Health, 93,* 1261–1267. doi:10.2105/AJPH.93.8.1261

Glazerman, S., Levy, D. M., & Myers, D. (2003). Nonexperimental versus experimental estimates of earnings impacts. *Annals of the American Academy of Political and Social Science, 589*, 63–93. doi:10.1177/0002716203254879

Glisson, C. (1989). The effect of leadership on workers in human service organizations. *Administration in Social Work, 13*(3-4), 99–116. doi:10.1300/J147v13n03_06

Glisson, C. (2002). The organizational context of children's mental health services. *Clinical Child and Family Psychology Review, 5*, 233–253. doi:10.1023/A:1020972906177

Glisson, C., Dukes, D., & Green, P. (2006). The effects of the ARC organizational intervention on caseworker turnover, climate, and culture in children's service systems. *Child Abuse & Neglect, 30*, 855–880. doi:10.1016/j.chiabu.2005.12.010

Glisson, C., & Green, P. (2006). The effects of organizational culture and climate on the access to mental health care in child welfare and juvenile justice systems. *Administration and Policy in Mental Health and Mental Health Services Research, 33*, 433–448. doi:10.1007/s10488-005-0016-0

Glisson, C., & Hemmelgarn, A. (1998). The effects of organizational climate and interorganizational coordination on the quality and outcomes of children's service systems. *Child Abuse & Neglect, 22*, 401–421. doi:10.1016/S0145-2134(98)00005-2

Glisson, C., Hemmelgarn, A., Green, P., & Williams, N. J. (2013). Randomized trial of the Availability, Responsiveness and Continuity (ARC) organizational intervention for improving youth outcomes in community mental health programs. *Journal of the American Academy of Child and Adolescent Psychiatry, 52*, 493–500. doi:10.1016/j.jaac.2013.02.005

Glisson, C., & James, L. R. (2002). The cross-level effects of culture and climate in human service teams. *Journal of Organizational Behavior, 23*, 767–794. doi:10.1002/job.162

Glisson, C., Landsverk, J., Schoenwald, S., Kelleher, K., Hoagwood, K. E., Mayberg, S., & Green, P. (2008). Assessing the organizational social context (OSC) of mental health services: Implications for research and practice. *Administration and Policy in Mental Health and Mental Health Services Research, 35*, 98–113. doi:10.1007/s10488-007-0148-5

Glisson, C., & Schoenwald, S. K. (2005). The ARC organizational and community intervention strategy for implementing evidence-based children's mental health treatments. *Mental Health Services Research, 7*, 243–259. doi:10.1007/s11020-005-7456-1

Glisson, C., Schoenwald, S. K., Hemmelgarn, A., Green, P., Dukes, D., Armstrong, K. S., & Chapman, J. E. (2010). Randomized trial of MST and ARC in a two-level evidence-based treatment implementation strategy. *Journal of Consulting and Clinical Psychology, 78*, 537–550. doi:10.1037/a0019160

Golden-Biddle, K., Reay, T., Petz, S., Witt, C., Casebeer, A., Pablo, A., & Hinings, C. R. (2003). Toward a communicative perspective of collaborating in research: The case of the researcher–decision-maker partnership. *Journal of Health Services Research & Policy, 8*(Suppl. 2), 20–25. doi:10.1258/135581903322405135

Goodman, K. W. (2003). *Ethics and evidence-based medicine: Fallibility and responsibility in clinical science.* Cambridge, United Kingdom: Cambridge University Press.

Gray, M., Plath, D., & Webb, S. A. (2009). *Evidence-based social work: A critical stance.* New York, NY: Routledge.

Green, J. W. (1995). *Cultural awareness in the human services. A multi-ethnic approach* (2nd ed.). Boston, MA: Allyn and Bacon.

Green, L. W., & Kreuter, M. W. (2005). *Health program planning: An educational and ecological approach.* Boston, MA: McGraw-Hill.

Greenhalgh, T., Robert, G., Macfarlane, F., Bate, P., & Kyriakidou, O. (2004). Diffusion of innovations in service organizations: Systematic review and recommendations. *Milbank Quarterly, 82*, 581–629. doi:10.1111/j.0887-378X.2004.00325.x

Haight, W. L. (2010). The multiple roles of applied social science research in evidence-informed practice. *Social Work, 55*, 101–103. doi:10.1093/sw/55.2.101

Hammersley, M. (2003). Social research today: Some dilemmas and distinctions. *Qualitative Social Work, 2*, 25–44. doi:10.1177/147332500300200103

Hannerz, U. (1992). *Cultural complexity: Studies in the social organization of meaning.* New York, NY: Columbia University Press.

Hannerz, U. (2000). *Flow, boundaries and hybrids: Keywords in transnational anthropology* (Working Paper WPTC-2K-02). Stockholm, Sweden: Stockholm University, Department of Social Anthropology. Retrieved from http://www.transcomm. ox.ac.uk/working%20papers/hannerz.pdf

Hansen, W. B. (2011). Was Herodotus correct? *Prevention Science, 12*, 118–120. doi:10.1007/s11121-011-0218-5

Hatch, J., Moss, N., Saran, A., Presley-Cantrell, L., & Mallory, C. (1993). Community research: Partnership in black communities. *American Journal of Preventive Medicine, 9*(6, Suppl.), 27-31.

Hatch, M. J. (1993). The dynamics of organizational culture. *Academy of Management Review, 18*, 657–693. doi:10.5465/AMR.1993.9402210154

Hawkins, J. D., & Catalano, R. F. (2002). *Investing in your community's youth: An introduction to the Communities That Care system.* South Deerfield, MA: Channing Bete.

Haynes, R. B., Devereaux, P. J., & Guyatt, G. H. (2002). Clinical expertise in the era of evidence-based medicine and patient choice. *Evidence-Based Medicine, 7*, 36–38. doi:10.1136/ebm.7.2.36

Heiwe, S., Nilsson-Kajermo, K., Olsson, M., Gåfvels, C., Larsson, K., & Wengström, Y. (2013). Evidence-based practice among Swedish medical social workers. *Social Work in Health Care, 52*, 947–958. doi:10.1080/00981389.2013.834029

Hemmelgarn, A. L., Glisson, C., & Dukes, D. (2001). Emergency room culture and the emotional support component of family-centered care. *Children's Health Care, 30*, 93–110. doi:10.1207/S15326888CHC3002_2

Higgins, J. P. T., & Green, S. (Eds.). (2011). *Cochrane handbook for systematic reviews of interventions* (Version 5.1.0). Retrieved from http://handbook.cochrane.org

Hoagwood, K., Burns, B. J., Kiser, L., Ringeisen, H., & Schoenwald, S. K. (2001). Evidence-based practice in child and adolescent mental health services. *Psychiatric Services, 52*, 1179–1189. doi:10.1176/appi.ps.52.9.1179

Hoagwood, K., & Olin, S. S. (2002). The NIMH Blueprint for Change report: Research priorities in child and adolescent mental health. *Journal of the American Academy of Child & Adolescent Psychiatry, 41*, 760–767. doi:10.1097/00004583-200207000-00006

Hofstede, G. (1991). *Cultures and organizations: Software of the mind.* New York, NY: McGraw-Hill.

Honig, M. I., & Coburn, C. (2008). Evidence-based decision making in school district central offices: Toward a policy and research agenda. *Educational Policy, 22,* 578–608. doi:10.1177/0895904807307067

Hopewell, S., Clarke, M. J., Lefebvre, C., & Scherer, R. W. (2008). Handsearching versus electronic searching to identify reports of randomized trials. *Cochrane Library.* doi:10.1002/14651858.MR000001.pub2

Hopewell, S., Loudon, K., Clarke, M. J., Oxman, A. D., & Dickersin, K. (2009). Publication bias in clinical trials due to statistical significance or direction of trial results. *Cochrane Library.* doi:10.1002/14651858.MR000006.pub3

Horwitz, S. M., Chamberlain, P., Landsverk, J., & Mullican, C. (2010). Improving the mental health of children in child welfare through the implementation of evidence-based parenting interventions. *Administration and Policy in Mental Health and Mental Health Services Research, 37,* 27–39. doi:10.1007/s10488-010-0274-3

Huberman, M. (1994). Research utilization: The state of the art. *Knowledge and Policy, 7*(4), 13–33. doi:10.1007/BF02696290

Huey, S. J., Jr., & Polo, A. J. (2008). Evidence-based psychosocial treatments for ethnic minority youth. *Journal of Clinical Child & Adolescent Psychology, 37,* 262–301. doi:10.1080/15374410701820174

Huey, S. J., Jr., & Polo, A. J. (2010). Assessing the effects of evidence-based psychotherapies with ethnic minority youths. In J. R. Weisz & A. E. Kazdin (Eds.). *Evidence-based psychotherapies for children and adolescents* (2nd ed., pp. 451–465). New York, NY: Guilford Press.

Hunter, J. E., & Schmidt, F. L. (2004). *Methods of meta-analysis: Correcting error and bias in research findings.* Thousand Oaks, CA: Sage.

Institute for Healthcare Improvement. (2004). The Breakthrough Series: IHI's collaborative model for achieving breakthrough improvement. *Diabetes Spectrum, 17,* 97–101. doi:10.2337/diaspect.17.2.97

Institute of Medicine. (2001). *Crossing the quality chasm: A new health system for the 21st century.* Washington, DC: National Academies Press.

Ioannidis, J. P. A. (2005). Why most published research findings are false. *PLoS Medicine, 2*(8), e124. doi:10.1371/journal.pmed.0020124

Israel, B. A., Eng, E., Schulz, A. J., & Parker, E. A. (Eds.). (2005). *Methods in community-based participatory research for health.* San Francisco, CA: Jossey-Bass.

Jamison, D. T., Breman, J. G., Measham, A. R., Alleyne, G., Claeson, M., Evans, D. B., . . . Musgrove, P. (Eds.). (2006). *Priorities in health.* Washington, DC: World Bank.

Jefferson, T., Rudin, M., Brodney Folse, S., & Davidoff, F. (2008). Editorial peer review for improving the quality of reports of biomedical studies. *Cochrane Library.* doi:10.1002/14651858.MR000016.pub3

Jinha, A. E. (2010). Article 50 million: An estimate of the number of scholarly articles in existence. *Learned Publishing, 23,* 258–263. doi:10.1087/20100308

Jonson-Reid, M., & Barth, R. P. (2000). From placement to prison: The path to adolescent incarceration from child welfare supervised foster or group care. *Children and Youth Services Review, 22,* 493–516. doi:10.1016/S0190-7409(00)00100-6

Joyce, W. F., & Slocum, J. W., Jr. (1984). Collective climate: Agreement as a basis for defining aggregate climates in organizations. *Academy of Management Journal, 27,* 721–742. doi:10.2307/255875

Judge, T. A., Thoresen, C. J., Pucik, V., & Welbourne, T. M. (1999). Managerial coping with organizational change: A dispositional perspective. *Journal of Applied Psychology, 84,* 107–122. doi:10.1037/0021-9010.84.1.107

Karger, H. J. (1983). Science, research, and social work: Who controls the profession? *Social Work, 28,* 200–205. doi:10.1093/sw/28.3.200

Kaska, S. C., & Weinstein, J. N. (1998). Ernest Amory Codman, 1869–1940: A pioneer of evidence-based medicine: The end result idea. *Spine, 23,* 629–633. doi:10.1097/00007632-199803010-00019

Kazi, M. A. F., Mantysaari, M., & Rostila, I. (1997). Promoting the use of single-case designs: Social work experiences from England and Finland. *Research on Social Work Practice, 7,* 311–328. doi:10.1177/104973159700700302

Kazi, M. A. F., & Wilson, J. T. (1996a). Applying single-case evaluation methodology in a British social work agency. *Research on Social Work Practice, 6,* 5–26. doi:10.1177/104973159600600101

Kazi, M. A. F., & Wilson, J. (1996b). Applying single-case evaluation in social work. *British Journal of Social Work, 26,* 699–717.

Kellam, S. G. (2012). Developing and maintaining partnerships as the foundation of implementation and implementation science. Reflections over a half century. *Administration and Policy in Mental Health and Mental Health Services Research, 39,* 317–320. doi:10.1007/s10488-011-0402-8

Kelly, M. P., & Moore T. A. (2012). The judgement process in evidence-based medicine and health technology assessment. *Social Theory & Health, 10,* 1–19. doi:10.1057/sth.2011.21

Kennedy, M. M. (1984). How evidence alters understanding and decisions. *Educational Evaluation and Policy Analysis, 6,* 207–226. doi:10.3102/01623737006003207

Klagholz, D. D., & Associates. (2005). *Starting early starting smart: Final report.* Retrieved from Healthy Families America website: http://www.healthyfamilie samerica.org/downloads/eval_hfdc_2005_final.pdf

Klein, K. J., & Sorra, J. S. (1996). The challenge of innovation implementation. *Academy of Management Review, 21,* 1055–1080. doi:10.5465/AMR.1996.9704071863

Knipschild, P. (1994). Systematic reviews: Some examples. *British Medical Journal, 309,* 719–721. doi:10.1136/bmj.309.6956.719

Kramer, T. L., & Burns, B. J. (2008). Implementing cognitive behavioral therapy in the real world: A case study of two mental health centers. *Implementation Science, 3,* 14. doi:10.1186/1748-5908-3-14

Kroeber, A. L., & Kluckhohn, C. (1952). *Culture: A critical review of concepts and definitions.* New York, NY: Vintage Books.

Landsverk, J., Brown, C. H., Chamberlain, P., Palinkas, L., Ogihara, M., Czaja, S., . . . Horwitz, S. M. (2012). Design and analysis in dissemination and implementation research. In R. C. Brownson, G. A. Colditz, & E. K. Proctor (Eds.), *Dissemination and implementation research in health: Translating science to practice* (pp. 225–260). New York, NY: Oxford University Press.

Latham, T. P., Sales, J. M., Boyce, L. S., Renfro, T. L., Wingood, G. M., DiClemente, R. J., & Rose, E. (2010). Application of ADAPT-ITT: Adapting an evidence-based HIV prevention intervention for incarcerated African American adolescent females. *Health Promotion Practice, 11,* 53S–60S. doi:10.1177/1524839910361433

Laupacis, A., Sackett, D. L., & Roberts, R. S. (1988). An assessment of the clinically useful measures of the consequences of treatment. *New England Journal of Medicine, 318*, 1728–1733. doi:10.1056/NEJM198806303182605

Lavis, J. N., Robertson, D., Woodside, J. M., McLeod, C. B., Abelson, J., & the Knowledge Transfer Study Group. (2003). How can research organizations more effectively transfer research knowledge to decision makers? *Milbank Quarterly, 81*, 221–248. doi:10.1111/1468-0009.t01-1-00052

Lewis-Fernández, R., & Kleinman, A. (1995). Cultural psychiatry: Theoretical, clinical and research issues. *Psychiatric Clinics of North America, 18*, 433–448.

Lindenauer, P. K., Rothberg, M. B., Pekow, P. S., Kenwood, C., Benjamin, E. M., & Auerbach, A. D. (2007). Outcomes of care by hospitalists, general internists, and family physicians. *New England Journal of Medicine, 357*, 2589–2600. doi:10.1056/NEJMsa067735

Lipsey, M. W., & Wilson, D. B. (1993). The efficacy of psychological, educational, and behavioral treatment: Confirmation from meta-analysis. *American Psychologist, 48*, 1181–1209. doi:10.1037/0003-066X.48.12.1181

Lipsey, M. W., & Wilson, D. B. (2001). *Practical meta-analysis*. Thousand Oaks, CA: Sage.

Lomas, J. (2000). Using 'linkage and exchange' to move research into policy at a Canadian foundation. *Health Affairs, 19*, 236–240. doi:10.1377/hlthaff.19.3.236

Lum, D. (1996). *Social work practice & people of color: A process-stage approach* (3rd ed.). Monterey, CA: Brooks/Cole.

Lundgren, L., Krull, I., de Saxe Zerden, L., & McCarty, D. (2011). Community-based addiction treatment staff attitudes about the usefulness of evidence-based addiction treatment and CBO organizational linkages to research institutions. *Evaluation and Program Planning, 34*, 356–365. doi:10.1016/j.evalprogplan.2011.02.002

Macaulay, A. C., Commanda, L. E., Freeman, W. L., Gibson, N., McCabe, M. L., Robbins, C. M., & Twohig, P. L. (1999). Participatory research maximises community and lay involvement. *BMJ, 319*(7212), 774–778. doi:10.1136/bmj.319.7212.774

Macdonald, G. (1999). Evidence-based social care: Wheels off the runway? *Public Money & Management, 19*, 25–32. doi:10.1111/1467-9302.00149

Machamer, P., Pera, M., & Baltas, A. (Eds.). (2000). *Scientific controversies: Philosophical and historical perspectives*. New York, NY: Oxford University Press.

MacKinnon, D. P. (2011). Integrating mediators and moderators in research design. *Research on Social Work Practice, 21*, 675–681. doi:10.1177/1049731511414148

Madison, S. M., McKay, M. M., Paikoff, R., & Bell, C. C. (2000). Basic research and community collaboration: Necessary ingredients for the development of a family-based HIV prevention program. *AIDS Education and Prevention, 12*, 281–298.

Manuel, J. I., Mullen, E. J., Fang, L., Bellamy, J. L., & Bledsoe, S. E. (2009). Preparing social work practitioners to use evidence-based practice: A comparison of experiences from an implementation project. *Research on Social Work Practice, 19*, 613–627. doi:10.1177/1049731509335547

Markham, C. R. (Ed.). (1877). *The voyages of Sir James Lancaster to the East Indies with abstracts of journals of voyages to the East Indies, during the seventeenth century, preserved in the India Office*. London, United Kingdom: Hakluyt Society.

Marshall, T., Rapp, C. A., Becker, D. R., & Bond, G. R. (2008). Key factors for implementing supported employment. *Psychiatric Services, 59*, 886–892. doi:10.1176/appi.ps.59.8.886

Marty, D., Rapp, C., McHugo, G., & Whitley, R. (2008). Factors influencing consumer outcome monitoring in implementation of evidence-based practices: Results from the National EBP Implementation Project. *Administration and Policy in Mental Health and Mental Health Services Research, 35*, 204–211. doi:10.1007/s10488-007-0157-4

McCabe, K., & Yeh, M. (2009). Parent–child interaction therapy for Mexican Americans: A randomized clinical trial. *Journal of Clinical Child & Adolescent Psychology, 38*, 753–759. doi:10.1080/15374410903103544

McFarlane, E., Burrell, L., Crowne, S., Cluxton-Keller, F., Fuddy, L., Leaf, P. J., & Duggan, A. (2013). Maternal relationship security as a moderator of home visiting impacts on maternal psychosocial functioning. *Prevention Science, 14*, 25–39. doi:10.1007/s11121-012-0297-y

McGuire, W. J. (1997). Creative hypothesis generating in psychology: Some useful heuristics. *Annual Review of Psychology, 48*, 1–30. doi:10.1146/annurev.psych.48.1.1

McKleroy, V. S., Galbraith, J. S., Cummings, B., Jones, P., Harshbarger, C., Collins, C., . . . the ADAPT Team. (2006). Adapting evidence-based behavioral interventions for new settings and target populations. *AIDS Education and Prevention, 18*(Suppl.), 59–73. doi:10.1521/aeap.2006.18.supp.59

McNeece, C. A., & Thyer, B. A. (2004). Evidence-based practice and social work. *Journal of Evidence-Based Practice, 1*(1), 7–25. doi:10.1300/J394v01n01_02

Mendel, P., Meredith, L. S., Schoenbaum, M., Sherbourne, C. D., & Wells, K. B. (2008). Interventions in organizational and community context: A framework for building evidence on dissemination and implementation in health services research. *Administration and Policy in Mental Health and Mental Health Services Research, 35*, 21–37. doi:10.1007/s10488-007-0144-9

Mihalic, S. F., Fagan, A., Irwin, K., Ballard, D., & Elliott, D. M. (2004). *Blueprints for violence prevention*. Washington, DC: U.S. Department of Justice, Office of Justice Programs, Office of Juvenile Justice and Delinquency Prevention.

Miles, M. B., & Huberman, A. M. (1994). *Qualitative data analysis* (2nd ed.). Thousand Oaks, CA: Sage.

Minkler, M., & Wallerstein, N. (Eds.). (2003). *Community-based participatory research for health*. San Francisco, CA: Jossey-Bass.

Miranda, J., Bernal, G., Lau, A., Kohn, L., Hwang, W.-C., & LaFramboise, T. (2005). State of science on psychological interventions for ethnic minorities. *Annual Review of Clinical Psychology, 1*, 113–142. doi:10.1146/annurev.clinpsy.1.102803.143822

Mitton, C., Adair, C. E., McKenzie, E., Patten, S. B., & Waye Perry, B. (2007). Knowledge transfer and exchange: Review and synthesis of the literature. *Milbank Quarterly, 85*, 729–768. doi:10.1111/j.1468-0009.2007.00506.x

Moher, D., Schulz, K. F., & Altman, D. (2001). The CONSORT statement: Revised recommendations for improving the quality of reports of parallel-group randomized trials. *Journal of the American Medical Association, 285*, 1987–1991. doi:10.1001/jama.285.15.1987

Mosteller, F., & Boruch, R. (Eds.). (2002). *Evidence matters: Randomized trials in education research*. Washington, DC: Brookings Institution Press.

Mullen, E. J., & Dumpson, J. R. (1972). *Evaluation of social intervention*. San Francisco, CA: Jossey-Bass.

Mullen, E. J., Shlonsky, A., Bledsoe, S. E., & Bellamy, J. L. (2005). From concept to implementation: Challenges facing evidence-based social work. *Evidence & Policy, 1*, 61–84. doi:10.1332/1744264052703159

Mullen, E. J., & Streiner, D. L. (2004). The evidence for and against evidence-based practice. *Brief Treatment and Crisis Intervention, 4,* 111–121. doi:10.1093/brief-treatment/mhh009

Murphy, S. A., Lynch, K. G., Oslin, D., McKay, J. R., & Ten Have, T. (2007). Developing adaptive treatment strategies in substance abuse research. *Drug and Alcohol Dependence, 88,* S24–S30. doi:10.1016/j.drugalcdep.2006.09.008

Nadeem, E., Olin, S. S., Hill, L. C., Hoagwood, K. E., & Horwitz, S. M. (2013). Understanding the components of quality improvement collaboratives: A systematic literature review. Milbank Quarterly, *91,* 354–394. doi:10.1111/milq.12016

National Association of Social Workers. (2008). *Code of ethics of the National Association of Social Workers.* Retrieved from http://www.naswdc.org/pubs/code/code.asp

National Board of Health and Welfare. (2011). *Svensk och internationell forskning om social interventioners effekter* [Swedish and international research on effects of social interventions]. Stockholm, Sweden: Socialstyrelsen.

Naylor, C. D. (1995). Grey zones of clinical practice: Some limits to evidence-based medicine. *Lancet, 345,* 840–842. doi:10.1016/S0140-6736(95)92969-X

Nevo, I., & Slonim-Nevo, V. (2011). The myth of evidence-based practice: Towards evidence-informed practice. *British Journal of Social Work, 41,* 1176–1197. doi:10.1093/bjsw/bcq149

Nigenda, G., & González-Robledo, L. M. (2005). *Lessons offered by Latin American cash transfer programmes, Mexico's Oportunidades and Nicaragua's SPN: Implications for African countries.* London, United Kingdom: DFID Health Systems Resource Centre. Retrieved from http://www.eldis.org/fulltext/verypoor/5_ningenda.pdf

Nutley, S. M., Walter, I., & Davies, H. T. O. (2007). *Using evidence: How research can inform public services.* Bristol, United Kingdom: Policy Press.

Oakley, A. (2000). *Experiments in knowing: Gender and method in the social sciences.* New York, NY: New Press.

Otto, H.-U., & Ziegler H. (2008). The notion of causal impact in evidence-based social work: An introduction to the special issue on what works? *Research on Social Work Practice, 18,* 273–277. doi:10.1177/1049731507313997

Palinkas, L. A. (in press). Causality and causal inference in social work: Quantitative and qualitative perspectives. *Research on Social Work Practice.*

Palinkas, L. A., & Aarons, G. A. (2009). A view from the top: Executive and management challenges in a statewide implementation of an evidence-based practice to reduce child neglect. *International Journal of Child Health and Human Development, 2*(1), 47–55.

Palinkas, L. A., Allred, C., & Landsverk, J. A. (2005). Models of research-operational collaboration for behavioral health in space. *Aviation, Space, and Environmental Medicine, 76*(Suppl. 1), B52–B60.

Palinkas, L. A., Fuentes, D., Finno, M., Garcia, A. R., Holloway, I. W., & Chamberlain, P. (2014). Inter-organizational collaboration in the implementation of evidence-based practices among public agencies serving abused and neglected youth. *Administration and Policy in Mental Health and Mental Health Services Research, 41,* 74–85. doi:10.1007/s10488-012-0437-5

Palinkas, L. A., Holloway, I. W., Rice, E., Fuentes, D., Wu, Q., & Chamberlain, P. (2011). Social networks and implementation of evidence-based practices in public youth-serving systems: A mixed-methods study. *Implementation Science, 6,* 113. doi:10.1186/1748-5908-6-113

Palinkas, L. A., Schoenwald, S. K., Hoagwood, K., Landsverk, J., Chorpita, B. F., Weisz, J. R., & the Research Network on Youth Mental Health. (2008). An ethnographic study of implementation of evidence-based treatments in child mental health: First steps. *Psychiatric Services*, *59*, 738–746. doi:10.1176/appi.ps.59.7.738

Palinkas, L. A., & Soydan, H. (2012). *Translation and implementation of evidence-based practice*. New York, NY: Oxford University Press.

Palinkas, L. A., Weisz, J. R., Chorpita, B. F., Levine, B., Garland, A. F., Hoagwood, K. E., & Landsverk, J. (2013). Continued use of evidence-based treatments after a randomized controlled effectiveness trial: A qualitative study. *Psychiatric Services*, *64*, 1110–1118. doi:10.1176/appi.ps.004682012

Pan, D., Huey, S. J., Jr., & Hernandez, D. (2011). Culturally adapted versus standard exposure treatment for phobic Asian Americans: Treatment efficacy, moderators, and predictors. *Cultural Diversity and Ethnic Minority Psychology*, *17*, 11–22. doi:10.1037/a0022534

Papanagnou, G. (Ed.). (2011). *Social science and policy challenges: Democracy, values and capacities*. Paris, France: UNESCO.

Pawson, R. (2002). Evidence-based policy: In search of a method. *Evaluation*, *8*, 157–181. doi:10.1177/1358902002008002512

Pawson, R. (2006). *Evidence-based policy: A realist perspective*. London, United Kingdom: Sage.

Petrosino, A., Boruch, R. F., Soydan, H., Duggan, L., & Sanchez-Meca, J. (2001). Meeting the challenges of evidence-based policy: The Campbell Collaboration. *Annals of the American Academy of Political and Social Science*, *578*, 14–34. doi:10.1177/000271620157800102

Petrosino, A., Turpin Petrosino, C., & Buehler, J. (2004). "Scared Straight" and other juvenile awareness programs for preventing juvenile delinquency. *Campbell Systematic Reviews*. Retrieved from http://www.campbellcollaboration.org/lib/download/13/

Petticrew, M., & Roberts, H. (2006). *Systematic reviews in the social sciences: A practical guide*. Malden, MA: Blackwell.

Popper, K. R. (1962). *The open society and its enemies* (Vols. I–II, 2nd ed.). London, United Kingdom: Routledge.

Popper, K. R. (1972). *The logic of scientific discovery* (Rev. ed.). London, United Kingdom: Hutchison.

Porras, J. I., & Robertson, P. J. (1992). Organizational development: Theory, practice and research. In M.D. Dunnette, & L. M. Hough (Eds.), *Handbook of industrial & organizational psychology* (Vol. 3, pp. 719–822). Palo Alto, CA: Consulting Psychologists Press.

Proceedings of the Conference on Improving the Teaching of Evidence-Based Practice in Social Work. (2007). *Research on Social Work Practice*, *17*(5).

Proctor, E. K., Knudsen, K. J., Fedoravicius, N., Hovmand, P., Rosen, A., & Perron, B. (2007). Implementation of evidence-based practice in community behavioral health: Agency director perspectives. *Administration and Policy in Mental Health and Mental Health Services Research*, *34*, 479–488. doi:10.1007/s10488-007-0129-8

Proctor, E. K., & Rosen, A. (2004). Concise standards for developing evidence-based practice guidelines. In A. R. Roberts & K. Yeager (Eds.), *Evidence-based practice manual* (pp. 193–199). New York, NY: Oxford University Press.

Raghavan, R., Inoue, M., Ettner, S. L., Hamilton, B. H., & Landsverk, J. (2010). A preliminary analysis of the receipt of mental health services consistent with national standards among children in the child welfare system. *American Journal of Public Health, 100,* 742–749. doi:10.2105/AJPH.2008.151472

Real, K., & Poole, M. S. (2005). Innovation implementation: Conceptualization and measurement in organizational research. In R. W. Woodman, W. A. Pasmore, & A. B. Shani (Eds.), *Research in organizational change and development* (Vol. 15, pp. 63–134). Oxford, United Kingdom: Elsevier.

Reid, P. T., & Vianna, E. (2001). Negotiating partnerships in research on poverty with community-based agencies. *Journal of Social Issues, 57,* 337–354. doi:10.1111/0022-4537.00217

Resnicow, K., Soler, R., Braithwaite, R. L., Ahluwalia, J. S., & Butler, J. (2000). Cultural sensitivity in substance use prevention. *Journal of Community Psychology, 28,* 271–290. doi:10.1002/(SICI)1520-6629(200005)28:3<271::AID-JCOP4>3.0.CO;2-I

Reynolds, A. J., & Temple, J. A. (1995). Quasi-experimental estimates of the effects of a preschool intervention: Psychometric and econometric comparisons. *Evaluation Review, 19,* 347–373. doi:10.1177/0193841X9501900401

Robinson, R. (1993a). Cost-effectiveness analysis. *BMJ, 307,* 793–795. doi:10.1136/bmj.307.6907.793

Robinson, R. (1993b). Cost–utility analysis. *BMJ, 307,* 859–862. doi:10.1136/bmj.307.6908.859

Rogers, E. M. (2003). *Diffusion of innovations* (5th ed.). New York, NY: Free Press.

Roos, N. P., & Shapiro, E. (1999). From research to policy: What have we learned? *Medical Care, 37,* JS291–JS305. doi:10.1097/00005650-199906001-00022

Rosen, A. (2003). Evidence-based social work practice: Challenges and promise. *Social Work Research, 27,* 197–208. doi:10.1093/swr/27.4.197

Rosenheck, R. A. (2001). Organizational process: A missing link between research and practice. *Psychiatric Services, 52,* 1607–1612. doi:10.1176/appi.ps.52.12.1607

Rousseau, D. M. (1977). Technological differences in job characteristics, employee satisfaction, and motivation: A synthesis of job design research and sociotechnical systems theory. *Organizational Behavior and Human Performance, 19,* 18–42. doi:10.1016/0030-5073(77)90052-6

Rubin, A. (2008). *Practitioner's guide to using research for evidence-based practice.* Hoboken, NJ: John Wiley & Sons.

Ruth, T., & Matusitz, J. (2013). Comparative standards of evidence in social work. *Journal of Evidence-Based Social Work, 10,* 285–298. doi:10.1080/15433714.2012.663660

Rycroft-Malone, J. (2008). Evidence-informed practice: From individual to context. *Journal of Nursing Management, 16,* 404–408. doi:10.1111/j.1365-2834.2008.00859.x

Rynes, S. L., Bartunek, J. M., & Daft, R. L. (2001). Across the great divide: Knowledge creation and transfer between practitioners and academics. *Academy of Management Journal, 44,* 340–355. doi:10.2307/3069460

Sackett, D. L., Richardson, W. S., Rosenberg, W., & Haynes, R. B. (1997). *Evidence-based medicine: How to practice and teach EBM.* New York, NY: Churchill Livingstone.

Sackett, D. L., & Rosenberg, W. M. (1995). The need for evidence-based medicine. *Journal of the Royal Society of Medicine, 88,* 620–624.

Sackett, D. L., Rosenberg, W. M. C., Muir Gray, J. A., Haynes, R. B., & Richardson, W. S. (1996). Evidence based medicine: What it is and what it isn't. *BMJ, 312,* 71. doi:10.1136/bmj.312.7023.71

Schoenwald, S. K., & Hoagwood, K. (2001). Effectiveness, transportability, and dissemination of interventions: What matters when? *Psychiatric Services, 52,* 1190–1197. doi:10.1176/appi.ps.52.9.1190

Schoenwald, S. K., Kelleher, K., Weisz, J. R., & the Research Network on Youth Mental Health. (2008). Building bridges to evidence-based practice: The MacArthur Foundation Child System and Treatment Enhancement Projects (Child STEPs). *Administration and Policy in Mental Health and Mental Health Services Research, 35,* 66–72. doi:10.1007/s10488-007-0160-9

Schoenwald, S. K., Sheidow, A. J., Letourneau, E. J., & Liao, J. G. (2003). Transportability of multisystemic therapy: Evidence for multilevel influences. *Mental Health Services Research, 5,* 223–239. doi:10.1023/A:1026229102151

Sells, S. B., & James, L. R. (1988). Organizational climate. In J. R. Nesselroade & R. B. Cattell (Eds.), *Handbook of multivariate experimental psychology: Perspectives on individual differences* (2nd ed., pp. 915–937). New York, NY: Plenum Press.

Shadish, W. R., Cook, T. D., & Campbell, D. T. (2002). *Experimental and quasi-experimental designs for generalized causal inference.* Boston, MA: Houghton Mifflin.

Shadish, W. R., & Ragsdale, K. (1996). Random versus nonrandom assignment in controlled experiments: Do you get the same answer? *Journal of Consulting and Clinical Psychology, 64,* 1290–1305. doi:10.1037/0022-006X.64.6.1290

Sheldon, B. (2003). *Brief summary of the ideas behind the Centre for Evidence-based Social Services.* Retrieved from University of Exeter website: http://www.ex.ac.uk/cebss/introduction.html

Sherman, L. W., Gottfredson, D., MacKenzie, D., Eck, J., Reuter, P., & Bushway, S. (1996). *Preventing crime: What works, what doesn't, what's promising.* Retrieved from National Criminal Justice Reference Service website: http://www.ncjrs.gov/works

Sholonsky, A., & Wagner, D. (2005). The next step: Integrating actuarial risk assessment and clinical judgment into an evidence-based practice framework in CPS case management. *Children and Youth Services Review, 27,* 409–427. doi:10.1016/j.childyouth.2004.11.007

Shortell, S. M. (2004). Increasing value: A research agenda for addressing the managerial and organizational challenges facing health care delivery in the United States. *Medical Care Research and Review, 61,* 12S–30S. doi:10.1177/1077558704266768

Shortell, S. M., Zazzali, J. L., Burns, L. R., Alexander, J. A., Gillies, R. R., Budetti, P. P., . . . Zuckerman, H. S. (2001). Implementing evidence-based medicine: The role of market pressures, compensation incentives, and culture in physician organizations. *Medical Care, 39,* 162–178. doi:10.1097/00005650-200107001-00005

Silverman, W. K., Pina, A. A., & Viswesvaran, C. (2008). Evidence-based psychosocial treatments for phobic and anxiety disorders in children and adolescents. *Journal of Clinical Child & Adolescent Psychology, 37,* 105–130. doi:10.1080/15374410701817907

Simpson, D. D. (2002). A conceptual framework for transferring research to practice. *Journal of Substance Abuse Treatment, 22,* 171–182. doi:10.1016/S0740-5472(02)00231-3

Smith, A. F. M. (1996). Mad cows and ecstasy: Chance and choice in an evidence-based society. *Journal of the Royal Statistical Society, 159,* 367–383. doi:10.2307/2983324

Smith, B. D. (2013). Substance use treatment counselors' attitudes toward evidence-based practice: The importance of organizational context. *Substance Use & Misuse, 48,* 379–390. doi:10.3109/10826084.2013.765480

Socialstyrelsen. (2011). *Svensk och internationell forskning om sociala interventioners effekter* [Swedish and international research on effectiveness of social interventions]. Stockholm, Sweden: Author. Retrieved from http://www.socialstyrelsen.se/Lists/Artikelkatalog/Attachments/18318/2011-4-17.pdf

Society for Social Work and Research Presidential Task Force on Publications. (2008). *Journal publication practices in social work.* Retrieved from http://www.sswr.org/PTFP%20final%20report%202008.pdf

Soliniś, G., & Bayá Laffite, N. (Eds.). (2011). *Mapping out the research-policy matrix: A report on the outputs from the first International Forum on the Social Science-Policy Nexus.* Paris, France: UNESCO.

Sosna, T., & Marsenich, L. (2006). *Community development team model: Supporting the model adherent implementation of programs and practices.* Sacramento, CA: California Institute of Mental Health. Retrieved from http://www.cimh.org/sites/main/files/file-attachments/cdt_report_0.pdf

Soydan, H. (1993a). *Det sociala arbetets idéhistoria* [in Swedish]. Lund, Sweden: Studentlitteratur.

Soydan, H. (1993b). A study of the history of ideas in social work: A theoretical framework. *Scandinavian Journal of Social Welfare, 2,* 204–214. doi:10.1111/j.1468-2397.1993.tb00040.x

Soydan, H. (Guest Ed.). (1998). Evaluation research and social work [Special issue]. *International Journal of Social Welfare, 7*(2). doi:10.1111/ijsw.1998.7.issue-2

Soydan, H. (1999). *The history of ideas in social work.* Birmingham, UK: Venture Press.

Soydan, H. (2008a). Producing knowledge for evidence-based practice and the future of social work research. In I. M. Bryderup (Ed.). *Evidence based and knowledge based social work* (pp. 173–184). Aarhus, Denmark: Aarhus University Press.

Soydan, H. (2008b). Applying randomized controlled trials and systematic reviews in social work research. *Research on Social Work Practice, 18,* 311–218. doi:10.1177/1049731507307788

Soydan, H. (2009). Evidence-based medicine and knowledge dissemination, translation, and utilization: Challenges of getting evidence-based treatments to patient care and service delivery. *Journal of Evidence-Based Medicine, 2,* 143–149. doi:10.1111/j.1756-5391.2009.01031.x

Soydan, H. (2010a). Politics and values in social work research. In I. Shaw, K. Briar-Lawson, J. Orme, & R. Ruckdeschel (Eds.), *The Sage handbook of social work research* (pp. 131–148). London, United Kingdom: Sage.

Soydan, H. (2010b). Migration. In T. Goldberg (Ed.), *Samhällsproblem* (pp. 231–271). Lund, Norway: Studentlitteratur.

Soydan, H. (Ed.). (2012). Shaping a science of social work [Special issue]. *Research on Social Work Practice, 22*(5).

Soydan, H., Jergeby, U., Olsson, E., & Harms-Ringdahl, M. (1999). *Socialt arbete med etniska minoriteter: En litteraturöversikt* [Social work with ethnic minorities: A literature review]. Stockholm, Sweden: Liber.

Soydan, H., Mullen, E. J., Alexandra, L., Rehnman, J., & Li, Y.-P. (2010). Evidence-based clearinghouses in social work. *Research on Social Work Practice, 20,* 690–700. doi:10.1177/1049731510367436

Sperber, E., McKay, M. M., Bell, C. C., Petersen, I., Bhana, A., & Paikoff, R. (2008). Adapting and disseminating a community-collaborative, evidence-based

HIV/AIDS prevention programme: Lessons from the history of CHAMP. *Vulnerable Children and Youth Studies, 3,* 150–158. doi:10.1080/17450120701867561

Spillane, J. P., Diamond, J. B., Walker, L. J., Halverson, R., & Jita, L. (2001). Urban school leadership for elementary science instruction: Identifying and activating resources in an undervalued school subject. *Journal of Research in Science Teaching, 38,* 918–940. doi:10.1002/tea.1039

Stoesz, D. (2010). Second-rate research for second-class citizens [Review of the book *Evidence-based social work: A critical stance,* by M. Gray, D. Plath, & S. A. Webb]. *Research on Social Work Practice, 20,* 329–332. doi:10.1177/1049731509347882

Straus, S. E., & McAlister, F. A. (2000). Evidence-based medicine: A commentary on common criticisms. *Canadian Medical Association Journal, 163,* 837–841.

Strauss, A., & Corbin, J. (1990). *Basics of qualitative research: Grounded theory procedures and techniques.* Newbury Park, CA: Sage.

Sundell, K., Ferrer-Wreder, L., & Fraser, M. W. (2013). Going global: A model for evaluating empirically supported family-based interventions in new contexts. *Evaluation & the Health Professions.* Advance online publication. doi:10.1177/0163278712469813

Sussman, S., Unger, J. B., & Palinkas, L. A. (2008). Country prototypes and translation of health programs. *Evaluation & the Health Professions, 31,* 110–123. doi:10.1177/0163278708315918

Swain, K., Whitley, R., McHugo, G. J., & Drake, R. E. (2010). The sustainability of evidence-based practices in routine mental health agencies. *Community Mental Health Journal, 46,* 119–129. doi:10.1007/s10597-009-9202-y

Swensen, S. J., & Cortese, D. A. (2008). Transparency and the "end result idea." *Chest, 133,* 233–235. doi:10.1378/chest.07-2101

Sztompka, P. (1990). Conceptual frameworks in comparative inquiry: Divergent or convergent? In M. Albrow & E. King (Eds.), *Globalization, knowledge and society* (pp. 47–58). London, United Kingdom: Sage.

Tabár, L., Gad, A., Holmberg, L. H., Ljungquist, U., Fagerberg, C. J. G., Baldetorp, L., . . . Pettersson, F. (1985). Reduction in mortality from breast cancer after mass screening with mammography: Randomised trial from the Breast Cancer Screening Working Group of the Swedish National Board of Health and Welfare. *Lancet, 325,* 829–832. doi:10.1016/S0140-6736(85)92204-4

Ten Have, T. R., Coyne, J., Salzer, M., & Katz, I. (2003). Research to improve the quality of care for depression: Alternatives to the simple randomized clinical trial. *General Hospital Psychiatry, 25,* 115–123. doi:10.1016/S0163-8343(02)00275-X

Ten Have, T. R., Joffe, M., & Cary, M. (2003). Causal logistic models for non-compliance under randomized treatment with univariate binary response. *Statistics in Medicine, 22,* 1255–1283. doi:10.1002/sim.1401

Theobald, G. W. (1937). Effect of calcium and vitamins A and D on incidence of pregnancy toxemia. *Lancet, 2,* 1397–1399. doi:10.1016/S0140-6736(00)83249-3

Trist, E. (1985). Intervention strategies for interorganizational domains. In R. Tannenbaum, N. Margulies, & F. Massarik (Eds.), *Human systems development* (pp. 167–197). San Francisco, CA: Jossey-Bass.

Tunis, S. R. (2007). Reflections on science, judgment, and value in evidence-based decision making: A conversation with David Eddy. *Health Affairs, 26,* 500–515. doi:10.1377/hlthaff.26.4.w500

Tylor, E. B. (1871). *Primitive culture: Researches into the development of mythology, philosophy, religion, art, and custom.* London, United Kingdom: John Murray.

U.S. Department of Health and Human Services. (2001). *Mental health: Culture, race, and ethnicity—A supplement to mental health: A report of the Surgeon General.* Rockville, MD: U.S. Department of Health and Human Services, Substance Abuse and Mental Health Services Administration, Center for Mental Health Services.

Valente, T. W. (1995). *Network models of the diffusion of innovations.* Creskill, NJ: Hampton Press.

Valente, T. W. (1996). Social network thresholds in the diffusion of innovations. *Social Networks, 18,* 69–89. doi:10.1016/0378-8733(95)00256-1

Valente, T. W. (2010). *Social networks and health: Models, methods, and applications.* New York, NY: Oxford University Press.

Valente, T. W., Hoffman, B. R., Ritt-Olson, A., Lichtman, K., & Johnson, C. A. (2003). Effects of a social-network method for group assignment strategies on peer-led tobacco prevention programs in schools. *American Journal of Public Health, 93,* 1837–1843. doi:10.2105/AJPH.93.11.1837

Valentine, J. C., Biglan, A., Boruch, R. F., González Castro, F., Collins, L. M., Flay, B. R., . . . Schinke, S. P. (2011a). Replication in prevention science. *Prevention Science, 12,* 103–117. doi:10.1007/s11121-011-0217-6

Valentine, J. C., Biglan, A., Boruch, R. F., González Castro, F., Collins, L. M., Flay, B. R., . . . Schinke, S. P. (2011b). Commentaries on replication in prevention science: A rejoinder. *Prevention Science, 12,* 123–125. doi:10.1007/s11121-011-0220-y

Wang, W., Saldana, L., Brown, C. H., & Chamberlain, P. (2010). Factors that influenced county system leaders to implement an evidence-based program: A baseline survey within a randomized controlled trial. *Implementation Science, 5,* 72. doi:10.1186/1748-5908-5-72

Webb, S. A. (2001). Some considerations on the validity of evidence-based practice in social work. *British Journal of Social Work, 31,* 57–79. doi:10.1093/bjsw/31.1.57

Weisz, J. R., Chorpita, B. F., Palinkas, L. A., Schoenwald, S. K., Miranda, J., Bearman, S. K., . . . the Research Network on Youth Mental Health. (2012). Testing standard and modular designs for psychotherapy treating depression, anxiety, and conduct problems in youth: A randomized effectiveness trial. *Archives of General Psychiatry, 69,* 274–282. doi:10.1001/archgenpsychiatry.2011.147

Weisz, J. R., Jensen-Doss, A., & Hawley, K. M. (2006). Evidence-based youth psychotherapies versus clinical care: A meta-analysis of direct comparisons. *American Psychologist, 61,* 671–689. doi:10.1037/0003-066X.61.7.671

Wells, K., Miranda, J., Bruce, M. L., Alegria, M., & Wallerstein, N. (2004). Bridging community intervention and mental health services research. *American Journal of Psychiatry, 161,* 955–963. doi:10.1176/appi.ajp.161.6.955

Wells, K. B, Staunton, A., Norris, K. C, & the CHIC Council. (2006). Building an academic-community partnered network for clinical services research: The Community Health Improvement Collaborative (CHIC). *Ethnicity and Disease, 16,* S1-3–S1-17.

West, S. G., Duan, N., Pequegnat, W., Gaist, P., Des Jarlais, D. C., Holtgrave, D., . . . Mullen, P. D. (2008). Alternatives to the randomized controlled trial. *American Journal of Public Health, 98,* 1359–1366. doi:10.2105/AJPH.2007.124446

Williams, C., Soydan, H., & Johnson, M. R. D. (Eds.). (1998). *Social work and minorities: European perspectives*. London, United Kingdom: Routledge.

Wilson, S. J., Lipsey, M. W., & Soydan, H. (2003). Are mainstream programs for juvenile delinquency less effective with minority youth than majority youth? A meta-analysis of outcomes research. *Research on Social Work Practice, 13*, 3–26. doi:10.1177/1049731502238754

Wisdom, J. P., Chor, K. H. B., Hoagwood, K. E., & Horwitz, S. M. (2013). Innovation adoption: A review of theories and constructs. *Administration and Policy in Mental Health and Mental Health Services Research*. Advance online publication. doi:10.1007/s10488-013-0486-4

Woltmann, E. M., Whitley, R., McHugo, G. J., Brunette, M., Torrey, W. C., Coots, L., . . . Drake, R. E. (2008). The role of staff turnover in the implementation of evidence-based practices in mental health care. *Psychiatric Services, 59*, 732–737. doi:10.1176/appi.ps.59.7.732

Yoo, J., Brooks, D., & Patti, R. (2007). Organizational constructs as predictors of effectiveness in child welfare interventions. *Child Welfare, 86*, 53–78.

Yoshioka, A. (1998). Use of randomisation in the Medical Research Council's clinical trial of streptomycin in pulmonary tuberculosis in the 1940s. *BMJ, 317*, 1220–1223. doi:10.1136/bmj.317.7167.1220

Zazzalli, J. L., Sherbourne, C., Hoagwood, K. E., Greene, D., Bigley, M. F., & Sexton, T. L. (2008). The adoption and implementation of an evidence based practice in child and family mental health services organizations: A pilot study of Functional Family Therapy in New York State. *Administration and Policy in Mental Health and Mental Health Services Research, 35*, 38–49. doi:10.1007/s10488-007-0145-8

Ziman, J. (2000). *Real science: What it is, and what it means*. Cambridge, United Kingdom: Cambridge University Press.

INDEX

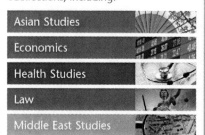